NORTHUMBERLAND

*The Political Career of John Dudley,
Earl of Warwick and Duke of Northumberland*

Barrett L. Beer

NORTHUMBERLAND
The Political Career of John Dudley,
Earl of Warwick
and Duke of Northumberland

The Kent State University Press

Publication of this book was assisted by the American Council of Learned Societies under a grant from the Andrew W. Mellon Foundation.

For
Jill, Peter, Caroline, and N. N.

Contents

Preface

John Dudley, Duke of Northumberland, is best known for his role in the abortive plot in 1553 to make Lady Jane Grey Queen of England. As the young King Edward VI lay dying, Northumberland attempted to divert the royal succession from Mary Tudor, eldest daughter of Henry VIII, to Lady Jane, who was married to his son, Guildford. After the plot had failed, Northumberland further discredited himself by renouncing the Protestant religion in a futile effort to save his life. Some writers have also held him responsible for the subsequent execution of Lady Jane, the innocent and virtuous young woman betrayed by the ambitions of her father, the Duke of Suffolk, and Northumberland. Generations of historians have chosen to view his career as little more than a period of preparation for the final catastrophic debacle. The result has been the creation of the legend of Northumberland the wicked duke, a legend that has survived for over four centuries.

The main purpose of this book is to re-examine Northumberland's political career as it unfolded from beginning to end. I have tried to look at events from Northumberland's perspective rather than from the perspective of persons writing after his death. Since it was not my intention to write a life and times biography or a history of the reigns of Henry VIII and Edward VI, religious, constitutional, and economic topics have been discussed only as they bear on the career of Northumberland. Greater weight has been given to contemporary documents than to those dating from a later period when it was convenient to hold him responsible for the failures of the reign of Edward VI. Imaginative writers have written more about Northumberland's character than can be learned from surviving evidence. For few men of the period is there conclusive documentation indicating the depth and intensity of religious convictions. Northumberland is no exception. Greed and political ambition often defy documentation as well. In practice historians ascribe good motives to persons whom they admire and evil ones to those they despise. Whenever possible I have allowed Northumberland to speak for himself even though many of his pronouncements cannot be taken at face value.

Throughout the course of my work I have been fortunate to have the advice and encouragement of Professor Lacey Baldwin Smith. Professors S. T. Bindoff, Joel Hurstfield, and Wallace T. MacCaffrey were extremely helpful and generous with their time during the early stages of research. The Marquess of Anglesey was kind enough to loan me materials from the Paget manuscripts. Among others who provided assistance, I would in particular like to mention Professors Lawrence S. Kaplan, C. Stewart Doty, and Martin J. Havran.

It is with sincere appreciation that I acknowledge grants from Northwestern University, the University of New Mexico, and the American Philosophical Society. These awards permitted me to spend more time in England working with manuscript sources than would otherwise have been possible.

Since much of this study is concerned with reinterpretation, I owe a heavy debt to Tudor historians who blazed the trails that I have followed. Whatever merit this study has derives in large part from those who have gone before; I stand responsible for all of the defects.

BARRETT L. BEER
February 24, 1973

NOTES ON THE ILLUSTRATIONS

1. EDWARD VI AND THE POPE   (P. 44)
    Unknown artist, *c.* 1548-49. National Portrait Gallery, London. John Dudley, Earl of Warwick is second on King Edward's left. According to Roy C. Strong, *Tudor and Jacobean Portraits* (London, 1969), I, 235, 344, this is the only authentic likeness of John Dudley.
2. JOHN DUDLEY, DUKE OF NORTHUMBERLAND   (P. 94)
    Unknown artist. By permission of Viscount De L'Isle, VC, from his collection at Penshurst Place, Tonbridge, Kent. This portrait cannot be substantiated.
3. KING EDWARD VI. EXCERPT FROM MY DEVISE FOR THE SUCCESSION   (P. 151)
    By permission of the Masters of the Bench of the Inner Temple, London.

NORTHUMBERLAND

The Political Career of John Dudley,
Earl of Warwick and Duke of Northumberland

I / The World
of John Dudley

John Dudley was a child of about six when his father, Edmund, was executed for treason. Although Edmund Dudley protested his innocence throughout his trial, he mounted the scaffold at Tower Hill, London, on August 17, 1510, and was beheaded. His crime was to have served the late King Henry VII too well as a crown official; he had worked too hard to assure the success of the first Tudor monarch's unpopular legal and financial policies, and his enemies in high places were legion. The young Henry VIII, hoping to begin a new reign on a wave of popular acclaim, had no reluctance in casting Edmund to the wolves, for there were others willing and able to do the King's bidding. Forty-three years later, in 1553, John Dudley, having advanced to the princely rank of Duke of Northumberland, retraced his father's steps to the scaffold and died for organizing the abortive plot to place Lady Jane Grey on the English throne. During the four decades separating the two executions, John Dudley rose from relative obscurity to become the leading figure in the government of Edward VI. Dudley's emergence as a major politician was unexpected, and his career forms one of the most remarkable chapters in the history of Tudor England.

The world of John Dudley combined the glitter and genius of

the Renaissance with the religious zeal of the Reformation. For all of Western Europe the sixteenth century was an era of change and uncertainty. The overseas voyages of the Spanish and Portuguese extended the horizons of Europe to Asia and the Americas. From Italy came new artistic and literary styles and an attitude of skepticism that challenged old beliefs. Erasmus, Prince of the Northern Humanists, reduced the wisdom of the past to mere folly. In Germany Martin Luther challenged the authority of the Pope, while the English martyr, Thomas More, preferred to die rather than forsake the Roman Catholic religion.

Dudley's contemporaries, in addition to Erasmus, Luther, and More, included Henry VIII. Before the death of Henry VII in 1509, the King had completed the restoration of the English monarchy and bequeathed his son a secure throne. Young Henry VIII, freed from his father's fears and anxieties, sought to give England a new style of leadership and aspired to be numbered among the great monarchs of Christendom. A man of restless energy, he has been termed "a prodigy, a sun-king, a *stupor mundi*."[1] By the 1530s Henry VIII's power permitted him to break with the Papacy and establish himself as the Supreme Head of the Church of England. The conflict between Henry and the Papacy stemmed from the Pope's refusal to grant the King a divorce from Queen Catherine of Aragon. Henry's motives for seeking the divorce included the pressing need for a male heir, disenchantment with his aging Queen, and above all infatuation with the vivacious Anne Boleyn. Once opened, the breach between England and Rome widened, and during the short reign of Henry's son, Edward VI, Protestantism became the official creed of the Church of England.

Behind the dramatic events and brilliant personalities of the early sixteenth century stood the grim realities of Renaissance political life. Never before had such opportunities for personal advancement existed, but at no time were the risks greater. Tudor kings demanded the impossible from their ministers and ruthlessly discarded those who outlived their usefulness. The price of failure—whether because of error, incompetence, or bad luck—was always disgrace and often the chopping block.

No family better illustrates the perilous aspects of Tudor politics than the Dudleys. Edmund was a lawyer and administrator of marked ability whose unpopularity made him a liability to Henry VIII; whether he was guilty of treason or not was virtually an irrelevant consideration. John Dudley, Duke of Northumberland, on the other hand, faced with the impending death of Edward VI, fatally blundered into promoting the claim of Lady Jane to the throne. While Northumberland was clearly guilty of rebellion and treason against Mary Tudor, he paid for the crimes with his own life and the temporary ruin of the Dudley family.

After the execution of Northumberland, few recognized the difficulties he had faced in reaching the decision to oppose the succession of Queen Mary, and almost everyone impugned his motives. Former friends and colleagues, scurrying to save their own lives, freely heaped abuse on the ruined duke. In later years chroniclers and historians alike portrayed him as the very embodiment of evil.[2] His entire life was seen as a sordid drama of intrigue and selfish ambition. As a result the legend of Northumberland the wicked duke was born, one that has survived for over four centuries.

John Dudley, despite his notorious reputation, enjoyed the distinction of descent from ancient and noble forbears. The family tree is traced through John de Sutton I (d. *c.* 1322), who inherited the estates of his wife, Margaret, whose family had held Dudley Castle in Worcestershire since the reign of Henry II.[3] John Dudley's grandfather was the younger son of a peer, John de Sutton, Lord Dudley. The grandfather, also named John Dudley, was a Sussex man having his seat at Atherington, a manor in the parish of Climping. He held a variety of local offices, including appointment as sheriff of Surrey and Sussex, and was elected to the House of Commons on several occasions, retiring after representing the borough of Arundel in the Parliament of 1491–1492. The terms of the elder John Dudley's will

Dudley Family Tree

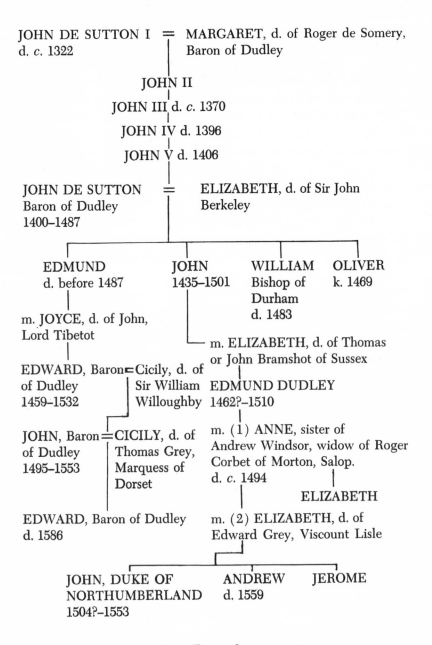

JOHN DE SUTTON I = MARGARET, d. of Roger de Somery,
d. c. 1322   Baron of Dudley

JOHN II

JOHN III d. c. 1370

JOHN IV d. 1396

JOHN V d. 1406

JOHN DE SUTTON = ELIZABETH, d. of Sir John
Baron of Dudley   Berkeley
1400–1487

EDMUND   JOHN   WILLIAM   OLIVER
d. before 1487   1435–1501   Bishop of   k. 1469
                              Durham
m. JOYCE, d. of John,   d. 1483
Lord Tibetot
                    m. ELIZABETH, d. of Thomas
                    or John Bramshot of Sussex
EDWARD, Baron=Cicily, d. of
of Dudley   Sir William   EDMUND DUDLEY
1459–1532   Willoughby   1462?–1510

JOHN, Baron=CICILY, d. of   m. (1) ANNE, sister of
of Dudley   Thomas Grey,   Andrew Windsor, widow of Roger
1495–1553   Marquess of   Corbet of Morton, Salop.
              Dorset   d. c. 1494
                                              ELIZABETH
EDWARD, Baron of Dudley   m. (2) ELIZABETH, d. of
d. 1586   Edward Grey, Viscount Lisle

JOHN, DUKE OF   ANDREW   JEROME
NORTHUMBERLAND   d. 1559
1504?–1553

Figure 1

leave little doubt that he was a man of considerable wealth in Sussex.[4] Edmund Dudley followed his father into Parliament, married well, and by his second wife, Elizabeth Grey, had three sons, John, Andrew, and Jerome.

Little is known about the early life of the young John Dudley and almost nothing of his brothers. John was probably born in 1504, for the act of Parliament which restored him in blood in 1512 described him as under eight years of age.[5] Before Edmund's death John lived in the comfort and security of the family home in Candlewick Street, London.[6] Later it is likely that he lived with his guardian, Sir Edward Guildford, squire of the body at the court of Henry VIII. John's mother was remarried to Arthur Plantagenet, a bastard son of the Yorkist King, Edward IV. The disgrace of Edmund was obviously a catastrophe for the family, for the wealth he had accumulated through service to Henry VII was swept away.[7] Nonetheless, the widow and sons escaped poverty and retained their ties with the aristocracy.

Family life dominated social relationships in the sixteenth century to a far greater extent than today. For this reason John Dudley's youth was closely connected with the affairs of his stepfather, Plantagenet, his cousins, the Lord Dudleys of Dudley Castle, and the Guildfords. Ties with the Guildfords were particularly important, for John married Jane, daughter and heiress of his guardian. Several of the Dudley children became almost as famous as their father. One son, Guildford, married Lady Jane Grey, while a daughter, Mary, was the mother of Sir Philip Sidney, the poet. Ambrose Dudley became the Elizabethan Earl of Warwick. Most renowned of all the Dudley children was Robert, Earl of Leicester, who established himself as the most celebrated Elizabethan courtier and nearly won the Queen's hand in marriage.

John Dudley, like his father, became a lawyer and used his profession for self-gain. Since land was the most important source of wealth during the Tudor period, an ambitious young man was obliged to accumulate as much property as possible, bending the law if necessary to suit his own purposes. To recover parts of his forfeited inheritance Dudley became involved in a number of highly complicated court actions.[8] He also requested the assistance of Thomas Cromwell, the great minister of Henry VIII, in safeguarding his wife's property from the designs of her Guildford relatives.[9] Young Dudley was not always the most scrupulous in his legal maneuvers, and he successfully wrested control of Dudley Castle from his inept cousin, John de Sutton, Lord Dudley.[10] Another victim was Plantagenet, Dudley's stepfather. On one occasion Dudley and Sir Edward Seymour, the future Lord Protector, connived to deprive Plantagenet of about £60 annual income.[11] That Dudley was a man on the make is undeniable, but it is also true that property disputes and prolonged litigation were common occurrences among the Tudor landed classes.

A man in Dudley's position could also improve himself by seeking advancement at court. Office-holding could be extremely profitable and was the recognized avenue to social betterment and political power. Dudley was probably introduced at court by his guardian, Sir Edward Guildford. In 1523 his career began with an appointment to a lieutenancy in the army. Dudley campaigned first in France, serving under the command of the King's favorite, the Duke of Suffolk, and was rewarded with a knighthood. Also receiving a knighthood was Dudley's comrade, Edward Seymour.[12] This campaign marked the beginning of their long association.

The succeeding years found Sir John Dudley actively serving Henry VIII at court and in the country. Before Christmas, 1525, Dudley and other young knights entertained the royal household in a "challenge of feats of arms."[13] Two years later he was included in the sumptuous entourage of Cardinal Wolsey traveling to France.[14] In 1532 the King's retinue at the Calais interview with Francis I of France included Dudley as well as the striking Anne Boleyn.[15] After Anne's coronation the following year, Dudley served as cup bearer to Archbishop Thomas Cranmer at the "Queen's board," and later bore gifts at the christening of the infant Princess Elizabeth. By 1537, when he was present at the christening of Prince Edward, Dudley had become an established figure at court.[16]

His local influence is seen first in Sussex, Surrey, and Kent where the Dudleys and the Guildfords had extensive lands. An appointment in 1532 to the office of joint constable of Warwick Castle and the acquisition of Dudley Castle extended Dudley's interests into the Midlands.[17] He entered Parliament for the first time in 1534, when he succeeded Sir Edward Guildford as member for Kent.

The most important achievement of Dudley's early career was to build for himself a military reputation that endured untarnished until the debacle of 1553. During the Pilgrimage of Grace in 1536, the most serious uprising during the reign of Henry VIII, Dudley was ordered to raise two hundred men and attend upon the King. Serving under the Duke of Norfolk, he assisted in the pacification of areas in the North that resisted the religious changes of the Reformation Parliament.[18] Dudley served at sea as well as on land and was appointed vice-admiral of a small fleet outfitted in 1537 to combat the piracy and coastal depredations of the Flemish. After successfully clearing the channel, Dudley was able to report to the King that he was once again respected as lord of the channel seas.[19]

Sir John Dudley was elevated to the peerage in 1542 as Viscount Lisle. The exact circumstances of his promotion were confusing even to contemporaries, inasmuch as the title should have descended to him by the right of his mother who was the daughter of Edward Grey, Viscount Lisle.[20] In fact Dudley's peerage was a new creation by letter patent of March 12, 1542. Magnificently clad in a fine surcoat and hood, "this noble knight" was led into the royal presence by Edward Seymour, Earl of Hertford, and Lord Russell. Sir Thomas Wriothesley read the letters patent with a high voice and gave the style of the new peer before Henry VIII sitting under the cloth of estate. Then the King, assisted by his council, placed the mantle upon Dudley. To the sound of blaring trumpets, the new Lord

Lisle withdrew to feast with the lords of England.[21] If the pomp and excitement of the occasion permitted a moment's reflection, John Dudley must have seen a new world of opportunity unfolding before him. He perhaps also considered how fully the son of an executed traitor had redeemed himself. Edmund Dudley had never been knighted; John had already climbed into the peerage.

II / Lisle and the Twilight of Henrician England

The last five years of the reign of Henry VIII witnessed the accession of John Dudley, Viscount Lisle, to political power. Serving the King on land, sea, and at court, he gained the experience required for greater responsibilities. Lisle's loyal and unswerving service over two decades atoned for the alleged crimes of his father and forced Henry VIII to recognize the wisdom of the first Tudor in favoring the Dudley family. Almost as old as the sixteenth century itself, Lisle was by no means a beardless boy in the 1540s; nor was his advancement meteoric. Yet, when Henry VIII died in 1547, Lisle and the King's brother-in-law, Edward Seymour, Earl of Hertford, were regarded as the two men most fit to rule.

Lisle apparently had no enemies before 1540 apart from unfortunates like Lord Dudley, who suffered from his legal machinations. His relations with the King's secretaries from Thomas Cromwell to William Paget and William Petre were good. After a military apprenticeship in 1523 under Charles Brandon, Duke of Suffolk, Lisle was held in high esteem by Henry VIII's closest personal friend. Thomas Howard, Duke of Norfolk, who was as much a permanent fixture in the Henrician political establishment as Suffolk, also had connections with the Dudleys. Lisle's brother, Andrew, was in Norfolk's service and held a position in the office of the lord treasurer by his favor.[1] Between Lisle and Hertford were close personal ties, which, if anything, grew stronger as the reign progressed. While all of these connections were important, they do not overshadow the simple fact that all political and military careers were ultimately dependent upon royal favor. Had this not been forthcoming, the son of Edmund Dudley would have lived out his days in political and social obscurity.

The channels through which Lisle rose to prominence are unique for the reign of Henry VIII. Unlike his father or Thomas Cromwell, Lisle was not primarily an administrator or bureaucrat. During the heyday of the Cromwell administration, he remained outside the reforming party but was on good terms with it. His career in no way depended on a blood tie with the royal family, as was the case with Suffolk, Hertford, and Sir William Parr, the brother of Henry's last Queen. Similarly, any effort to demonstrate that he gained power through the acquisition of key offices is doomed to failure. The positions he held during the 1530s included the joint constableship of Warwick Castle, master of the armory of the Tower, vice-admiral, and master of horse to Anne of Cleves. Surely, it would be difficult to select a collection of less promising posts. Even after his creation as viscount, admission to the august board of the Privy Council, and election to the Garter, his most lofty office was that of lord high admiral, admittedly a position of great importance in wartime, but one that had never figured prominently as a stepping-stone to political eminence.

Lisle is likewise singularly uncomfortable in the standard sociological categories of rising middle class, rising or declining gentry, or ancient feudal aristocracy. The de Suttons of Dudley Castle certainly belonged to the ancient nobility, but Lisle's grandfather, John Dudley, Esq., of Sussex was a solid member of the gentry. Edmund Dudley, on the other hand, might be described as one of the rising bourgeoisie, if it were not for his noble forebears. But there was nothing bourgeois about Lisle, who was above all else a soldier and courtier; his business interests always occupied a subordinate position. While he acquired vast landed property, he never represented any particular region nor did he behave like a territorial magnate. It is clear then that none of the usual sociological formulas will adequately explain Lisle's career. The alternative is to analyze the events leading to his political ascent.

During the last years of Henry VIII, English politics were strongly influenced by the King's war policy. Lisle and other military leaders assumed greater responsibilities as foreign and domestic affairs became almost inseparable. Henry VIII, determined to further his ambitions in Scotland, depleted his country's resources and jeopardized its financial stability. The failure of James V of Scotland to meet Henry at York in September 1541 led to hostilities between the two countries and eventually between England and France. Alternating hot and cold war, continuing until Henry's death, forms the background against which Lisle's career must be viewed.

In 1542 conflict along the Scottish border offered Lisle new challenges and opportunities. Shortly after his elevation to the peerage, he was sent northward as commissioner to Berwick and the borders of Scotland. Arriving early in May 1542, Lisle and Sir Richard Southwell examined fortifications on which twenty thousand marks had been spent and found that these works did not answer the King's expectations.[2] The first attacks on the Scots were launched later in the summer without much success. A force led by Sir Robert Bowes was actually defeated at Haddonrig, while the main army led by Norfolk, son of the victor of Flodden, succeeded in doing no more than burning Roxburgh and Kelso and twenty villages. Lisle was not involved in these campaigns and was back at court by the beginning of October where he participated in the creation of the Irish chieftain, Conn O'Neill, as Earl of Tyrone.[3] Nevertheless, he returned to the Border again before the end of 1542 and replaced Hertford as lord warden. This was the first of a long and fateful series of exchanges of positions between the two old colleagues.

Hertford had been anxious to be relieved and had written the Privy Council some rather cryptic comments about his potential successors on October 30, 1542:

> In case you would know my opinion who were more meet at this present to furnish the said room, sure I am that there is neither my Lord of Norfolk, Mr. Comptroller [Sir John Gage], nor Mr. Brown being demanded on their allegiances, but can declare that there is neither my Lord of Cumberland by reason of his lands, kindred, and alliance, my Lord Parr being of great possession and kindred in these parts, my Lord Lisle who is already furnished for that he should have gone into France, nor yet my Lord Dacres, if the King's majesty did so accept him; by my considerations well pondered, every of them are more meeter to serve in this case than I.[4]

From York, Norfolk, the lieutenant general, and the council of the north wrote Hertford that he was being replaced by the Earl of Rutland, but since he was physically unable to hold the position, they urged Hertford to remain and suggested that the Earl of Cumberland was better qualified for the post than Rutland.[5] At Hampton Court on the same day, November 8, Sir Thomas Wriothesley wrote to Hertford that Lisle would receive the appointment and assured him that "I shall lay my hands so about me as he shall be with you soon upon the end of this month having already dispatched the letters for the levying of his men."[6] A third letter of the same date from the King to Norfolk and his aides made the appointment official. Henry VIII thought Cumberland young and inexperienced. Lisle, on the other hand, was well-qualified but of "small experience on the Borders"; therefore, the King ordered Cuthbert Tunstall, Bishop of Durham, to remain in the North to aid and advise Lisle.[7]

Scotland was clearly a new venture for Lisle. Like Hertford, he had no territorial influence along the Borders and was thus very much the King's man. In time of crisis the King wanted men upon whom he could depend in strategic posts, and he was slowly realizing that some of the burden of leadership previously exercised by Norfolk and Suffolk would of necessity have to be shouldered by younger men.

Wriothesley fulfilled his promise to Hertford because Lisle arrived on schedule before December 1, 1542.[8] In preparation for his coming, arrangements were made by Tunstall to levy 2000 men for the winter. Norfolk had commanded Cumberland to ready 5000 spearmen and archers to attend on Lisle, but the earl protested that he was "without the precincts of all the three borders" and could not carry out the order without the King's license.[9] Meanwhile, the military question was resolved in a decisive and dramatic manner. At Solway Moss on November 24, a Scots army of some ten thousand, commanded by Sir Oliver Sinclair, the favorite of James V, was disastrously defeated by a force less than a third its size under the English deputy warden, Sir Thomas Wharton. This humiliating defeat was the last for James V, who died three weeks later, leaving as his heir the newly born Princess Mary under whose rule Scotland found even less peace and quietness.

With the immediate threat removed, Lisle's duties as lord warden centered more on routine matters of diplomacy and military preparedness. His orders included the grim responsibility of sending a number of Scots prisoners to row as slaves in the galleys. He and Hertford informed the Privy Council that "upon consultation, reasoning, and debating of diverse considerations and causes rising among us thereupon, it is thought good unto us all to forbear and not to put in execution the said proclamations" until the latter had explained to the councillors "such inconveniences as thereby might ensue." It is not clear whether Lisle and Hertford were motivated by humanitarian considerations or whether they merely feared reprisals by the Scots and their French allies. A few weeks later Lisle revealed a measure of chivalry and perhaps a touch of humility when he advised Henry VIII that he would not resume hostilities against the Scots until he received further orders since it did not seem "to the King's honor to make war upon a dead body, or a widow, or a suckling, his daughter, especially at the time of his funeral."

Lisle quickly discovered a large number of his troops to be unfit for active military service. In many cases, their horses were spent, and the men did nothing more than consume badly needed victuals. To remedy the deteriorating situation Lisle, with Hertford's advice, dispatched 1,100 troops to their homes, keeping only those who were able to engage actively in combat.[10]

Henry's policy was to exploit the victory at Solway Moss and the timely death of James V to the utmost, first by means of an English party in Scotland and eventually by a marriage treaty between his son, Prince Edward, and the infant princess Mary. Loyal to the King's wishes, Lisle supported diplomatic maneuvers at the Scottish court, although he recognized better than the King the political limitations of intrigues that were unsupported by substantial military force:

> No perfect reformation will ever be had until the King has all that part of Scotland on this side of the Frithe [Firth of Forth] on the East and on this side of Dunne Bretayne [Dumbarton] on the West.
> To take it would be "an acceptable deed before God, considering how brutally and beastly the people now be governed" and the effusion of Christian blood which has happened every 20 or 24 years and ever shall until the marches are set to these limits.
> Oh, what godly act should it be to your excellent highness to bring such a sort of people to the knowledge of God's laws, the country so necessary to your dominions by reason whereof so many souls should live also in quietness.[11]

So long as England lacked the strength to do more than ravage border towns and rout poorly led troops, Scotland would remain free to ally herself with France and follow an independent policy. Lisle's boldness was not altogether typical of the man, yet it reflects his military training and a practical and methodical approach to a question rarely faced directly by the King and his councillors. Lisle's awareness as early as 1542 that a successful Scottish policy also required religious innovations, albeit of an unspecified sort, suggests his own appreciation of the situation to be more sophisticated than might be expected from a military commander. In February of the following year, he urged Arran, the Regent of Scotland, to "let slip among the people" the Bible in English "whereby they may perceive the truth" and offered to get copies in England if Arran could not supply them himself.[12]

After only five weeks of service as lord warden, Lisle learned from the King that he had been appointed lord high admiral of England because of his "good endeavors and earnest desire to do . . . true, faithful, and acceptable service."[13] Once again he followed on the heels of Hertford, who vacated the position upon being advanced to great chamberlain. So that Lisle might continue on the Borders, the King temporarily appointed Sir Francis Bryan of the privy chamber to be vice-admiral and commanded him to sail to the Firth of Forth with ten ships to harass Scottish trade. Lisle remained in the North through April, 1543, to assure that the rapport he had established with Arran might bear all possible fruit, but his importance was diminished in February with the arrival at Newcastle of the Duke of Suffolk, the King's lieutenant.[14]

Lisle's correspondence from the Borders sheds valuable light on a personality all too frequently shrouded behind formal rhetoric. Lisle often called attention to his own inadequacies and at times supported them with enough elaboration and logic to suggest that his modesty was not feigned. His reply to Hertford's letter announcing his appointment as lord high admiral contains a typical example of self-effacement; Lisle declared himself most "unmeet and unworthy," but pledged to do his utmost to serve the King.[15] Such statements may be used to underscore his self-righteousness and false modesty, but they are better explained as accepted literary devices commonly found in the correspondence of the period. Quite different was Lisle's reaction to the departure of Bishop Tunstall, president of the council of the North, who provided invaluable counsel to the lord warden. On January 21, 1543, Lisle complained to the King that "These affairs had more need of such a wise head

as my Lord of Durham is than twenty such as I am, wherefore
I most humbly beseech your excellent highness to have in respect the insufficiency of my capacity. . . ."[16] The next day he
repeated the same fears and anxieties to the council, begged
them to send him advice, and added a most revealing observation:

> Your lordships'doth know my bringing up, I have never been
> practised nor experimented in no matters of council before this
> time. At my first coming hither it was open war; it was then more
> easier to conduce those affairs than these which be presently in
> hand. Therefore knowing mine own infirmity and the fear that it
> puts me in day and night, lest anything should pass through my
> negligence contrary to the King's majesty's pleasure, I can no less
> of my bounden duty and for mine own discharge, but still to
> trouble your lordships herewith.[17]

In this statement Lisle was specific enough to leave little
doubt about the sincerity of his sentiments. Negotiations of
the greatest importance to Henry VIII were underway to bring
about the marriage treaty that would unite the two kingdoms
under Tudor rule. To assure his success the King had gone to
inordinate lengths in promoting an English party in Scotland
that would restrain the French faction of Cardinal Beaton.
Lisle's experience in diplomatic affairs was limited, and Scotland was a new field of operations for him. Thus, it cannot be
doubted that the absence of Tunstall was a matter of genuine
concern. In reminding the council of his education or, as he put
it, "my bringing up," Lisle assumed their familiarity with his
lack of legal and literary training and with the misfortune that
had troubled his childhood. To forget the fate of his father was
impossible for John Dudley, and throughout the reign of Henry
VIII, he was continually devoted to proving his loyalty and
freedom from ambition. Obsessed with the terrifying thought
that he might incur the King's disfavor through error, he
stressed the "insufficiency of my capacity," and told the council of his constant fear "lest anything should pass through my

negligence contrary to the King's majesty's pleasure." In spite of his long presence at court, Lisle regarded himself as little more than a soldier and as one who, in the best of all worlds, would have preferred to remain, like his grandfather, a mere country gentleman. Shortly after Lisle wrote these letters to the King and council, Suffolk arrived in the North to relieve him of the burdensome responsibility. Lisle was therefore freed from the heavy yoke of duty, but in the future there would be fewer of Henry VIII's old stalwarts to rescue him, and within four years the great King himself would be gone.

Lisle's return to Westminster was greeted with new marks of favor and political power which he must have coveted highly. He was sworn a member of the Privy Council, the most powerful organ of Tudor government, on April 23, 1543, along with Sir William Paget, who also became one of the two principal secretaries. At the same time he was elected to the Order of the Garter after being nominated by all members present and voting, including Norfolk, Hertford, Audeley, and Russell. Also elected were William, Lord Parr, brother to Catherine Parr, and William Paulet, Lord St. John, the master of wards.[18] Lord Parr replaced Lisle as lord warden of the marches to allow the latter personal charge of affairs at sea for the remainder of the year.[19] The sequence of events following Lisle's return raised him to heights hitherto unknown to a member of the Dudley family and could not be interpreted as anything less than a promotion for work well done in Scotland during the past winter. Lisle's doubts about his ability were as yet unfounded.

During the summer months, Henry VIII's Scottish policies suffered a severe setback. The Treaties of Greenwich, agreed on July 1, resolved both everything and nothing at all. While the marriage and peace agreements superficially embodied the English demands, they were in practice mere scraps of paper, inasmuch as Henry neither gained control over Princess Mary nor severed the Scottish alliance with France. Even worse, the treaty helped provoke a political reaction in Scotland that saw the return of Cardinal Beaton and the French party to power.

Once again Henry faced the combined hostility of France and Scotland. The English fleet under Lisle's command, perhaps reflecting the frustration of the kingdom as a whole, managed to do little more than engage in harassing encounters with the French. A small fleet under Sir Rice Manxell met the French in July and had what Lisle described to the King as a good fight. Operations continued through November when bad weather began to curtail all activities.[20]

The year 1544 heralded the beginning of the close of Henrician England, although the King himself would have been the last to recognize it. During his last years, Henry was preoccupied with the massive attack of Hertford and Lisle on the perfidious Scots and with his own invasion of France. Both events conjured up fond memories of the past when, as a young man, Henry led a victorious English army into Tournai and rejoiced over the destruction of the Scottish host at Flodden. But not even the mighty Henry VIII could will history to repeat itself; for behind the facade of similarity, important changes were afoot that no man could direct or control.[21]

The changes taking place during the twilight of Henry's reign not only altered the political scene, but also substantially accelerated Lisle's advancement. The emergence of John Dudley as the second most powerful man in the realm after the death of Henry VIII was a direct consequence of the events of these years. The death of the King's brother-in-law, Suffolk, was one sign of the passing of the old order. Henry himself showed numerous signs of old age and physical decline, and the advancing age of Norfolk foretold a less active role for the noble who had served faithfully since the days of Wolsey. Men of Lisle's generation were called forth to assume greater responsibilities. Not only Lisle, but Hertford, Surrey, the son and heir of Norfolk, Paget, and others stood on the threshold of greater political power. The opportunities of these men increased with each passing year. Moreover, there was a strong undercurrent of Protestantism, subservient enough to the iron will of Henry, but ready to blossom forth when the barriers to radical reform fell.

As in the past, religious changes were seized upon by politicians for their own advantage. Finally, the hopes and fears of the future, both in politics and religion, centered more and more on the young prince, who most likely would ascend the throne as a minor and thereby create difficulties never before encountered by the Tudor dynasty. The men who controlled the prince at the moment Henry died would monopolize political power and rule England.

Henry's growing corpulence and disabled leg were the symbols of the expiring generation. Formerly a robust man, the King found it increasingly difficult to ride, and in the final year he had to be conveyed in a sedan chair and borne up and down stairs by a mechanical "device." Nevertheless, Henry did not let go of the reins of power and refused to admit that he was dying despite rumors predicting his death as early as September 1546.[22] The death of Suffolk, who was believed by William Thomas, author of *The Pilgrim*, to be "of more familiarity with the King than any other person," in 1545 at the age of sixty-one deprived the King of one of his oldest colleagues and forced him to find new company. While Henry was recovering from a fever of a few days duration in March 1546, Van der Delft, the Imperial ambassador, reported that the King passed "the time playing cards with the lord admiral and other intimates."[23] To what extent Lisle stepped into Suffolk's position is not clear, but their names were suggestively connected in a diplomatic dispatch announcing the latter's death: "Suffolk is dead and the Admiral is increasing in influence."[24]

The other prominent member of the old order, Norfolk, was seventy-three years old in 1546 and had seen the fortunes of his family gradually decline since the execution of Catherine Howard. Wise enough not to stake the whole future of the house of Howard on his frivolous and brilliant son, Surrey, the aged duke tried unsuccessfully to diversify his family's political ties through a marriage alliance with the Seymours. In May 1546 Norfolk asked the King "to help that a marriage might be had between my daughter and Sir Thomas Seymour," the son of

Hertford. He also suggested marriages between his grandchildren and the Seymours.[25] During the reign of Edward VI, it must have been a ruined and unhappy old man who, imprisoned in the Tower, learned of the marriage of Hertford's daughter, Anne, not to a Howard, but to the eldest son of John Dudley.

In 1544 the future was probably the brightest for the Earl of Hertford, the uncle of Prince Edward. He held no position of supremacy, but was highly esteemed by the King and Queen Catherine Parr. Hertford, the oldest of Lisle's contemporaries was a soldier and courtier well versed in the affairs of state. A survey of Hertford's widely varied activities during the final years suggests that the King wanted him in the most important and responsible positions at all times. While the King was in France besieging Boulogne, the key charge was obviously in England where a trusted and capable man was required to assure domestic tranquility and to keep a watchful eye upon developments in Scotland. So it was that the Queen was named Regent with a council composed of Hertford, Cranmer, Wriothesley, Thirlby, and Petre,[26] of whom Hertford was the only one competent to deal with either civil or foreign insurrections.[27] The Regency council held broad powers including a commission to sign bills in the King's name. After the King returned home to celebrate the addition of Boulogne to the realm, the diplomatic situation became critical as charges and countercharges were exchanged between Henry and Charles V in which each accused the other of violating the terms of the alliance against France. Hertford and Bishop Gardiner, the wily and skillful student of Wolsey, were dispatched to Brussels to meet representatives of the Emperor while other councillors negotiated with the French. Neither mission achieved much success, and the war continued through 1545.[28]

After English troops under Sir Ralph Evers rode into an ambush at Ancrum early in 1545 and fled in disarray like the Scots at Solway Moss, the Scottish situation clearly called for the strong hand of Hertford, who was in France. Ordered back to England and dispatched northward by the King, Hertford made a show of English strength by extensive devastation along the Border, and at the same time he prepared to counter an expected French invasion. The details of this campaign reveal Hertford not as a mild-mannered social reformer and idealist, but as a hard-fisted spoiler of Scotland. On October 25, he wrote to Paget and "marveled" to find Scots garrisons remaining along the Border "since all is so razed, spoiled, and burnt." Henry was well pleased with Hertford's accomplishments and rewarded him with notes of appreciation and eagerly sought-after land grants.[29]

In the following year French attacks on Boulogne required Hertford's further attention; apparently the King felt that the situation demanded a more experienced commander than the Earl of Surrey, who had failed to distinguish himself during the winter of 1545–1546. The defenses of the town were found to be in poor condition since the old fortifications had never been completed and "new devices were not able to be perfected in 1546." Hertford and Lisle, who was commander-in-chief of naval forces, inspected all the fortifications and authorized the necessary work.[30] The large army that Hertford brought over from England succeeded in keeping Boulogne in English hands, but the indecisive skirmishing that occupied the summer months clearly showed that both the English and French were exhausted and ready for peace. Henry was determined to hold his newly won prize, and the French, seeing no immediate threat of further English conquests, decided to cut their losses and negotiate in good faith.

While Hertford was the eldest of the group of aspiring courtiers and councillors, the Earl of Surrey at twenty-nine (in 1546) was the youngest. A poet of rare ability, Surrey often lapsed into a hazy dream world that curiously combined medieval chivalry and renaissance ribaldry. Wild drunken escapades with his aristocratic cronies through the streets of London offered a striking contrast to the military capabilities he possessed while serving under his father. Rewarded with an independent command at Boulogne in 1545, Surrey hoped to delight the King with sparkling victories that would catapult him to greater glories. But something went wrong. Most of the council in London, including his father, the Duke of Norfolk, were anxious to end a war that was pushing the country to the brink of bankruptcy.[31] To make matters worse, Surrey's attack of January 7, 1546, resulted in 205 killed in the English army. A contemporary, Elis Gruffydd, a member of the garrison at Calais, explained the defeat as the result of low morale from poor food and lack of pay, but "chiefly because of the earl their leader, whose head and heart were swollen with pride, arrogance, and empty confidence in his own unreasoning bravery."[32] The grumbling of a mere Welshman might be discounted or even dismissed were there no other evidence in existence. However, the dispassionate letter of Paget relieving Surrey of his command on February 20 tends to confirm Surrey's Welsh antagonist. Paget wrote, "For your reputation you should gain experience and peradventure do some notable service, in revenge for the loss of your men at last encounter with the enemies."[33] In short, Paget was telling Surrey that his best hope was to request a subordinate position in Hertford's army. Lord Herbert, the perceptive seventeenth-century scholar, remarked that Surrey "did so little satisfie our King (who lov'd no noise but of victory) that he ever after disaffected him; for which cause also he was shortly removed."[34] Surrey's star reached its zenith with the appointment to Boulogne. He returned to England not in full disgrace, but reduced to modest stature.

In addition to Hertford and Surrey, the most important men of Lisle's generation included Wriothesley, William Parr, Earl of Essex, Sir Thomas Seymour, and the two secretaries, Paget and Petre. The senior and more important of the latter, Paget, already a "master of practices," had risen under the expert tutelage of Gardiner and held a key position as secretary to the King. Except when annoyed by a bothersome case of piles, Paget represented the vigorous, efficient, sensible bureaucrat at his best.[35] While his proximity to the royal ear made him indispensable to all members of the council, he enjoyed no independent position or status as *alter rex*. Henry VIII had one master in Cardinal Wolsey and a potential one in Cromwell; during his last years, he refused to allow power to devolve upon any single councillor. A year older than Paget was the forty-one-year-old chancellor, Thomas, Lord Wriothesley, an ex-protegé of Cromwell, who leaned toward conservatism but was unable to wield decisive power.[36] The influence of both Parr and Seymour was in large measure due to their family ties with the crown. Brother to Queen Catherine, Parr had been educated at Cambridge under Cuthbert Tunstall and was best known as a soldier. Potentially the most dangerous of this group was Seymour, the younger brother of Hertford and, of course, an uncle to Prince Edward. He served with distinction at sea under Lisle's command, but entertained larger ambitions, which included a long-starved passion for Queen Catherine, a fondness for Princess Elizabeth, and interests in supplanting his brother as prospective guardian to Edward.[37]

Very little is known about the religious views of Lisle and his lay colleagues in the council. In later years Lisle described himself as one who labored mightily for the Protestant cause and suffered great dangers for his convictions. There is, however, no contemporary evidence that he risked his life or career for religious considerations. His knowledge of theology was superficial, and we may assume that his religion, like that of most of his countrymen, was the same as the King's. The passage of the Six Articles in 1539 retarded the progress of the Reformation and allowed Gardiner to represent Henry as an anti-papal Catholic when the diplomatic situation required. Yet there remained a powerful undercurrent of reformist and humanistic concern over the godly task that had been interrupted with the fall of Cromwell.

There has been a tendency to exaggerate the degree to which politics were divided along strictly religious lines. Differences between Lisle and his colleagues and the so-called "conservative" party of Norfolk and Gardiner were neither well defined nor continuous during the reign of Henry VIII; and it is questionable whether the word *party* can be applied to more than the small group of bishops, clerics, and educated laymen who were fully engulfed in the religious struggle. The great difficulty in interpreting a religious conflict is the fact that both sides claim divine justification for their cause and see the hand of the devil guiding their opponents. This polarization of religious parties had its fullest political impact only later in the sixteenth century when Catholics were fired with the Tridentine theology circulated by Jesuitical enthusiasts, and Protestant fanatics drew strength from the horrors of the Spanish Inquisition in the Netherlands and the writings of John Foxe. In the 1540s Lisle, as well as "conservatives" like Gardiner and Norfolk, obeyed the theological dictates of Henry VIII. Norfolk, for example, had condemned More and Fisher to death, crushed the Pilgrimage of Grace, and accepted monastic lands. The concept of "religious party" was an invention of Elizabethan Puritans and must be used with great caution during the earlier period.

Contemporaries regarded Queen Catherine and Archbishop Cranmer as the focal points of the Protestant cause at court. The Queen, although not a full-fledged humanist in the Erasmian sense, was one of the best educated women of a generation in which female intellectuals were highly suspect. Her *Prayers or Meditacions* (1545) can scarcely be classed as an heretical tract since preceding the prayers is a sixty-page meditation borrowed from the *Imitation of Christ*; nevertheless, the Queen later became fully identified with the reforming tradition.[38] Her intimates at court included the Countesses of Hertford and Lisle, who probably shared her religious convictions.[39] The Spanish chronicler described Catherine as "quieter than any of the young wives the King had had, and as she knew more of the world, she always got on pleasantly with the King, and had no caprices, and paid much honor to Madam Mary and the wives of the nobles."[40]

Why the King allowed Gardiner and Lord Chancellor Wriothesley to draw up articles of treason against Catherine is unknown. Learning of the plot to remove her, the Queen drew upon all of her many female charms, and succeeded in regaining Henry's favor. She promised to meddle no more in religion, but the King insisted, "Not so (by St. Mary), . . . you are become a Doctor, Kate, to instruct us." Her persistence in renouncing religious zeal pleased the King, who closed the affair saying, "Then we are perfect friends again." When Gardiner, Wriothesley, and forty of the guard arrived to take Catherine to the Tower, the King angrily turned them away. In relating this episode Lord Herbert observed that "Winchester, who (it was thought) chiefly endeavoured her ruin, did himself not long after fall into the King's disfavor."[41]

The Henrician religious compromise was clearly threatened from both sides during the years 1544 to 1547, and it is a mistake to conclude that either ideology was on the threshold of total victory. The King himself leaned toward the earlier humanistic reform tradition, which he supported throughout his reign. After Reginald Pole's withdrawal to the Continent, the humanistic tradition in England came to acquire strong Protestant leanings.[42] The religious issue in Germany was also far from decided. The Emperor had notions of church reform that ran contrary to those of the Pope, and in 1545 the Council of Trent had only begun its deliberations. The Lutheran princes, still hopeful of winning Charles V to the cause of reform, were not to suffer crushing defeat at his hands until the summer of 1547. And the Jesuits (founded in 1540), the strong arm of militant papalism, were only in their infancy. Consequently, so long as Henry reigned, there could be only one religious party, the party of the King, with two wings constantly modulating themselves to keep in tune with the changing fortunes of the Reformation.

For Lisle and Englishmen of all classes and religious persuasions, the hopes and anxieties of the future centered on the young Prince. In large measure the destiny of England was determined by the King's decision to give his heir a humanistic education. Henry had long kept in touch with university scholars through Dr. William Butts, his personal physician, who in the spring of 1544 recommended that John Cheke, a fellow of St. John's, Cambridge should become one of Edward's tutors. Cheke, a man possessed of great intellectual powers, was said "to have laid the very foundations of the [new] learning in that college." He had held a Greek lectureship from the King; among his students were Roger Ascham, Sir Thomas Smith, and William Cecil.[43] The choice of tutors for the Prince reflected Henry's own inclination toward humanistic religious reform, and, whether he willed it or not, the Prince grew into a staunch and even priggish Protestant. Cheke's stimulating teaching coupled with a pleasant family life, presided over by the Queen and a doting father, contributed to Edward's intellectual and social development.

As the uncle of the Prince, Hertford held a unique position among the King's councillors. He had only to continue in high favor with Henry and await the accession of his nephew. If Hertford did no more than hold his own, he stood in a strong position to become guardian of the next King and had excellent opportunities for full political authority during the minority. His success required no plots, intrigues, nor even much overt action. The possibilities of ecclesiastical rule in the future were slight, for Gardiner had never received the complete confidence of Henry VIII, and Cranmer clearly lacked the capacity for political leadership. Lisle must have recognized Hertford's potential power, and he continued close ties with the comrade with whom he had first campaigned in 1523.

Lisle commanded large numbers of men and ships in his capacity as lord high admiral and increased his influence during the war years of 1544 to 1546.[44] Preparatory to the invasion of Scotland in 1544, there was the shuffling of commanders that was becoming a veritable leitmotif of Henrician strategy. The King wrote Suffolk in the North at the end of January that he was being replaced by Hertford "to the intent you might prepare yourself to pass over with us into France." For the more important of the two ventures of the year, Henry VIII wanted the old stalwarts once again at his side. Suffolk and the aging, but indefatigable Norfolk headed up what was to be the King's last conquest on the Continent, while the Scottish campaign was consigned to Hertford, the most experienced of the younger commanders. Before it was clear that Suffolk would leave the North, he requested the "help and counsel" of Hertford, Lisle, and Sir John Gage, comptroller of the household. If Lisle could not be spared, he wished the King would send William Parr, Earl of Essex, in his place. "In this part," Suffolk explained, "I ensure your grace there is but little help of such men as shall be requisite for such an enterprise." The toughened old veteran knew the value of first rate commanders and had unsuccessfully requested Lisle's services the previous September.[45]

Edward Hall's account of the combined land and sea attack gives the impression of precise coordination between Hertford and Lisle. "This year the King sent a great army into Scotland by sea, and he made the Earl of Hertford lieutenant general of the same and the Viscount Lisle, high admiral, which valiant captains so sped them that the third day of May the lord admiral arrived with all his fleet which was 200 sail in the Fryth, where he landed divers of his men and there took divers vessels. . . ."[46] What escaped the chronicler's eye was a curious incident which, had it taken a different course, might have ended the career of John Dudley. The admiral left Harwich with ten sail on March 25; five days later Hertford wrote to the Privy Council that Lisle's arrival at Tynemouth was awaited and expressed concern over a storm that might have delayed him. Hertford reported to the King on April 1 and again on April 4 that Lisle had still not arrived, and because of this the army under his command could not attack.[47] Had the admiral perished at sea? Or had he been taken prisoner by the French? Lisle's arrival on April 20, nearly a month after his departure, was anticlimactic. Hertford and Lisle, having made the rendezvous, merely informed Henry VIII that the whole fleet had arrived, and stated, "Now we make all haste we can to set your majesties' army to the sea."[48] If Lisle made any written explanation of his

delay, it has disappeared along with so much other vital information about the man.

Lisle led the English fleet into Leith, bearing on the foretop
mast of the "Rose Lyon" a flag of St. George's cross. Landing
about two miles from the city, Hertford took command of the
whole force while Lisle led the forward troops. Defended by
six thousand Scots, Leith fell to the English after "three great
battles," and yielded "such riches" as the invaders thought not
to have found in any town of Scotland. Lisle, marching the victorious army onward to Edinburgh, passed through the suburbs
to the principal gate of the city, which was well fortified with
men and ordnance. According to Hall, the ordnance was "shot
off so fast" that some of the English were killed in the streets
while others began to "shirk and retire." Lord William Howard
was struck with an arrow above the cheek, but it was "so faint
and weakly shot that he was little hurt." Hertford had hoped
that Edinburgh would surrender to him; when it did not he was
determined "utterly to ruinate and destroy the said town by
fire, which thing immediately was attempted, but because
night was come, the army withdrew to their camp." On the following day the army "set fire where none was before, which continued that day and two days after burning." Both Holyrood
Abbey and House were burnt and devastated. The massive
Castle of Edinburgh, however, remained impregnable, and the
commanders had to content themselves with pillaging the city
and the surrounding countryside.[49]

With the King's mission of destruction completed, Lisle
was no longer required in the North. As he returned, no further
opportunities for devastation were neglected. Lisle informed
Henry VIII that he had appointed certain ships "to sail along
the coast towards St. Andrews, and as they pass with the 'Galie
Subtle' and their boats to set some good number of men aland
to burn such towns and villages on the coast as they may conveniently."[50] He also promised to deal with any French ships
that might be found. For all of his exertions Lisle received the
gratitude of the King and continued to be held in high per-

sonal esteem by his immediate superior, Hertford, who wrote of him to Henry:

> I can do no less than to recommend him unto your highness as one that has served you hardely, wisely, diligently, painfully, and as obediently as any that I have seen, most humbly beseeching your majesty that he may perceive by your highness that I have not forgotten his good service.[51]

Lisle next turned to sweep the channel free of French merchantmen, as Henry VIII's army crossed over to besiege Boulogne. The royal navy, Henry's own cherished creation, fought with distinction under the lord admiral, and it was this force according to James A. Williamson, that played "the decisive part in shaping and terminating the war."[52] The town and castle of Boulogne capitulated on September 14, 1544, surrendering all artillery, powder, and munitions. Lisle was chosen to remain through the winter and supervise the building of fortifications against French counter-attacks. Numbering some 5500 men and officers, the garrison included 1353 hackbutters, many of whom were German mercenaries. The force was plagued by shortages of food about which Lisle complained desperately to the council at Calais. Back in England, the King grew anxious about the building of ditches and bulwarks and questioned Lisle's use of supplies. By the end of November, Lisle was able to report considerable progress. In a letter to Henry, he stated that the victuals were in good condition and that "Base Boulogne" was beginning "to be a handsome town again." The ditches and trenches constructed about it drew the moisture out of the streets and proved "a great health and cleanness."[53]

The following year witnessed the threat of a massive French invasion. Hertford was sent to Boulogne where he appointed Sir Thomas Poynings to replace Lisle. The King wanted the admiral to take personal charge of the fleet, because the enemy was preparing "to enter the seas with a main army 'to invade our dominions and impeach our enterprise.' "[54] In June 1545

Lisle struck the first blow and launched an ambitious but unsuccessful naval attack. "He proposed to convert 30 merchantmen, which had been brought to the Downs as prizes, into fire ships and to send them in with the tide upon the enemy's anchorage at Havre. The prizes designed for this purpose escaped in a storm, but Lisle, not choosing to be disappointed, sailed without them and ventured himself into the Seine, within shot of the French."[55] Lisle's ships fired their guns, and the French galleys came out to attack. After two assaults the smaller galleys could no longer withstand the rising wind and the rages of the sea. The English fleet, on the other hand, feared shallow water and returned to Portsmouth.[56]

Lisle deployed the fleet the next month at Portsmouth to resist the main French thrust near the Isle of Wight. The *Henry Grace à Dieu*, a large ship of a thousand tons, carried Lisle's flag. The situation was perilous enough to require the presence of the Privy Council and the King himself, who took Van der Delft on board the flagship to meet Lisle. The ambassador later wrote to Charles V that "the admiral received me very cordially, and asked me to dinner for the following day, when I was very handsomely entertained." The combined English naval and land forces successfully drove off the French invaders, in spite of the loss of the *Mary Rose*, which sank with her captain and most of those on board. Later another attempted invasion was thwarted along the Sussex coast. In September, Lisle led a successful attack on Treport in Normandy. Although this town was a minor objective, it was burned together with three or four nearby villages, several homes of the aristocracy, and an abbey. Some twenty ships in the haven of Treport were also burned. Having lost only three men, Lisle returned unresisted to England.[57] Lisle won no great naval victory during 1545, but through his efforts and those of his countrymen, the French invasion was a miserable failure.

The final year of the war and of Henry's reign was not fruitful militarily. Since Hertford and Lisle were both anxious to end hostilities, they jointly recommended an attack on Estaples to "annoy" the enemy and "thereby the sooner have peace." Hertford was again in France with an army of 30,000 men, while Lisle prepared a fleet "a third more powerful" than the one that had frustrated the enemy the previous year.[58] Most of the planning for the defense of Boulogne was arranged by the two veterans, occasionally with the help of Sir Thomas Seymour, the vice-admiral. In March Lisle was rewarded with the lavish title, "Lieutenant General of the Army and Armada upon the Sea in outwards parts against the French."[59]

Soon afterwards Lisle and Paget had a misunderstanding about admiralty funds. Paget found the treasury of the admiralty could not account for £2000 and asked Lisle, "If you know where it is bestowed, you will write to me thereof." Lisle replied that he had received only half that amount and had spent it on new coats and wages. He admitted borrowing £2000 but "on his own name," and he claimed to have repaid the same. Defending his integrity, Lisle declared, "Other than this I never meddled with his majesty's money, nor never desired to meddle with any of his highness's money, I can so evil keep my own." This apparently satisfied Paget and ended the investigation. That no hard feelings lingered was evidenced by Paget's comment only a month later that Lisle was "a worthy gentleman and given to serve the King as much as any man I ever saw."[60]

The diplomatic history of these years is a series of confused and contradictory double-dealings and intrigues on the part of all concerned. Henry invaded France in alliance with the Emperor, who deserted him by signing a separate peace with France at Crêpy on September 18, 1544. The English attempted to revive the Imperial alliance the next year. At the same time, however, Richard Bucler, secretary to Queen Catherine was sent into Germany to negotiate secretly with the Lutheran princes.[61]

Until late in 1546 Lisle was highly regarded by the King's untrustworthy Imperial allies. Van der Delft was invited in November 1545 to stand as sponsor at the baptism of Lisle's daughter, Lady Catherine Dudley. The godmothers of the child represented both religious groups; the one being Princess Mary and the other the widowed Duchess of Suffolk. The ambassador particularly enjoyed his conversation at the christening with Mary, who showed hìm "much honor and compliment" and spoke very well "in various languages."[62] Early in the next year Van der Delft referred to Lisle in a letter as one who "at present deals well and promptly with our claims."[63] Soon afterwards Lisle's brother, Andrew, was sent by Henry to carry a gift from the King to the Queen Dowager of Hungary. Van der Delft wrote to the Queen telling her of Andrew Dudley's departure and advised that since Lisle "is said to have on several occasions favored the subjects of the Emperor," she should thank him through his brother.[64]

Lisle's most significant diplomatic task was to negotiate a peace with France that would permit Henry to retain Boulogne. Together with Paget and Dr. Nicholas Wotton, Dean of York and Canterbury, Lisle held talks with the French admiral and President Raymond of the Parlement of Rouen. Treachery and stalling tactics retarded progress, and, at one point, Lisle told Henry that "no trust" should be given to the overtures of Francis I. Yet it was clearly recognized that both countries needed peace badly.[65] During the protracted negotiations, Lisle found time to hunt hare with Raymond and feast with Secretary Paget on "red deer" and delectable puddings, which the admiral "liketh well." On May 12, 1546, Paget complained that Lisle had left the parley for the Downs and interrupted negotiations with the French admiral, who would meet with no one else since he had begun talks with Lisle. Paget reprimanded Lisle for this saying, "You asked my advice and I send it; but I see that great men sometimes ask advice only for 'manners' sake." Lisle immediately retorted that he had been ordered by the King to take command of the navy but was returning to rejoin Paget after transferring the command to Lord William Howard. He had also made certain improper statements about Henry's willingness to accept French terms and desire to stall for time. He begged Petre, the junior secretary, to "wropp upp my follys to gythers and kepe theym to your selffe." Lisle similarly resented Paget's whispering special information to Raymond. One explanation for the difficulties between the two long-time allies may have been Paget's illness. Neither the dispute nor the sickness were serious, however, and Lisle wrote afterwards to his colleague, "I am glad you have taken the purge. The ladies and all the rest received your recommendations with thanks and long for your return."[66]

Peace was finally concluded by the Treaty of Camp, which was signed on June 7, 1546, by Lisle, Paget, and Wotton. The terms of the treaty permitted the English to hold Boulogne for eight years when the French would buy it back for two million gold crowns. Henry, whose conquests Lisle praised as "a memory to the world," was satisfied with the outcome and thanked the negotiators for their accomplishments.[67]

Lisle's next assignment was to travel to Paris to obtain Francis' signature on the treaty. Headed by Lisle, the embassy included thirty dignitaries, the most notable of whom were Wotton, Tunstall, Sir Henry Knyvet, the Earl of Rutland, and Andrew Dudley. On July 18, the party was welcomed everywhere with presents of wine and wild fowl. Several delays were required enroute because of diplomatic complications developing out of the French admiral's reciprocal embassy to London. Bishop Tunstall's age was used as an argument for the late arrival in Paris. Arriving only on July 25, Lisle's delegation was met and banqueted at the abbey of St. Denis. A few miles from the city M. de Lavall, "one of the greatest inheritors in all France," greeted the English with sixty gentlemen; later they were met by the provost of the merchants and many burgesses on horseback. Lisle wrote that "a great supper" was prepared at their lodgings and on the following day a banquet, "all at the town's cost." In the evening Cardinal de Medon entertained the embassy in the Louvre. Lisle remarked on the following day, "The Cardinal of Medon made us great cheer last night, with meat and drink, and good company of ladies and gentlewomen, but the plays and pastime were spoilt by the crowd." The cardinal excused this by calling attention to the "devotion the people had to see the Englishmen which came with so joyful news unto them."[68]

At Fontainebleau Francis impressed Lisle and his compatriots with the splendors of the French court and made their cheer "exceeding great." In accepting the treaty the King acknowledged the whole royal title of Henry except "King of France," which would have been utterly impossible. "In the chapel the French King himself read the oath with a loud voice declaring Henry, Defender of the Faith, and Supreme Head of the Church of England and Ireland in presence of six cardinals and 'divers others'. . . ." Francis then showed Lisle, Tunstall, and Wotton his library with books translated from Greek and feasted them at another great banquet. The whole affair was an unqualified triumph.[69]

On the return trip Lisle sent a most amusing note to his wife via Paget. The secretary must have smiled as he read: "As I lack leisure to write to my wife, I shall desire you to make her my recommendations; and where she wrote for some goldsmith's work from Paris, I pray God I may have enough to bring home myself. I assure you this journey hath been extremely chargeable, after such sort as I think I shall be fain to hide me in a corner for seven years after. I have borrowed here in Paris almost £500 and all little enough."[70] We are left wondering whether Lisle lacked courage and required Paget as an intermediary in handling his wife.

The King rewarded Lisle for his military and diplomatic achievements with generous land grants. He was clearly one of the two most capable and trusted commanders in the realm. His rather meager conquests fail to elevate him to the ranks of the great seamen such as Drake, Hawkins, or Howard of Effingham, but we may assume that Henry would not have depended upon him so heavily had better admirals been forthcoming. As a diplomat Lisle gained needed experience and acquitted himself well. His growing importance was further reflected by regular, but not constant, attendance at meetings of the Privy

Council. Obviously, Lisle's long tours of duty outside England precluded as active a role in domestic politics as would have been possible in peacetime.

The year 1546 contained a sequence of events which might have indicated, at least superficially, that the political fortunes of Lisle, Hertford, and their colleagues were in danger; but which in fact merely confirmed their positions. John Hooper, the future Bishop of Gloucester, wrote from Strassbourg in January what appeared to be an accurate description of the English religious situation, for indeed Catholic beliefs "were never before held by the people in greater esteem than at the present moment."[71] So it seemed to the reformer lodged on the Rhine. The rumors circulating about yet another royal divorce led to the attack on Queen Catherine, but talk about the growing favor of the Duchess of Suffolk came to nothing.[72] Protestant pessimism was strengthened by the failure of Cranmer's plans for further religious reform. And most apparent to observers from overseas and to later writers like John Foxe was the wave of religious persecution.

The arrest and subsequent execution of the heretic Anne Askew cast a shadow of suspicion over her intimates at court, who included the Countess of Hertford and the Duchess of Suffolk. In response to Sir Richard Rich's examination, Anne replied that she knew no others of her sect, and when questioned specifically about the ladies of the court, she answered, "If I should pronounce anything against them, that I were not able to prove it." She stubbornly and defiantly refused to recant even after Lisle, Parr, Gardiner, and Nicholas Shaxton, Bishop of Salisbury, tried to persuade her to abandon her fanatical course. Lisle, who was abroad part of the time, played the role of an orthodox Henrician; along with Gardiner he entreated Anne to confess the truth of transubstantiation.[73]

Explanation of the outburst of religious persecution in the summer of 1546 is difficult, if not impossible. The return of Gardiner from abroad furnishes only a partial answer at best, as does Dr. Edward Crome's intemperate sermon against the doctrine of purgatory. The diplomatic scene likewise provides only limited insight. Before peace had been concluded with France, it was necessary for England to make an appearance of orthodoxy in order to strengthen the Imperial alliance. But peace was signed with France on June 7, eliminating the need for further Imperial courtship. Thus diplomatic reasons hardly required Anne's execution on July 16, unless it is argued that the Treaty of Camp was only tentative and subject to violation by both parties. Henry VIII's life-long policy of keeping several balls in the air comes the closest to offering an acceptable explanation. The King had never been averse to sacrificing human life for reasons of state, and there was no reason for granting the fanatical Anne Askew special consideration. And should the persecution of Protestantism cease to be advantageous, he could always turn to the German princess, who had been consulted the previous year, and parade forth the Queen and his devoted Archbishop Cranmer.[74]

Lisle returned from the French mission on August 12 and was present in the Privy Council the next day.[75] Ignoring the peace treaty, Ambassador Van der Delft still believed the fortunes of the Imperial alliance were high. He wrote on the 16th that the principal members of the council, Gardiner, Wriothesley, and Paget were firmly attached to Charles V and that there was no indication of a Protestant alliance. Four days later Lisle's counterpart, the French admiral, arrived in England to receive Henry's ratification of the peace treaty. In the course of the celebration and pomp, Lisle and the admiral became involved in a quarrel concerning a captured French galley. The King only offered to restore the hull of the galley, but not the slaves since they had already been given their liberty. Lisle and the admiral had "warm words, but they ended friendly." The amity of the admirals notwithstanding, a renewal of the war threatened. On September 10, Lisle inspected ships in the Thames that were being equipped and armed in haste, and reports circulated that men were being levied in Kent.[76] The dispute centered around French unwillingness to demolish forti-

fications near Boulogne, and the subsequent English reinforcement of the town's garrison.

It was at this point that Van der Delft realized for the first
time the winds of change and reversed his earlier appraisal of
Lisle. He had sent no reports between August 16 and September 3, when he wrote that "certain persons had come into great
favor with the King, whom I wished were as far away as they
were last year;" these persons were Lisle and Hertford. Ten
days later the ambassador discovered a Protestant party led
by Lisle and Hertford which was rapidly gaining favor with
the King. What had happened to cause the ambassador's
about-face? Gardiner was still active and in apparent favor.
Neither Surrey nor his father had been sent to the Tower. The
best answer is that the ambassador saw for the first time the
strength of Hertford's position, Lisle's favor with the King, and
the undercurrent of reform that had not been extinguished by
a few spectacular persecutions. He may have overlooked these
men because they had been out of the country so much in the
past two years. But where would he expect to find the King's
top military commanders in time of war? Indeed, Van der
Delft had become the victim of his own self-deception;[77] he
simply had failed to realize that Henry VIII could play a double game and take both sides seriously.

Although the war scare gradually subsided, the peace continued to be uneasy. On September 19, the French ambassador
wrote Francis that Hertford was displeased by the rumors of
war preparations and had explained that the Boulogne garrison was merely undergoing a routine reinforcement. The ships
that were being armed under Lisle's supervision were actually
intended for Scotland where the English were being pillaged.
Lisle himself became ill and withdrew from court into the
country to recover. At a meeting of the council at his house in
London on the 20th, he was too ill to peruse a letter concerning
admiralty affairs and asked Gardiner, Wriothesley, and the
other members to proceed as they thought proper. Four days
later it was announced that he would be away for a month.

Only on November 1 did he return to the Privy Council. The French ambassador had another explanation for Lisle's absence, and remarked that he had been away "because of a blow he gave to the Bishop of Winchester in full council, for which he has been in trouble and danger."[78]

Lisle played no decisive role in the final three months of the King's life. He continued in high favor with the King and maintained his previous connections with Hertford and Paget. There is indeed little contemporary documentary evidence suggesting a plot, a coup, or any kind of cloak-and-dagger proceedings during this period. Even Ambassador Selve, who usually had his ear to the ground, qualified his references to "dissension" in the council and inquiries about treasonous statements with the comment, "Writes thus, but cannot vouch for it."[79] Van der Delft completed his about-face when he wrote that neither Lisle nor Hertford had "ever been very favorably disposed" toward the interests of the Emperor. He did testify to their growing influence and popularity, a discovery that was hardly of staggering significance at the end of December. Moreover, he curiously connected the termination of religious persecution with the growth of heretical sects and predicted that steps would be taken "in favor of getting rid of the bishops."[80]

Much of the speculation about the sinister designs of a Protestant party centers around the arrest and trial of the Earl of Surrey and his father. This thesis presumes that Henry could not have eliminated the Howards without the assistance and conspiracy of powerful members of the council such as Hertford, Lisle, and Paget, a contention hardly consistent with the King's previous facility for removing persons threatening the Tudor monarchy. A better explanation is that Surrey simply destroyed himself and his father in an unwise scheme to regain the position of prominence his father had lost through old age and to advance himself to heights his own achievements had not warranted. His crime was primarily against the royal person, not members of the council. While Hertford and Lisle might assume that time was on their side, Surrey was forced to show his hand in the last months or stand idly by and watch power slip away.

Testimony presented during the trial was filled with vague, incomplete, and often suggestive statements that tempt the imagination of the historian. Early in July, Lisle wrote to Paget that he had received a letter from Surrey containing "so many parables that I do not perfectly understand it" and requested that the letter be shown to the King. The deposition of Hugh Ellis at the trial offers more possibilities for speculation, for he knew about "discord" between Surrey and Lisle to whom "he did write his mind in a letter." Likewise tempting is the peculiar reference: "Things in common: Paget, Hertford, Admiral, Denny." But where does all of this lead? Absolutely nowhere. The preponderance of evidence suggests that Surrey committed an overt act of treason under existing law and expressed a desire to gain control of the Prince before the King was dead. Lisle's role in the whole affair was that of a privy councillor and juror, neither more nor less.[81]

The execution of Surrey, the disgrace of his father, and Gardiner's poorly timed quarrel with the King helped decide the issue of Edward's minority in favor of some form of collective rule with strong possibilities for a Protectorate under Hertford.[82] Before learning of Henry's death, the former Imperial ambassador, Chapuys, who had left England twenty months before to re-enter retirement, observed that Hertford and Lisle would have "the management of affairs, because, apart from the King's affection for them, and other reasons, there are no other nobles of a fit age and ability for the task." It would be difficult, if not impossible, to present any analysis of the structure of politics at the death of Henry VIII that would be more plausible than that of Chapuys. After Hertford there was not a single man in the kingdom whose proven capacity for leadership exceeded that of Lisle. Of the future no one could be certain, and no one knew this better than Eustace Chapuys, for his long experience had taught him that the English are "so changeable and inconsistent that they vary, I will not say from year to year, but every moment."[83] The next reign would also bear out this prophecy.

III / John Dudley,
Earl of Warwick,
and the Protectorate

When Henry VIII died in January 1547 the crown passed to
his son, Edward VI, who was nine years of age. It was possible
for a child to inherit the throne and reign, but he obviously
could not rule. In the crisis that followed, Lord Lisle, as well as
others holding office under the deceased king, had the responsibility of providing leadership in the absence of royal initiative.
The immediate situaton was complicated by Henry's last will
and testament which attempted to organize his son's government. Although the political crisis was temporarily resolved by
the creation of the Protectorate, instability threatened throughout Edward's six-year reign.

The events immediately preceding and following the death of
Henry VIII have been the subject of both controversy and confusion, but this has not been due to a dearth of serious historical scholarship. At the turn of the century, A. F. Pollard
addressed himself to the question and was followed at nearly
equal intervals of thirty years by Kenneth Pickthorn and L. B.
Smith.[1] The difficulties centered on an event and a document:
the passing of the King at two of the morning on Friday, January 28, 1547, and the royal will. Did Henry recognize that his
life was drawing to a close during the hectic final years of the

1. EDWARD VI AND THE POPE

reign? What kind of political legacy did he wish to bequeath to his son? In answering these questions one is confounded by a lack of conclusive evidence. As Smith has suggested, the activities at the end of the reign augured life, not death. The old King, far from preparing himself for the grave, was in fact planning new aggression into Scotland and contemplating a diplomatic revolution that would have had far-reaching political and religious implications. Within England leadership was passing into the hands of Hertford and Lisle, who had become prominent only since the fall of Cromwell. The formidable Howard family was ruined by the folly of the gifted Surrey, while the future influence of Stephen Gardiner, Bishop of Winchester, outside his own diocese seemed seriously impaired. With the two experienced commanders, Hertford and Lisle, firmly in harness and the old chieftains either weakened or removed, the country was ready to embark on any military schemes that were attractive to Henry VIII.

If the will did little more than confirm the political tendencies of the past, it nevertheless raised a host of related questions. The document itself is unambiguous.[2] It named as councillors for the minority of Edward VI all of the leading figures of the Henrician council except Gardiner and, of course, Norfolk, who was under sentence of death. The most curious aspect of the will was the exclusion of the Stuarts from the succession in favor of the Suffolk line, but this was of no immediate significance since three heirs of Henry's body had prior claims. More important is the question of the King's intent in drawing up the will. Did the despotic old man, as Pollard believed, hope to rule from the grave through his appointed council? Or, as Smith argued, was the will a sword of Damocles suspended over the heads of ambitious councillors and courtiers by which Henry hoped to control the various personalities in the council? Of the two alternatives the Smith thesis makes better sense with one small amendment: That is, besides being a political instrument, the will was probably not intended to be the King's last testament, but merely a temporary expedient pending an expected recovery. If the date of signing is assumed to be January 27, rather than December 30, there is a further possibility that the King had no time to prepare a final will even had he wished to do so.

The will was modeled on a previous version and provided for heirs by Queen Catherine or another wife. Certainly a man who knew he was dying would be unlikely to entertain the prospect of begetting future children (unless he assumed conception had already taken place) or the sheer fantasy of another spouse. Moreover, provisions for the council were unrealistic in that there was no arrangement for replacing those who might become ill or die before Edward came of age. Among the most prominent men named were Cranmer, Paulet, Russell, and Tunstall, all of whom were as old or older than the King himself. Each, by the standards of the sixteenth century, was living on borrowed time and might be expected to be removed from the scene in the near future. The fact that all managed to outlive the young King can hardly be attributed to Henry's political acumen. Regardless of what may be said against Henry the man and the King, few have regarded him as a fool. Yet, if the will is to be regarded as a political testament for his son and the Tudor dynasty, it would be hard to acquit him of bungling and dereliction of duty. It is more plausible to believe that down to his very last hours Henry VIII was too stubborn and egotistical to envisage a future in which he would not rule.

As astute a politician as Henry knew full well that the success of the Tudor monarchy was predicated upon strong personal rule by the sovereign. His failure to provide a mature heir created a problem for which his experience provided no remedy. Fear of a return to fifteenth-century disorder helps to explain the King's proceedings of the 1530s as well as Henry's reluctance to plan for the succession of his son. Events in Scotland after Solway Moss only underscored the danger, and the Scottish solution of a Regency was no solution at all. Although the question of a minority was unique for the Tudors, it had been a stumbling block for an orderly succession in the recent past. The King could find little comfort or assurance in recalling the history of the reigns of Henry V or Edward IV. Henry V had hoped to safeguard his dynasty by appointing his younger brother, Humphrey, Duke of Gloucester, to be Regent during the minority of Henry VI. The magnates of the first Parliament of the new reign proceeded to reject the deceased King's plan and to grant limited and ambiguous powers to Gloucester under the title of a Protectorate. This defiance of Henry V's will only emphasized the wisdom of the adage, "woe to the land where the King is a child." Edward IV followed the logic of Henry V in entrusting the care of Prince Edward to Richard, Duke of Gloucester. Again the greatest misfortune befell both the dynasty and the country.

The political situation in 1547 was not analogous to the fifteenth-century minorities, because both Henry V and Edward IV had brothers to whom a Regency might be granted. Henry VIII had none. The only mature person of the blood royal at his death was the thirty-one-year-old Princess Mary, who had never been active in government and was assigned no responsibilities during the minority of her younger brother. Queen Catherine, the only mother Edward had ever known, had been appointed Regent in 1544 when Henry invaded France. Yet being only stepmother to the heir, she was in no position to play the role of Elizabeth Woodville at the death of Edward IV. It was surprising, however, that both Mary and Catherine were excluded in the will from any participation in the minority government. Hertford, like Earl Rivers, was uncle to a young King and held a position in the country not unlike that of Gloucester in 1483. But the experience of the Yorkist era scarcely offered a model worthy of imitation. Of all the possibilities the one chosen, that of a balanced council operating on the principle of majority rule, made the least sense. It was not based upon historical precedent, nor was it a realistic solution to the problem of a royal minority in the sixteenth century.

Neither the anomalies of the will nor the compelling question of the King's intentions for the minority had a direct effect upon Lord Lisle. His position after Henry's death was, strictly speaking, the same as it had been before. Lisle had been an influential member of the council and, by the terms of the will, merely retained his former status. There is not a scrap of contemporary evidence to suggest that he rejoiced at the death of the old King because it would allow him greater realization of lifelong ambitions, or that he harbored in the dark recesses of a scheming mind a grand design for a *coup d'état* to overthrow the Seymours. As he had written Paget slightly over a year before, he regarded it as his duty "to offer continual service."[3] For this Lisle had been well rewarded by Henry VIII. If he had any feelings beyond genuine remorse for the loss of a benevolent sovereign, he may have breathed a sigh of relief that he was spared the humiliation his father had suffered at the accession of the second Tudor monarch.

Lisle, like prolific men of all ages, had to provide for a growing family. Only with great difficulty had the heir of Edmund Dudley accumulated landholdings sufficient to allow him to offer continual service to the crown. By 1547 Lisle had a landed interest in some twenty-six counties in England plus holdings in Wales.[4] In addition to building a family estate, a good sixteenth-century father was expected to arrange marriages for each of his offspring, secure promising positions for his sons and sons-in-law, if required, and in general look out for any members of the family who might be less well-placed than himself. The family of John and Jane Dudley numbered five sons and two daughters in 1547. The eldest, named after his father, was known successively as Lord Lisle and the Earl of Warwick during the reign of Edward VI. The next three sons, Ambrose, the Elizabethan Earl of Warwick, Robert, Earl of Leicester, and Guildford, future husband to Lady Jane Grey, eventually rivaled their father in renown. The family also included a fifth son, Henry, and the daughters, Mary, mother of Sir Philip Sidney, and Catherine. Closely connected to the family circle was Lisle's devoted brother, Andrew, who saw service as a diplomat, soldier, admiral, and as a handyman about the court. All of the children became marriageable during Edward's reign, and Andrew, a bachelor, was probably a perennial candidate for matrimony.

Lisle's advancement under Henry VIII had not been rapid, but it had been a steady ascent in which courtly recognition and military experience led to ever-increasing political power. He had chosen his friends wisely. His colleague, Hertford, possessed the key to continued favor during the young King's minority, while Paget had the staying power of a shrewd, calculating politique. If Gardiner and the Howards were in fact Lisle's enemies, these too had been well-chosen; for Henry VIII removed both potential threats by his last acts.

Whether Lisle liked it or not, his position after the death of the King could not be identical to what it had been before. Henry VIII's death left a gaping hole in the Tudor constitution and created an inevitable political vacuum. Each of the leading members of Edward's council was thrust into the forefront of politics in a way that was totally impossible under either Henry VII or Henry VIII. Therefore, from the moment of the King's death, Lisle's position and future were fundamentally changed without the least stirring on his own part.

The political maelstrom in which he found himself at the accession of Edward VI is one that has been often described, but rarely analyzed.[5] Unless a preliminary attempt is made to determine the substance of politics, however incomplete it may be, the realities of the reign and the role of the Dudleys will remain irretrievably obscured and confused. The best recent studies of Tudor politics have been concerned with the lower strata of activity, primarily with questions of patronage and parliamentary representation. As valuable and necessary as this work is, it sheds very little light on the mechanics of politics at the policy-making level. Moreover, before 1558 the House of Commons did not regularly initiate legislation; nor was Lord Chesterfield's advice to his son two centuries later, that "you must first make a figure there if you would make a figure in your country," relevant to Lisle's age.[6]

Tudor England was ruled by the King and Privy Council, and councillors like Lisle were only intermittently concerned with parliamentary elections and management. Leading politicians exercised power by a careful distribution of patronage, but the crown possessed the greatest power to advance men to high office, as evidenced by the career of John Dudley and his rise through the favor of Henry VIII. During the reign of Edward VI, the wealth of the crown was more than adequate to sustain and enrich the chief ministers. Hertford and Lisle did not have to engage in direct competition for offices or lands; there was enough for both. The men at the top lived in a world completely divorced from those who had to struggle desperately for an appointment as humble as keeper of a royal woods. They played for higher stakes and were not always offered the luxury of retirement to the country or blissful oblivion.

The men holding positions of greatest responsibility by no means constituted a monolithic group. Some moved in and out of office with the ease of those of lesser rank. In 1553, for example, Northumberland was the only peer executed for attempting to divert the succession to Lady Jane Grey. William Paulet, Marquess of Winchester, succeeded Somerset as lord treasurer in 1550 and retained the position until his death in 1572, notwithstanding his support of Northumberland and his return to Roman Catholicism under Mary. The same is true of John Russell, Earl of Bedford, who served as lord privy seal under both Edward and Mary. William Parr, Marquess of Northampton, on the other hand, spent the Marian years in a political wilderness only to be reinstated by Elizabeth. Even Henry Grey, Duke of Suffolk, father of Lady Jane and ally of Northumberland, was not executed until after Wyatt's rebellion. Others like the Earls of Cumberland and Rutland were only periodically involved in the responsibilities of the central government and more often confined themselves to the shires where they held lands. Few of the Edwardian nobles belonged to the ancient feudal aristocracy; the only peer in the council with a peerage of twelve years standing was Henry Fitzalan, twelfth

Earl of Arundel. During the short reign former principal secretaries were elevated to baronies and earldoms. Humble families were dignified with greater rapidity than at any other time in the sixteenth century. The highest positions involved the greatest responsibility and risk, a fact well illustrated by recalling that each of the three dukes created during Edward's reign, Somerset, Northumberland, and Suffolk, was executed.

The Tudor system—if the expression means anything at all—was rule by a strong monarch manipulating Parliament and the council in the interests of the state. With the throne occupied by a nine-year-old boy, the whole system automatically was abrogated. Faced with a minority, every councillor found himself without the necessary experience to rule, since there had been no prior opportunity to exercise real power and initiative. In previous centuries conciliar government had been almost always weak, and it was unlikely that the council of equals established by the King's will would be more successful. Power tends to concentrate in the hands of a single man or a small oligarchy; and since Henry VIII was in as good a position to understand this as any man of his age, the terms of the will are even more incomprehensible. Henry had groomed no successor, nor was there among the council designated by the will an astute statesman of long experience. The best man available was probably Gardiner, Bishop of Winchester; yet the King ruled the wily Winchester out of the will. Chapuys, writing from retirement, dubbed Hertford and Lisle as the two most fit to rule during the minority. Perhaps he should have added that they were merely the best of a poor lot.

Not one of the councillors named in the King's will were of the caliber of Cardinal Wolsey or Thomas Cromwell. Until the death of Suffolk and the fall of the Howards, Hertford could scarcely qualify as the first soldier of the realm. In statesmanship, his experience was only slightly greater than that of Wriothesley. Lisle was even less qualified than Hertford to assume the role of *alter rex*. A survey of the other councillors only confirms the judgment of Chapuys. Surely it was clear long before

1547 that Cranmer lacked the political capacity to out-maneuver Gardiner, to say nothing of becoming another Wolsey. Paget and Paulet were primarily administrators and diplomats, while Russell, Parr, and Arundel were perhaps less able to provide leadership than Hertford and Lisle. Thus, in a political situation requiring the highest qualities of statesmanship, the whole nobility of England could supply no one as competent as Gardiner —who had been disqualified by the late King. The political vacuum was, therefore, twofold: At the summit, the heir of the mighty Henry was a child of nine. Within the council existed the greatest dearth of talent since Henry VII picked up the crown of Richard from the bloody battlefield of Bosworth.

Our understanding of the political situation in 1547 has been hindered by misuse of the word *party*. A. F. Pollard, the historian most responsible for creating the traditional picture of the early Tudor period, as well as later writers, thought of political parties in a way not unlike the Whig historians, who were criticized so effectively by Sir Lewis Namier and his disciples. During the reigns of Henry VIII and Edward VI there are generally presumed to be only two parties or factions. The names of the groups vary: At one point Catholics struggle against Protestants. Cromwellians do battle against conservatives led by Gardiner and Norfolk. The reformer theologians vie with humanistic legalists, while the Protestant party overthrows the Howards. After the death of Henry VIII, the faction of Hertford and Lisle executes a *coup d'état* against a party that might be called the Wriothesley new conservatives. And finally the Seymours are destroyed by the clique of Dudley, which curiously had the strength to accomplish its nefarious deed despite the fact that it "alienated or outraged nearly every section of the upper classes."[7] In all of this, the Whiggery is of a rather mild form inasmuch as some recognition is given to the existence of personal groups that are constantly changing. What is troubling, however, is the premature appearance of the two-party system and an over-simplified approach to Tudor politics. What is required is a thorough study of the substance of politics from 1485 to 1558.

The most that can be attempted here is an examination of these assumptions during the reign of Edward VI, viewed from the perspective of the political career of John Dudley.

One of the most difficult questions for political historians is that of motivation. Why did men like Dudley become involved in politics, and why did they reach the highest positions? The first query appears on the surface to be the least difficult, for Old Testament prophets and more than a few recent writers explain man's quest for power in terms of innate wickedness, greed, and selfish ambition. With a minimum of modification, this approach can be applied to Lisle by arguing that he coveted titles and offices to satiate his appetite for power and to enhance the wealth of the Dudley family. So easy a formula assumes that political ambition is evil, and that the ambitious man must necessarily pervert justice and ride roughshod over the righteous. It also omits the element of risk as a deterrent to self-destroying ambition and presumes that an individual will be satisfied with nothing but the highest position.

To sustain the original sin theory of political motivation, it would be necessary to present evidence of a consciously conceived plan of personal and family aggrandizement. Dudley's moral perversity can only be established if he conspired to overthrow men who were effectively executing the legitimate functions of government. At each stage in his career from his entry into the Privy Council to his alteration of the succession in 1553, it must be shown that he was dissatisfied with his position and yearned for more wealth and power. If the surviving evidence will not support these views, other explanations must be considered. There is always the possibility that a man may be moved by wholly praiseworthy motives. On the other hand, Dudley may have been forced into acts against his own wishes by events demanding leadership that no one else was willing or able to exercise. Responsibilities far beyond his capacity may have been thrust upon him. Troubled and confused by the rush of political crises, Dudley may have lost touch with reality and acted irrationally against his own legitimate interests and those of his family. All of these contingencies can only be resolved by a dispassionate examination of the evidence and by an acceptance of the dictum that the simplest explanation is not necessarily the most correct.

The alleged *coup d'état* by which Hertford became Protector is the logical point of departure.[8] A workable definition for a *coup d'état* is "a sudden exercise of force whereby the existing government is subverted" or "an unexpected stroke of policy." If this is accepted, it is difficult to see how the events of January 28–31, 1547, fit these requirements. Whatever Hertford may have done in establishing himself as Protector, he clearly did not use force in the usually accepted sense, nor was an existing government subverted. The Regency council of equals called for by the will existed only on paper and did not need to be overthrown. The leadership of any real or supposed conservative groups had been removed by Henry VIII, not by his councillors. Moreover, nothing could have been more expected. Those in any way acquainted with history were readily familiar with the ample precedents for one-man rule during a minority. Even the aged Chapuys, writing from retirement in distant Louvain, and his earnest, but mediocre successor, Van der Delft, saw the direction events were moving before learning of the King's death.[9] For a genuine *coup* to take place, it would have been necessary for Mary to have seized control of her brother or for Gardiner and Norfolk to have overthrown both the will and the council. More precise terminology demands the less dramatic appellation of political reorganization or, to use a modern idiom, a reshuffling of the cabinet—in this case the Privy Council.

Events during the days immediately following the death of Henry VIII are poorly recorded, and even contemporaries differed about what took place. The tale of the Spanish chronicler has nothing but its boldness to commend it; written after Hertford had become Duke of Somerset, this account alleges that Henry sent him for the Prince, who was fifteen miles from London, on the day before he died. Hertford left with three hundred horse, but was informed before he could return that the

King had died. Later during Somerset's imprisonment, the chronicler related a conversation between the Duchess and Dudley wherein the latter said, "Duchess, you well know that I was the cause of your husband's being made Protector." Wriothesley's *Chronicle* provided a simple explanation showing, if nothing else, that contemporaries were even less sure of their facts than modern historians, for it states that the position of Lord Protector was ordained in the King's will. Laboring under an additional burden of time, Sir John Hayward was convinced that Hertford had been elected Protector.[10]

While the King lay dying in the early hours of Friday morning, January 28, Hertford took a walk with Paget in the gallery where the two held "some serious conference" regarding the future government. Hertford left to inform Edward, after advising Paget of the high place he would have in the future, "being the next of kin to the young King." Inasmuch as the death was not officially disclosed until Monday morning, security arrangements were put to a test that later governments would be hard pressed to equal. Judging from ambassadorial reports, Hertford and the council were remarkably successful in maintaining the cloak of secrecy. As late as Monday, the French ambassador was uncertain of the King's death and could do no better than report a false rumor from the son of the Venetian secretary that the King had died on Thursday, January 27. Yet, he was correctly informed that Hertford would be the "chief" councillor. Van der Delft wrote to Charles V describing how royal dishes were even borne out to the sound of trumpets in an attempt to disguise the King's death, and he added that a passport was necessary to send his letter since all roads were closed. To the Queen Dowager of Hungary, the ambassador repeated the widespread rumor: "It is whispered already that the leading man will be the Earl of Hertford, who, indeed, occupied that position before the death of the late King."[11]

A royal death brought forth an incredible variety of conjectures about what was or would shortly be taking place. Fact and fiction were freely intermingled. As early as the end of December, Van der Delft believed the majority of Englishmen were committed to "perverse sects" and favored getting rid of the bishops. Such a prediction was only one hundred years wide of the mark, but his guess that some wanted Bishop Gardiner committed to the Tower was much more quickly corroborated. Chapuys was equally unable to comprehend the spirit of the English Reformation in spite of his long residence in the country. Like Van der Delft, he forecast doom to the episcopal hierarchy; the next Parliament would divest the bishops of their property and authority and leave them with nothing but pensions from the King's coffers. This diabolical plan, it was said, had been conceived by Hertford through the teachings of Cromwell and had presumably undergone an abnormal period of gestation.[12]

The French ambassador saw the danger of an insurrection in the interval between Henry's death and the coronation and gave this as the reason for Edward's presence in the Tower after his return to London. Although it is difficult to see what parties would have been prepared to resist the accession of Henry's only son, Van der Delft's problems in sending a message out of London also suggest a tense atmosphere.[13] The most likely candidate to lead an opposition, Norfolk, was reported executed by Van der Delft on the same day that the extreme security measures were observed. Foreign ambassadors were expected to supply masses of intelligence and regularly did so without a great deal of scrutiny. Amongst the wild speculations and gossip, grains of truth would inevitably emerge; then the conjecturer would become a sage.

The death of the King was officially announced to Parliament at eight o'clock Monday morning, January 31, by Lord Chancellor Wriothesley. Paget then read selected portions of the will, having been previously advised by Hertford not to disclose the full contents.[14] An hour later Cranmer, Wriothesley, St. John, Russell, Lisle, Tunstall, and others rode out of Westminister Palace to proclaim the death publicly. Hertford did not arrive with the King until three in the afternoon. Shortly thereafter the executors met and agreed upon the formation of the Protectorate. It is uncertain whether this was the first meeting after Henry's death, because Hertford had written Paget from Hertford early in the morning on the 29th that "the contents . . . [of the will] shall be declared unto them on Wednesday in the morning at the parliament house, and in the meantime we to meet and agree therein, as there may be no controversy hereafter." Hertford's reasons for sending this message so soon after his departure are a mystery. If an early meeting of the executors took place, Hertford could not possibly have been there, and his advice to delay informing the Parliament two more days went unheeded. In spite of these uncertainties and the initial hesitancy of Wriothesley and Sir Anthony Browne, the appointment of Hertford as Protector was virtually a foregone conclusion to which the council agreed unanimously on Monday.[15]

More than a month passed before the new regime was fully legalized. Although Edward gave assent to the appointment of his uncle on February 1, doubts about the powers of the Protector led to two confirmations the following month. The most notable signature missing from both of these documents was that of Lisle, then Earl of Warwick.[16] Early in February came the long list of promotions said by Paget to be the wish of the late King. Hertford headed the list with a dukedom, a fitting recognition of his political ascendancy. William Parr, Earl of Essex, became Marquess of Northampton while Lisle, Wriothesley, and later Russell and Paulet all received earldoms.* Baronies were granted to Sir Thomas Seymour, Sir Richard Rich, and Sir Edmund Sheffield. Duly advanced in rank and dignity, the councillors witnessed the coronation of Edward on February 20.[17] The pomp and ceremony of the occasion were cut because of the young King's age and health, but all of London had its opportunity to rejoice at the beginning of what was expected to be a long and glorious reign. Besides the feasting, proces-

---

*Thomas, Lord Wriothesley became Earl of Southampton. William Paulet, Lord St. John was later created Earl of Wiltshire and Marquess of Winchester. John, Lord Russell later became the first Earl of Bedford.

sions, and other pleasantries, other matters required attention. All of those who held land of the King by service were commanded to "attend upon his majesty's person royal at the time and day of his grace's coronation to do, exhibit, and minister to his highness their several services, duties, ministries, and offices."[18] Arrangements for the proceedings were the responsibility of Southampton, Warwick, Shrewsbury, Northampton, together with two justices. These commissioners constituted themselves as a court and met with landholders before the coronation. In feudal theory, the King's prerogatives over his tenants were considerable; in practice landholdings were the most secure and important source of wealth a subject might possess.

Warwick, a trusted personal friend, cooperated closely with Somerset during the first months of the reign. Following a pattern established under Henry VIII, the younger man succeeded the Protector in offices as each advanced. Accordingly, he became lord great chamberlain, but interrupted the sequence by relinquishing the post of lord admiral to Thomas, Lord Seymour. The precise activities and movements of Warwick cannot be established during this crucial period. He attended the council regularly until the middle of March; two months later he represented Somerset at the christening of Ambassador Van der Delft's infant son. That his intimacy with the Protector continued there can be no doubt. Besides the dubious testimony of the Spanish chronicler, Guaras said that Warwick was the "most intimate friend" of Somerset and counselled him "in all things."[19]

The two brothers, Somerset and Seymour, were on less friendly terms. Somerset's opposition to his brother's interests in Princess Mary led to a marked deterioration of whatever brotherly love they had for each other. Warwick, according to a secondhand story, felt bold enough to intervene in their quarrels. Using strong language against Seymour, he urged abandonment of the marriage scheme and explained that Seymour had been admitted to the council against the wishes of the late King. "Be content, therefore," said Warwick, "with the honor done to you for your brother's sake and with your office of lord high admiral which I gave up to you for the same motive; for neither the King nor I will be governed by you; nor would he be governed by your brother, were it not that his virtues and loyalty towards the King and the kingdom make him the man fittest to administer the affairs of the country during the King's minority."[20] This stern admonition is said to have had such a powerful effect that Seymour at once made up his quarrel with Somerset although he later turned to new schemes. Such evidence casts Warwick in the role of family friend and honest broker and suggests that his intimacy with the brothers was of a degree that allowed intervention in fraternal disputes.

Warwick's growing influence was demonstrated not only by offices and titles, but also by the attention given him by Van der Delft. By February 10, the ambassador assumed the four leading men of the realm were Somerset, Warwick, Wriothesley, and Paget, each of whom would be striving for his own advancement. While Somerset and Warwick would enjoy the "honors and titles of rulers," Wriothesley and Paget would have the "entire management of affairs." In his efforts to keep on good terms with all, Van der Delft served as godfather to Warwick's youngest child. He saw the possibility of jealousy between Warwick and Somerset mainly because of the two men's differing characters. Warwick was a man of "high courage," who would not willingly submit to his colleague. He was also believed to be held in higher esteem both by the people and the nobles than Somerset owing to his liberality and splendor. The Protector, on the other hand, was looked down upon by everyone as a dry, sour, and opinionated man. This contrast in personalities is unusual in that it attributed to Warwick qualities of liberality and popularity generally assigned to Somerset. Five months later, the ambassador, for undisclosed reasons, revised his opinion of Warwick's character. The new image was that of a man lacking in ambition and unwilling to take the risk of opposing the Protector. Accordingly, Warwick would content himself with the preeminence he presently enjoyed, that of ranking before all but

Somerset. Van der Delft felt Warwick would not persevere in the management of affairs, nor would he be able to support the work that was unable to tire his superior.[21]

Little opposition was voiced against the Protector by the councillors during the first year of the new regime. There was no reason why there should be any. From the outset the four leading men were Somerset, Warwick, Southampton, and Paget. The harmony between the first two was based on long-standing comradeship. Paget, it was believed, cooperated out of affection, while Southampton did so out of fear.[22]

The influence of Sir William Paget during this period can scarcely be exaggerated. At one point he was regarded as the "person most in authority." During the last years of Henry VIII, Paget formed close ties with both Warwick and Somerset. Indeed, Paget enjoyed a special relationship with the Protector as a confidential advisor. The Paget Letter Book, preserved in the Northamptonshire Record Office, reveals the detailed and often critical advice that Paget sent to Somerset. Suitors for the Protector's favor often wrote directly to Paget because of his intimacy. It was to Paget that Warwick turned for assistance in obtaining Warwick Castle. Paget was willing to do all that he "might conveniently" and later helped Warwick secure other favors from the Protector.[23]

The most important potential dissident, Lord Chancellor Southampton, reluctantly acceded to the formation of the Protectorate. But, if he cooperated with Somerset only out of fear, he cooperated nonetheless and fell by his own folly. The attempt to relieve himself of the duties of office by appointing civilian deputies would have brought charges of criminal malfeasance by more modern standards. Under Somerset's lenient rule the offender was merely deprived of office on March 5, confined to his house, and fined. Probably before the end of 1547, the fine was cancelled, and Southampton was restored to the Privy Council.[24]

A continuing state of cold war between England and both France and Scotland provided ample opportunities for military service to Warwick and other members of the Dudley family. Lord Edward Dudley, cousin to Warwick, served under Lord Grey on the council of Boulogne. In February 1547 he spent part of his wages for improving the fortifications of the base town and afterwards petitioned Paget for his own advancement. Another cousin, Henry Dudley, the future conspirator against Queen Mary, was captain of the guards at Boulogne. Sir Hugh Paulet, who had been sent as a commissioner to survey the pale of Boulogne, described to Warwick the lively activities displayed in the town in celebration of the King's coronation and remarked, "Mr. Henry Dudley is not so much noted as his worthiness in these exercises hath notably deserved." During one event in the tourney Dudley, clad in silk and carrying a staff garnished with colors, "passed round about the field" with Sir Thomas Palmer, who became one of Warwick's most devoted followers.[25]

In a more strategic position was Andrew Dudley, Warwick's brother. Named admiral of the King's fleet "addressed into the North Seas," he was charged to harass and annoy the Scots and French. When he wrote to his superior, Lord Admiral Seymour, in March 1547 for instructions and assurance that he would receive his share of the booty, Dudley had succeeded in capturing a host of enemy marines and several ships. Two years later the council learned that influential merchants in Hamburg had suffered losses of ships and supplies at his hands. So serious was their petition for redress that the council was advised to give satisfaction lest the aggrieved Hamburgers refuse to furnish ships then needed by the English. Unlike his kinsmen, Warwick was at this time occupied as a peacemaker. With Seymour, Russell, and Paget, he successfully negotiated a defensive league with France. But any hopes of a lasting settlement were quickly dispelled after Henry II, who became King upon the death of Francis I on March 31, refused ratification.[26]

The invasion of Scotland, begun in September 1547, was caused by a combination of old and new grievances.[27] Before his death Henry VIII was preparing further military action against his traditional enemy; in this sense the campaign of 1547 was simply the execution of previously formulated policy. Yet there were new elements to be reckoned with, for England and France were formally at peace at the beginning of the year and the negotiations of Warwick and his colleagues paved the way for a defensive alliance. The whole situation changed when the accession of Henry II brought the house of Guise to power in France. In Scotland Mary of Guise, the widow of James V and mother of Mary Queen of Scots, supported by Henry II, gained ascendancy over her rivals and sought to bind her country more closely to France. Moreover, with the fall of St. Andrew's Castle in July, which harbored John Knox and the murderers of Cardinal Beaton, the French gained a strong military hold on the country. Faced with this deteriorating situation plus the failure of diplomacy, Somerset resolved to invade.[28]

The Protector instructed Warwick to muster troops on August 24 and have the whole force at Berwick before the 31st.[29] Naval units were under the command of Edward, Lord Clinton, admiral of the fleet, assisted by Andrew Dudley.[30] The Protector himself arrived on the 27th at Newcastle where he met Warwick. A week later the army crossed the border led by Warwick with 3000 foot, followed by the main body of 4000 under Somerset, and a rear guard of 3000 under Lord Dacres. The diarist, William Patten, who heaped uncritical praise on all of the English commanders, was particularly impressed that Warwick "did camp in the field with the army" on the night before departure; he did not say where Somerset lodged. He further observed of Warwick that very few things had been achieved in the recent Scottish wars "wherein his lordship has not been either the first there in office or one of the foremost in danger." His heroism and "accustomed valiance" showed forth during an attempted ambush by the Scots in a thick mist on September 7. Charging one of his attackers 240 yards at spear point, Warwick and a small band forced all of the attackers to flee. "His wonted worthiness saved his company and discomforted the enemy;" soon afterwards he overtook Somerset, "being as then set at dinner," and delivered the prisoners that had been taken. Two days later Warwick's predilection for gallantry got the upper hand and led him into an act of reckless daring. The Earl of Huntley, the Scottish chancellor, rashly challenged Somerset to personal combat. The Protector refused saying he was of "such estate, as to have so weighty a charge of so precious a jewel, the governance of a King's person. . . ." The excitement of the moment was too great for Warwick, and he offered to fight Huntley himself in place of the Protector. "Nay," replied Somerset restraining his subordinate, "the Earl of Huntley is not meet in estate with you, my lord." Warwick persisted with his request but was wisely refused.[31]

The English army at Pinkie was opposed by a larger Scottish force confident of victory and well located to resist an assault. Choosing to attack rather than defend their impregnable position, the Scots momentarily turned the English left and had revenge for Flodden and Solway Moss within their grasp. At the crucial point Warwick "did very nobly encourage and comfort" his men to counterattack the enemy right, and he bade them, "Pluck up your hearts and show . . . [yourselves] men." Victory was in their own hands, if they would abide by it, Warwick exclaimed, as he pledged to live and die with his men. Other units were courageously rallied by Somerset, and the Scots saw victory turn into catastrophe. Before sunset on September 10, the army fled toward the outskirts of Leith and Edinburgh, and the Earl of Huntley was a prisoner in the English camp. Estimates of the Scottish dead varied from an exaggerated high of 12,000, to a low of 6,000. Patten described the battlefield in terms reminiscent of Gettysburg or Verdun:

> Some with legs off, some but hough [ham-strung] and left lying half dead; other, with the arms cut off; divers, their necks half asunder; many, their heads cloven; of sundry, the brains pasht out; some others again, their heads quite off.

The next phase of English operations included occupation of a number of strategic points and plundering the countryside.

Although the troops spoiled the nearby Abbey of Holyrood, Somerset took "pity" on Edinburgh, presumably recognizing from experience the utter futility of occupying the city without besieging the castle. Andrew Dudley was knighted by the Protector and dispatched with Lord Clinton to occupy the Castle of Broughty Craig at the mouth of the River Tay near Dundee.[32] When the Protector returned to London, he modestly refused the city's proposal for a triumphal entry. Pinkie raised the prestige of both Somerset and Warwick; of the two, however, Warwick had shown his abilities more brilliantly, a fact that was slowly gaining recognition.[33]

Warwick, remaining behind to negotiate with the Scots, learned that the Earl of Bothwell, captured at Pinkie, was willing to deliver his house, the Hermitage, to Edward VI if Somerset could find him a suitable English wife. Bothwell's tastes were several cuts above the ordinary; those considered most suitable were the Duchess of Suffolk, Princess Mary, and Princess Elizabeth. According to Warwick, the vain Scot would accept merely permission to see the ladies "as though if he liked them, they would not mislike him."[34]

The capture of Broughty Craig, announced on September 24 by Lord Clinton and Sir Andrew Dudley, began a long and fruitless military adventure.[35] Appointed captain, Dudley began the arduous task of fortifying the place against a threatened siege by the Earl of Angus. Although Dudley's base of operations remained insecure against mutiny owing to the bad state of the garrison and provisions, an attack was launched on Dundee. The English believed the Scots would gladly submit were it not for the "fear of great men and the priests." The surrounding territory of Angus and Fife appeared ripe for religious reform; to assist in the conversion, "a good preacher and books and testaments" were requested. Dundee surrendered before the end of December, but fear increased daily of French intervention. Dudley warned the Protector of great talk that France, the Emperor, and the Pope would declare war against England and wrote to William, Lord Grey, of great power coming from France to take the young Queen and besiege Broughty Craig.[36]

The English successes in Scotland diminished with the beginning of the new year. Differences among commanders and a continuing shortage of supplies led to the abandonment of Dundee. On February 5, 1548, Lord Grey gave Dudley permission to return to Protector Somerset, but he remained at his post for another month. At this point Dudley apparently turned over his command to Sir John Lutrell, who had distinguished himself earlier at Pinkie under Warwick and more recently abandoned the nearby fortress of Inch Colm.[37] The arrival of 6,000 French troops in June sealed the already impending defeat of the English; yet the affair was not so quickly ended. The stronghold of Haddington provided an excellent base for operations into the surrounding area, and the Scots were by no means united in their allegiance to Henry II. The seige of Haddington by a combined Franco-Scottish army, begun in July 1548, failed to yield the desired results. By the spring of 1549, however, Hume Castle, Broughty Craig, and other places were lost.[38] Revolts in the West and in Norfolk further weakened the English cause, and in September Haddington was evacuated. Once again efforts to control Scotland had failed. Somerset, like Henry VIII, could defeat Scottish armies in the field even when the advantage lay with the other side, but neither could achieve the desired political end. England continued to lack the resources and perhaps also the military competence to conquer and subjugate the weaker nation. With or without the aid of France, the vagaries of fortune seemed to have decreed the survival of Scotland as an independent nation, notwithstanding the armies sent to destroy her.

The first Parliament of Edward's reign met on November 4, 1547, after the victory over the Scots at Pinkie. The repeal of the Six Articles and the passage of a new treason act foreshadowed an era of religious and political reform. Nevertheless, the rate of change was moderate, and more was left undone than was done. Warwick was never listed present during the sittings of the House of Lords. His name was listed next to last among the earls after the Protector, the great officers of state, and the marquesses. There are, however, enough discrepancies for the session in the *Lords Journal* to raise doubts about its reliability in reporting attendance.[39] While any statement about Warwick's activities during this session of Parliament must be based on conjecture, it seems likely, judging from the past rather than anticipating the future, that his sympathies were on the side of Somerset's reforms.

The surviving record of Warwick's career is more sparse for 1548 than for any year after he became a privy councillor. Extant letters reveal that he was in and out of the London area throughout the year and never far from the political pulse of England. In March, Ambassador Selve wrote Henry II about a doctor who had treated Warwick for a bad leg all winter, and two months later he again commented that Warwick was continually ill, but still influential in advising the Protector on matters of war. Inasmuch as Warwick was quite active between indispositions, the ailments may have been chronic or of several different types. From this point forward he was increasingly troubled by poor health.[40]

There was also some evidence of discord between Warwick and Somerset. After his appointment as president of the council in Wales, Warwick wished to name John Gosnold to a position currently held by a Mr. Townsend by life patent. He wanted Townsend to withdraw, but advised against breaking "any of the King's grants by letters patent," because "by such example the like may happen to me and others hereafter."[41] Apparently Warwick expected Somerset to encourage Townsend's resignation; when this did not happen, he felt greatly offended and complained that others were gaining favor with the Protector at his expense. His grievance further suggests that Somerset had first promised to assist him and later reconsidered. This incident was probably little more than a small ripple in a large sea, for Warwick and Somerset were on their usually good terms both before and afterwards.[42]

The correspondence of Warwick with William Cecil, secretary to the Protector, underscores both Cecil's growing influence and the Protector's regal pretensions.[43] Cecil began to occupy a position of intermediary between Warwick and the Protector much like that of Sir William Paget, who, during the last years of Henry VIII, often maintained contact between the King and his councillors. Whereas Lisle and Hertford had regarded each other as equals, there now was a tendency for Warwick to approach Somerset through his servants, Cecil and Sir John Thynne. A close friendship quickly developed between Warwick and Cecil, as might be expected, since both were devoted to the interests of the Protectorate throughout its first years. On one occasion Warwick thanked "gentle Master Cecil" for his "friendly remembrance of my suit to my Lord's grace." A few weeks later he sent "very hearty thanks" for Cecil's "gentle friendship showed . . . in all my affairs." Requests for land grants were still made directly to the Protector, but Cecil was generally used for less important matters. In July Warwick asked that the surgeon of Boulogne be permitted to remain with a certain lady, who was in great danger because of ill treatment by London surgeons and risked having her leg sawed off. Later the same month, he requested the appointment of one of his chaplains to a prebend in Canterbury held by Nicholas Ridley, Bishop of Rochester.[44]

In spite of the pique Warwick may have felt from time to time, he had by no means lost his influence with Somerset and passed into eclipse. Sir Henry Long's request to the Protector for a lease in January 1548 shows Warwick's importance as a go-between. Long said he had previously written to Somerset about the matter and received a reply from Thynne, stating that the duke "had then no time to take order of the same." To better his chances of favor, Long emphasized, "It may please your grace to understand that I have written unto my Lord of Warwick desiring his lordship to be a mean for me unto your grace whereby I trust the sooner to know your grace's pleasure."[45]

One explanation for Warwick's use of Cecil as an intermediary may have been the ill health that forced him to express in writing what in other circumstances would have been communicated directly to the Protector. Fabyan's *Chronicle* describes the "great mortality in London" during the year and the instructions to curates concerning burial of the dead. This infection may have affected the Dudley household in September, when Warwick wrote Somerset that his wife "had had her fit again more extreme that she had any time yet," and that he intended to go to Greenwich, but would "keep Holborn for a while" on account of sickness. He fell ill while at the Earl of Southampton's house with "such a dampish savor [sic]" that he believed himself "stricken to the heart." His stomach was very weak, and he had not eaten "so much meat as a little chicken." By November 27, he was sufficiently mended to take his place in Parliament and to play an active role throughout December and January. Warwick's name also appeared on a council directive in December, but the following month he again referred to his health.[46]

The great questions of the second session of Parliament were religious. Fortunately much more is known about the role of Warwick, whose attendance was quite regular according to the *Journal*. His growing power is revealed by the *Journal's* cold formality; after November 28, 1548, Warwick was listed first among the earls, and by March 6, 1549, his name stood near the top as "comes Warwick, Magnus Camerai." During the famous debate in December 1548 over the real presence, Warwick's two speeches left little doubt about his religious leanings. Throughout the last years of Henry VIII, he had been included among those favoring reform, and as early as December 1547 Van der Delft was reporting to Charles V that mass was no longer celebrated in his house.[47] But, besides establishing Warwick's religious views of the hour, the debate did little to flatter his reputation as a man of learning.

The principal bishops, who discoursed upon the subtleties of the holy communion, included Cranmer, Ridley of Rochester, Holbeach of Lincoln, and Goodrich of Ely for the reformers; and Tunstall of Durham, Bonner of London, Heath of Worcester, Day of Chichester, Skyp of Hereford, Rugg of Norwich, and Thirlby of Westminster for the conservatives. To this auspicious and learned assemblage of divines must be added three laymen, Somerset, Warwick, and Sir Thomas Smith. On the first day Warwick was the last speaker. Having suffered in silence while the ecclesiastics waxed long and loud he must have been bored and finally shocked into a realization of the futility of disputation, when Thirlby solemnly advised the audience that:

> The book which was read touching the doctrine of the Supper was not agreed on among the bishops, but only in disputation; lest the people should think dishonesty in them in argument against their own deed that they [had set their] hands unto.
> And for his part did never allow the doctrine.

Showing his support for Cranmer and the reformers, Warwick replied that such was "a perilous word" to be spoken. He felt Thirlby "worthy of displeasure" for having "in such a time when concord is sought for, . . . cast such occasions of discord among men." Warwick may have been angered at the conservative's recalcitrance; he may, like all non-theologians, have been dismayed at the overfine distinctions and nice logic; he most assuredly remembered and cherished Henry VIII's famous exhortation to the clergy "to give example to the rest and to agree especially in their teaching—which seeing there is but one truth and verity, they easily do, calling therein for the aid of God."[48]

Warwick again spoke toward the end of the second day in the midst of a dialogue between Heath and Ridley. Heath contended, "All the old doctors grant a conversion of the bread," and asked, "Wherein is the bread converted? Is it in the bread?"

Ridley replied, "It is converted into the body of Christ," and followed with the question, "how are we turned in baptism?"

Ridley then said, "Even as glass receiveth the light of the sun, but the stone cannot, for it may not pierce through it, so the evil man cannot receive the body."

The rather weak analogy offered by Ridley impressed Warwick, who asked Heath, "Where is your scripture now, my Lord of Worcester? Me think because you cannot maintain your argument neither by Scripture nor doctors, you would go now with natural reason and sophistry." The most pertinent observation that can be made about Warwick's contribution would be that it was irrelevant to what had immediately passed. If nothing else, he proved that he had been listening to the debate, because the previous speakers had been buttressing their arguments with St. Peter, the Acts, St. Augustine, and St. Chrysostom; presumably, he believed the last statements of Heath were sophistical. Besides revealing Warwick out of his element in the debate, the speech offers little scope for interpretation. If spoken with clenched fist and piercing eye, the words would be those of an angry and violent man. On the other hand, if offered with a gentle smile and twinkling eye, the speech would have been regarded, at least by Warwick, as an example of his cleverness and wit. No one bothered to reply to him, and Cranmer picked up the debate as though Warwick had never spoken. The bishops undoubtedly would have preferred to settle the question of the sacrament by themselves and would have shed no tears had Warwick and the other laymen withdrawn.[49]

Warwick spoke no more during the debate, but was present in the House of Lords on January 15, 1549, when the first act of uniformity was passed. Only three lay peers, Derby, Dacres, and Windsor, joined with seven bishops in opposing the reform. Parliament continued until March 14 when it was prorogued to the following November. Up to this point all evidence of Warwick's participation in reform proceedings, with the exception of the enclosures' question, indicated his support for the Protectorate.

The issue of enclosures, usually cited as a prime source of ill-feeling between Warwick and Somerset, raises several difficult questions. In 1548 Somerset appointed a commission headed by the zealous reformer, John Hales of Coventry, to investigate enclosures in the Midlands. According to John Strype, reports of Hales' activities came to Warwick's attention while in Warwickshire, and "he grew much displeased with Hales, who acted very honestly in this commission and favorably to the commons." Warwick's complaint against Hales has apparently not survived. Hales, however, wrote Warwick in August 1548 and defended his action. He had heard that Warwick was "highly displeased" with him for investigating enclosures "in this troublesome time" and for kindling and stirring the commons against the nobility and gentlemen. Hales maintained that he had not incited the people to violence and offered to explain everything to Warwick in person. The only evidence of inquiries in Warwickshire by the commissioners on enclosures, Dugdale's notes of the inquisition of 1549, contains no mention of complaints against the Earl of Warwick. The next year a letter from Warwick to Cecil, dated June 18 by the latter, complained about plowing up a park. "Surely if it had not been for my lords' pleasure," said Warwick, "I would not have suffered so much 'dispit' of them as to let them plow the fairest ground in all the park and to use the thing so much to their own advantage."[50] The letter did not attack Hales by name; nor did it single out Somerset for reproach. Warwick was unquestionably annoyed by these events. Whether his anger had political significance is an open question.

Although Warwick never made a comprehensive statement of his views on enclosure, he was almost certainly opposed to Hales' reforms. Warwick's sympathies undoubtedly lay with men of property who enclosed to make their lands more profitable. Since Parliament had been unresponsive to the Protector's requests for enclosure legislation, Warwick was by no means the only one with misgivings. Tudor England was an agrarian society in which political power rested in the hands of property holders who were determined to utilize their lands as they saw fit. The landlords of England placed their own interests before those of the poor and down-trodden. Any politician or aspiring social reformer who ignored this vested interest faced not only frustration but possible ruin.

IV / The Fall of
the Protectorate

The Protectorate faced a series of crises in 1549 from which it never recovered. First, a bitter quarrel between Protector Somerset and his brother, Thomas, Lord Seymour, leading to the latter's execution for treason, weakened the regime's moral authority at the highest level. During the summer, revolts in the West of England and Norfolk destroyed what was left of the government's prestige. When Somerset himself fell from power in October, Warwick emerged as the dominant figure in English politics.

The story of Lord Seymour's decline and fall is well known and has been treated in detail elsewhere.[1] What needs to be emphasized here is the family character of the controversy and the role of Warwick. It would be scarcely an exaggeration to assert that the Seymour affair aptly points out the domination of Tudor politics by family interests. As younger uncle to the King, Seymour became jealous of his brother and through marriage joined forces with Catherine Parr, the Queen Dowager, who lost her political influence after the death of Henry VIII. Both believed themselves denied their rightful positions. The marriage fanned the flames of family discord, and the Duchess of Somerset sustained an affront to her dignity when the Queen

Dowager took precedence over her at court. Catherine nicely summed up this aspect of the quarrel in a letter to Seymour, "[The Protector] has this afternoon a little made me warm. It was fortunate we were so much distant, for I suppose else I should have bitten him. . . . What cause have they to fear having such a wife."[2] Seymour hoped his unborn child would revenge "such wrongs as neither you nor I can at this present" and intimately wished his wife's "good diet and walking" would keep the child "so small that he may creep out of a mousehole."[3]

Two minor figures in the Seymour affair, the Marquesses of Dorset and Northampton, were also motivated by family interests. Henry Grey, Marquess of Dorset, the father of three daughters in the royal succession, was first attracted to Seymour's scheme to marry Lady Jane to the King; later another plan of family aggrandizement caused him to favor the marriage of Lady Jane and Lord Guildford Dudley. The involvement of Northampton, brother of the Queen Dowager, was on a much lower plane. Northampton was at least willing to listen to his brother-in-law, Seymour, because of a strong sense of devotion to his sister and a grudge against Somerset for refusing to recognize his second marriage. As early as September, 1547, Seymour wrote in favor of Northampton to Somerset and asked that various offices of his deceased father be granted to him.[4]

Warwick certainly had nothing to gain by the fall of Seymour, unless it is assumed that he harbored a complex and long-range plan to destroy the Seymour family. Those arguing along these lines meet not only with a complete lack of documentation, but also with a rejection of logic. In the first place Warwick already outranked Seymour and had nothing to gain by his fall. If he were plotting against the family, he would surely have tried for larger game and joined with Seymour in overthrowing the Protector. Warwick enjoyed almost as long a friendship with Seymour as with Somerset. In the letter of September 1547 to the Protector, who was in Scotland, for example, Seymour asked to be remembered to Warwick and remarked that "my Lady [of Warwick] is also merry."[5] Moreover, the appointment of Andrew Dudley as admiral the same year could hardly have taken place without the approval of Thomas Seymour.

Actually, Seymour turned against Warwick because he was a friend of the family and wished to preserve harmony, which to Seymour meant the *status quo*. Van der Delft learned from Paget shortly after Henry's death how Warwick had prevailed on Seymour to be content with the position of lord high admiral and to serve the King and Protector loyally. In his deposition to the council after hearing about Seymour's ambitions, Warwick said he had warned him that Somerset would "set the said lord admiral fast in the Tower." To this sound advice, Seymour madly answered that he would thrust his dagger in anyone who tried to restrain him. Sir William Sherington, the corrupt treasurer of the Bristol mint, suggested in his testimony that Seymour turned against Warwick because of his loyalty to Somerset:

> And when he came to Bristol, he would say: this is my Lord Protector's, and of other, that is my Lord of Warwick's, to the which two, this examinate knows he had no great affection.

Seymour knew the forces of Warwick would stand with the Protector in any conflict between the two. The same assumption was also behind Seymour's request to Dorset to keep his house in Warwickshire, for it was a country full of men who would undoubtedly rally to the bear and ragged staff. When Dorset said his house there was nearly down, Seymour urged him to make repairs and establish himself in force.[6]

The bizarre and absurd schemes unraveled before the council raised doubts about Seymour's mental competence. Viewed in the most sympathetic light, they reveal him to be a political tactician on a level with the Earl of Surrey or Perkin Warbeck. By Tudor standards of justice, his guilt could not be denied. Had the Protector made an exception for his brother, his own integrity would have been undermined. But by permitting the only possible sentence—death—he did the same thing. Therein lay the tragic dilemma.

That the execution of Seymour on March 20, 1549, was the first of a series of worsening calamities befalling Somerset was accepted before the time of Sir John Hayward, the seventeenth-century biographer of Edward VI. Defamed as "a blood-sucker, a murderer, a parricide, and a villain," the hapless Protector was nearly overwhelmed by revolts in the West and in Norfolk and finally deposed by a conspiracy of the council in October. Opposition to Somerset can be found as far back as the last years of Henry VIII. After 1547 the advice of Sir William Paget can be cited to show the wise counsel that went unheeded. While it is indeed tempting to portray the fall of Somerset as inevitable, such an approach oversimplifies an extraordinarily complicated sequence of events. Both the chroniclers and historians were all too willing to disregard the greater wisdom of John Foxe, who wrote, "How the matter fell out between the Lord Protector and certain other Lords, I know not. . . ."[7]

The strongest cross-current is a highly important correspondence between Warwick and Somerset's unpopular ally, Sir John Thynne. Beginning in March 1549, Warwick sent a series of letters to "my loving friend Sir John Thynne, Knt., steward to my Lord Protector's grace," seeking assistance in acquiring land. Warwick was anxious for quick action since he was anticipating service away from London, presumably in Scotland. When he learned Somerset would not grant one of his requests, Warwick was disappointed, but promised Thynne, "It becometh me not to sue any further for it." A few days later he received a "good answer" from Somerset concerning an unnamed request for which he had good cause to think himself "bound to his grace." Warwick concluded, "So shall the same be most assured of my faithful heart and service during my life." "In all my requests," he told Thynne, "I will prefer my lord's pleasure, commandment, and surety before my desires as knoweth God."[8]

Warwick made the following comment to Thynne on April

22 concerning an office that had recently been filled by the Protector:

> Albeit indeed I have more largely preferred myself towards it than ever I intend to do for any other while I live; for I have made sundry motions for it much against my nature to do and ashamed that it might be thought that I did "hable" myself to it, being so great an office and meet for the best man in the realm under my lord himself. And that made me the more ashamed to seem to labor for it or to presume to "hable" myself for it. When it was offered unto me, then could not my lord with his honor give it unless his grace should have seemed to have done another man much injury, which I would have been most loth he should have so done for me. But I speak not for any intent that I would you should any further travail with his grace in this for me, for I hold me as well content as he whosoever he be that his grace has given it unto.[9]

It is, unfortunately, not clear what office is referred to. The best possibilities are lord high admiral, vacant after the execution of Lord Seymour, and master of the horse, formerly held by Sir Anthony Browne, who died in 1548. Warwick would hardly have praised his former position so highly, nor does it seem that master of the horse should have been such a coveted post. The fact that these remarks—so revealing in nature—were made to Thynne suggests a degree of intimacy scarcely expected between a ranking councillor and the servant of another.

The correspondence gives every impression that Warwick and the Protector shared each other's confidence until it closed on July 12, 1549. At the end of April, a group of councillors met with Warwick at Esher where further requests were made to Somerset. The main purpose of the gathering is unknown, but with Somerset and Thynne in attendance it could not have been of a conspiratorial nature, unless Somerset was ignorant of a cabal forming in his very presence. Warwick's petitions flowed in a steady stream and were by no means always granted. At one point he was maneuvering for Hatfield, the residence of Princess Elizabeth, and proposing that Thynne help her find "some other place agreeable to her desire." Even when Somerset "did somewhat stick" at his wishes, Warwick remained hopeful that further favors would be forthcoming. Thynne was always profusely thanked for his labors: "I wish it lay in me to do you some thing in recompence of part of your friendship, but when the power wanteth, the good will shall be always ready." Had there been any lack of mutual trust, Warwick would never have sent Thynne a list "of such manors as I desire to exchange for my land in Kent" on June 22 with the plea, "I pray you let not every man see these names of these manors." The tenor of the letters is, if anything, more friendly than that of the previous year, when Warwick told Cecil that his honor had been disregarded by the Protector's actions. Somerset not only kept Warwick's good will, but also favored Sir Andrew Dudley. Nor is there any hint that the Protector became puffed up with pride and conceit, and treated his fellow councillor with contempt or condescension.[10]

While the majority of Warwick's requests were for his own aggrandizement, exceptions may be found. Men seeking personal favors frequently bore letters of recommendation from a patron, and by following this common practice Warwick was neither exceptional nor over-generous. For example, Warwick asked Thynne to show a Mr. Peckham "your lawful favor in such suits and business as he has with you."[11] During the previous year he had advanced Henry Mackerel, the King's physician, to Cecil for a position at court held by a "sickly" old man. By 1549, Mackerel was dead after receiving favor, and Warwick supported a new (unnamed) candidate, who more than any other man in London was able "to execute and discharge the room."[12] Were more known about these individuals, the motives of Warwick for befriending them might prove to be selfish; yet Warwick was powerful enough to throw a few scraps to a worthy man without requiring compensation.

The fattening of Warwick through the favor of Somerset was by no means unique. Thomas Wriothesley, Earl of Southampton and deposed lord chancellor, was the Protector's most powerful potential enemy before the crisis of October. Nevertheless, Somerset asked him in June to negotiate with the French, only to be refused on grounds of ill health. Within three days after learning Southampton was "vexed by divers infirmities," Somerset released him from duty. For this he was duly thanked: "You shall never have cause to repent of your goodness toward me." But Southampton was not content merely to return to his country home and mend. "May it please you to remember my suit for the house," he wrote to the Protector, "which is now ten times more important than before, both because I am utterly destitute and because unless I know where to rest in the winter, I shall not be able to lay in my provision of hay, coals, and wine."[13] Thus as late as June 1549 both Southampton and Warwick, the two most powerful leaders in the revolt against Somerset, thought they were in high favor with him.

Also ailing at this time was Warwick. It was rumored in February that he would lead an army into Scotland to revive the declining English fortunes, but in July he still lingered in London recovering from what Van der Delft described as a long illness. By then Scotland had to be sacrificed for crucial interests nearer home. On July 12, Warwick wrote Thynne that he was sorry to hear of "the continual trouble" of Somerset with "these uproars" and explained his own inactivity. He would have come to the Protector with advice and counsel, if he had had "either notice or knowledge" of the need even though he "should have been the worse all my life after." Confined to Ely Place with a stomach ailment, he had met only with Rich and St. John. If Somerset harbored any doubts about his condition, Warwick referred him to the duke's own secretary, Thomas Fisher, to whom he declared his "estate, which is such that conveniently I cannot come abroad this day." On the morrow Warwick vowed to "adventure" to Somerset regardless of the consequences. His letter described conditions in Warwickshire where rebels were preparing "to spoil" the town of Warwick. The castle, although "a very slender house of strength," had been placed in readiness. Warwick not only asked all of his servants and friends "to repair towards me," but pledged to "live and die" wherever the Protector commanded him and pray "for the staying of the fury of this people."[14]

The fury of the people shook the Protectorate at its foundation during the summer months. Peasants rose to pull down enclosures, which had been condemned by the commissioners. In Devon and Cornwall, the *Book of Common Prayer* was rejected with vehemence of frightening proportion. True to his own conscience, Somerset advocated a policy of moderation and pardon, for he believed many of the rebels had genuine grievances. By so doing he violated cardinal principles of Tudor rule. Both Henry VII and Henry VIII learned that to yield to popular outcries was a sign of weakness, destructive to the power and prestige of the crown. While campaigning in Scotland, Somerset had been schooled in the proper Tudor tradition and had proved himself a master thereof, but, when faced by his beloved countrymen in 1549, his nerve failed. What to Victorian humanitarians was the virtue of gentleness, was to sixteenth-century political realists the sin of cowardice and dereliction of duty.

Lord Russell was sent to quell the Western revolt, and his immediate objective was to relieve the beleaguered city of Exeter. He was faced with a shortage of men and received the promise of the Protector and council on July 22 that Warwick "shall be in order to depart towards you" within two days. Warwick, however, remained in London until at least July 28, when he was sent not to the West, but northward; in his stead Russell was to be reinforced by the forces of Sir William Herbert. For the moment Russell was left to his own devices, and the frequent letters from Somerset and the council offered much sympathy but little real assistance: "That all should be well causes us to write. And how wise and valiant captain a man is, yet to hear the counsel of another can do no hurt. And we think us to have some experience in these things." Difficulties were even encountered in levying troops in the county of Somerset where the Protector's prestige should have been great. From the Protector and council came the sage advice that too many supplies were required and that shot and arrows would simply be returned by the enemy, if used too freely. At times the council seemed confused and lacking in authority. The dispatch of July 28 fell between the poles of hopeful advice and an order:

"Wherefore we pray you to consider these things amongst other, and so to take order accordingly."[15] While Somerset and the council fussed and prated at Westminster, the future of Edwardian England lay with the men in the field.

Russell's army marched out of Honiton and met heavy resistance between Clyst St. Mary and Topsham. By August 5, victory was at hand. The next day Russell was joined by Herbert's Welsh, who arrived "too late for the work, but soon enough for the play," and entered Exeter. Again the city's proud motto, "Semper Fidelis" bestowed by Henry VII, was justified. Somerset and the council sent "most hearty thanks" to Russell and the mayor and gentlemen of Exeter for their successes, but differences soon developed between the Protector and the victors. The councillors were critical of Russell's large council of the West and advised "the having of many councillors shall not only be troublous to them that be called, but also may breed a confusion in the affairs." The council was to be limited to Lord Grey, Herbert, Sir Andrew Dudley, John Paulet, Sir Hugh Paulet, and Sir Thomas Speke. In dealing with the defeated insurgents, a confusing policy of alternating harshness and leniency was followed. Realizing his earlier errors, Somerset now favored immediate execution of the ringleaders. Many believed Robert Paget, "a head and captain of rebellion" and brother of Sir William, should be spared, but Somerset personally ordered otherwise. "Yet in this case of such treason as this," he said, "it behoveth us most of all to show indifferent justice and, especially, considering that we have not spared our own brother in matters concerning the . . . King's majesty's person." A few days later the Protector, joined by Rich, St. John, Petre, and surprisingly Archbishop Cranmer again entreated Russell, "We have now resolved you shall cause him [Paget] to suffer as others. . . ."[16]

The increasing burden of military expenditures forced the Protector to urge the strictest economies upon Russell. Extra troops, especially horsemen, were to be sent to Warwick in Norfolk. By the end of August, Somerset fully realized the financial difficulties of which Paget had warned him earlier. He and the council gently chided Russell, " 'My lord, if you knew as much as we do herein presently see (and yet you can well guess it) what divers and sundry occasions the King's majesty has to employ both men and money,' you would exercise greater economies."[17]

For the sake of a clear-cut explanation of Russell's adherence to Warwick and his associates in October, it would be desirable to show that the disputes were entirely between a vacillating and confused Protector and a rugged field commander faced with restoring law and order. Alas, such was not the case. When Russell was stoutly reprimanded on September 10, for his "proceedings in the gift of the lands and goods of the rebels in Devonshire and Cornwall," the signatures on the letter included not only those of Somerset, Cranmer, St. John, Petre, and Sadler, but also that of Warwick, who had recently returned after his victory over Kett. The councillors did not want Russell to think "we conceived any ill opinion either of corruption or of wrong doing in you, whom we all know to be of much honor," but they opposed his alteration of the amnesty proclamation. "We do not think that any man should lose lands or goods before he be attainted of the crime." Furthermore, the council felt that Russell's men "might have been well-stayed from going to the people and that by these gifts, the multitude of the common people, seeing their lands and goods given from them, were thereby made the more desperate and much the more stirred to follow their devilish enterprise." The order to discharge redundant horsemen "for the diminishing of the King's majesty's charges" was also repeated over Warwick's signature.[18]

A few days later Somerset and the council (excluding Warwick) cautioned Russell to show moderation and "as much quietness and as little offence . . . to the common people as may be." But the tone of the correspondence changed dramatically on September 18. Writing from Syon, the Protector learned that Robert Paget had not been executed as ordered over a month ago. Somerset believed his own honor was impugned, because of talk that "we should consent to the death of our own brother and now would wink at him." Accordingly, Paget was to suffer "without delay." The long and revealing series of communiques to Russell ended September 25 with another personal letter from Somerset; the letter demanded two more executions and mysteriously ordered Russell and Sir William Herbert to return to London about October 8 "for matters of importance."[19] Given the advantage of hindsight, these matters of importance seem obvious, but is it possible that Somerset foresaw or staged the proceedings that ended his rule?

Occurring simultaneously was the Norfolk rebellion headed by Robert Kett, a life tenant of Warwick at Wymondham. The revolt was a protest against enclosures and social injustice. Although Somerset's sympathies were on the side of the insurgents, he was obliged to support the military action demanded by the nobility and gentry. Troops led by Northampton, who was instructed "to avoid the fight," suffered abysmal defeat and were driven from Norwich with heavy losses. The Protector was displeased with his performance and considered assuming the leadership himself. Considerable confusion and apparent indecision ensued in selecting a new general. Warwick, who was first to reinforce Russell in the West, was sent northward sometime between July 28 and August 10, probably after the council learned the fate of Northampton. A proclamation of the latter date gave command in Norfolk to Somerset. Two days later the Protector changed his mind, and it was decided that Warwick would assume the charge. The reasons for Somerset's remaining in London are unknown, but it has been suggested that he shrank at the thought of letting the blood of the peasantry.[20]

After reaching Warwick Castle about August 10, Warwick wrote "gentle Master Cecil" to thank the Protector and council for appointing him to lead the shires of Cambridge, Bedford, Huntingdon, Northampton, Norfolk, and Suffolk. "I do think myself much bounden," he said, "to my Lord's grace and the council for enabling me to receive so great a charge, so I cannot but wish that it might please the same to permit and suffer my Lord Marquess of Northampton to continue still in the force of his commission." It is not clear whether he knew then that he would have supreme command, or whether, as at Pinkie, he would serve under Somerset; in this letter he was solely concerned with the discredited Northampton. Warwick believed he had "by misfortune received discomfort enough" and advised his re-employment lest this "might give him occasion to think himself utterly discredited, and so for ever discourage him." He continued, "I shall be as glad for my part to join with him, yea, rather than fail, with all my heart to serve under him for this journey, as I would be to have the whole authority myself; and by this means his grace shall preserve his heart, and 'hable' him to serve hereafter, which otherwise, he shall be utterly in himself discouraged [to do]. I wish that no man for one mischance or evil hap, to the which we be all subject that must serve, should be utterly abject, for if it should be so, it were almost a present discomfort to all men before they go to it since those things lie in God's hand."[21]

Warwick's army of some 6000 foot and 1500 horse advanced eastward, passing through Cambridge and Newmarket, and arrived at Wymondham on August 22. The force included two of his sons, Ambrose and Robert, whose presence committed the fortunes of the Dudley family to success. His brother, Sir Andrew, was serving in the West under Russell. Also in the party were some of Warwick's old followers and confederates, Sir Thomas Palmer, Sir Thomas Gresham, Sir Edmund Knyvet, and Sir Andrew Flammock plus Northampton. Warwick stayed at the house of Gresham at Intwood, three miles from Norwich.

His policy was to offer pardon, but to employ force if refused. After Kett rejected terms excluding himself, Warwick successfully seized the city. In the marketplace his army hanged at least forty-nine rebels for whom the city records show burial cost 3s. 9d; others received pardon and were ordered home. The issue was still undecided, for Kett's men remained encamped outside Norwich on Mousehold Heath, while supporters still within the city captured valuable munitions. Some of the more faint-hearted asked Warwick to leave the city, as Northampton had done earlier. He refused saying, "I will first suffer fire, sword finally all extremity before I will bring such a stain of infamy and shame either on myself or you." With these words he drew his sword, as did the rest of his nobles, and commanded, "after a warlike manner," that "they should kiss one another's swords, making the sign of the holy cross." By oaths and solemn promises, the men pledged themselves not to leave Norwich before they had "utterly banished the enemy or else, fighting manfully, had bestowed their lives cheerfully for the King's majesty."

Warwick, joined by reinforcements, marched out of Norwich to attack Kett at Dussindale on August 27. A curious omen, it is said, foretold the rebels' doom. A snake leaping out of a rotten tree sprang directly into the bosom of Kett's wife, an event which—besides discomforting Mrs. Kett—struck fear into the hearts of the superstitious. Once again before ordering an advance, Warwick sent Palmer and Knyvet to parley with the enemy. Terms were refused, and the day was quickly decided in favor of Warwick's superior army. The flight of Kett broke the rebels' spirit; those remaining received a generous offer of pardon.

In victory Warwick could afford to be magnanimous. Restraining those who wanted mass slaughter, he demanded no more than that the defeated rebels be good plowmen and "harrow their own lands." Warwick remained in Norwich for about two weeks during which the city fathers, having recovered their courage, heaped praises upon him and his followers. His insignia, the bear and ragged staff, was erected at all the city gates, and the city enacted that on every succeeding August 27, a commemoration of its deliverance should be held. According to city records, his victory continued to be honored as late as 1667.[22] Unfortunately, no correspondence comparable to the one between the council and Russell has survived to illustrate relations between Warwick and the Protector. General satisfaction with Warwick's achievement and moderation was, however, expressed in a letter from the Protector and council to Sir Philip Hoby. It stated, "So you shall understand that in Norfolk the living God has so wrought by the wisdom and manliness of my Lord of Warwick that they also are brought to subjection." A member of the Norfolk gentry complained of his losses of bullocks and sheep and of Warwick's hangings. The determination of Warwick to keep all ordnance and spoil for the King disappointed some, but almost all admitted having been treated fairly, if not generously. "I asked my lord for my two pieces of brass," one man said; "but I cannot have them at his hand; yet he is very gentle to me."[23]

Law and order had been restored in England by the beginning of September. Compromise and conciliation had failed; it was the sword that brought peace. Faced with the most dangerous crisis since the Pilgrimage of Grace in 1536, the country had been saved by its soldiers. Both Warwick and Russell, as well as their lieutenants, risked their lives, reputations, and fortunes in the field of combat. In Norfolk Warwick suffered heavy casualities to say nothing of the destruction wrought among the populace. Criticism was heaped upon Lord Russell, on the one hand, for excessive reprisals and, on the other, for delay in executing a rebel and traitor. The rebellions discredited the leadership of the Protector. The work of the enclosures commission first brought down the wrath of the nobles and gentry; by September it could be cited as a fundamental cause of the revolts. After the commons were in arms, the Protector's sincere offers of pardon fell on deaf ears. Even the *Book of Common Prayer* was not welcomed with open arms, as its supporters had hoped. When the fury abated, the Protector, still true to his ideals, pressed for free and general pardon and was staunchly opposed by many of the council.[24] Until midsummer he had carried most of his colleagues with him because his program contained promise and marked a welcome departure from the harshness characteristic of Henry VIII's reign.

But Henry's regime, based on that of his father, was in tune with the political realities of the sixteenth century, while the Protector's was not. In spite of its virtues, the Protectorate was a failure, at best only a noble experiment and a fond hope. Had

Somerset recognized this and trimmed his sails accordingly, he might have weathered the storm. Unfortunately for him and for England, he failed in the hour of crisis and proved himself a political bungler. The victories of Warwick and Russell owed nothing to his leadership. If anything, he had been more of a liability than an asset. Remaining in London he revealed the full extent of his incapacity by his harassment of Russell and by his vacillation in dealing with Kett. Outside of England his record was even poorer. The victory over the Scots at Pinkie had been in vain, and on the Continent France pressed her advantage.

In all these affairs the counsel of Somerset's friend, Sir William Paget, was ignored. From the beginning of the Protectorate, Paget sent detailed letters of advice concerning both specific policy decisions and general problems of government. Paget's forthright approach leaves no doubt that he initially enjoyed Somerset's complete confidence. As early as February 2, 1549, Paget's correspondence began to convey a sense of alarm and urgency. He sent unequivocal warnings about foreign policy, finance, and social unrest and feared he was becoming a Cassandra or prophet of doom. A month later Paget felt Somerset had "conceived some displeasure" toward him; and while he continued to send his advice, it is clear that Somerset was committed to an independent line of action. Sir Thomas Smith, servant to Somerset and secretary to the King, also "lamented this miserable estate of our commonwealth."[25] When the end came, friend and foe alike could see the inadequacies of Somerset's rule. Judged impartially on its achievements alone, the Protectorate deserved to fall.

To complicate matters further, personal animosities and jealousies were raised against Somerset. While others risked all in the field, he bided his time in safety. To some his sympathies for the poor seemed feigned, as he grew rich and built the splendid residence of Somerset House. In spite of Sir John Thynne's apparent good relations with Warwick, Somerset's unpopular steward was a definite political liability as was the duchess, who was blamed for many of her husband's failings.[26] Although we do not have his own word for it, the best evidence suggests that Warwick broke with Somerset while serving in Norfolk or shortly thereafter. An anonymous observer in the service of Somerset, writing in the early Elizabethan period, referred to hostile daily letters between the two men in August.[27] These letters have not survived. The writer constantly called Warwick the Duke of Northumberland but, nevertheless, appears to have a thorough enough grasp of details to give his account credibility. He suggested that Warwick began "to move" the nobility accompanying him against Somerset "calling him secretly, to such of his acquaintances as he might trust, a coward, a breaker of promises, a nigard, covetous, and ambitious. . . ." Every gentleman "fell in a great liking of the Duke of Northumberland" because of his fortitude, and after returning victoriously he was refused further grants by the Protector. The details of the dispute would be greatly illuminated by the lost correspondence. If these letters resembled the exchange between Somerset and Russell, Warwick's loss of confidence in his friend would be readily understood.

The anonymous account is partially supported by Van der Delft's awareness at the same time of general opposition to Somerset in the council. The ambassador learned from Princess Mary that there was much rivalry and division in the council, because Warwick, Southampton, Arundel, and St. John resisted the formation of a "new council," presumably composed of the Protector and his personal minions. By September 15, Van der Delft knew of a split in the council and ill feeling between Warwick and the Protector and had been asked by Paget to bring the Earl "round to a better disposition regarding religion." A week later, he believed the fall of the Protector was imminent. Even the devoted Paget wavered after a dispute with the Protector; he complained that Somerset had become so suspicious that he could not see two councillors speaking together without becoming jealous. Sometime between September 15 and 23, Warwick met with the ambassador at the latter's house in the country. Warwick discussed his discontent with Somerset and said the time was ripe for Charles V "to come forward as the King's father." After the conversation, Van der Delft believed Somerset was under the influence of his wife and regarded Warwick the more flexible of the two. When the Protector had been deposed, Van der Delft alleged to have learned in confidence from Warwick that "he would not so soon have let a hand to this undertaking to succour the realm had it not been for the talk he had with me when he came to see me in the country."[28]

The confrontation between Somerset and the Privy Council is a dramatic and well-documented historical episode. Sometime before October 5, the Protector realized the widespread opposition to his rule within the council. On that date he issued a proclamation against that body and ordered the commons to arm themselves and repair to Hampton Court to defend the King.[29] By this act Somerset not only seized the initiative, but also declared a virtual state of war against the Privy Council of England. The morning of the following day saw almost the entire council assembled at Warwick's residence, Ely Place. Before the day was over, their numbers included Warwick; Rich, the lord chancellor; St. John, the great master; Arundel, lord chamberlain; Secretary Petre; Southampton; Northampton; Shrewsbury; Sussex; and other lesser personages. The most notable late comer was Petre, who remained with the council after he was sent to them by the Protector. In response to Somerset's propaganda, the councillors issued their own proclamation, "Let the people know the truth," it rang out urging all to rally to them, not the traitorous Somerset, for the King's safety. In a letter addressed to the King, they alleged the Protector was "too much given to his own will" and would not hear reason. It was their hope to have "gently and quietly spoken with him in these things, had he not gathered force about him."[30]

The councillors responded to Somerset's military challenge by issuing an appeal to the city of London. Somerset, also fully aware of the city's importance, sent a request for assistance bearing the King's signature. Both letters, according to the Journal of the Court of Common Council, were "plainly and distinctly read and the whole contents and effects of either of them by the commons in the said Common Council assembled." The opposing communiques were "deliberately debated and pondered"; and finally the council agreed to join "with the said lords for the defense, safeguard, and maintenance both of the King's Majesty's person and of this his grace's city of London." This decision of the common council on October 7, gave the privy councillors the moral support of the city and led to a commitment of one thousand armed men.[31]

From the beginning Somerset's opponents had the better position. His supporters included only Paget, Cranmer, and Smith, in addition to his household servants. Any hope of success lay in his possession of the King and in an appeal to Russell, who had not appeared as requested with his veteran troops. The charges and countercharges gave rise to a host of wild and irresponsible rumors that were discountenanced to Russell. Somerset denied that he was in the Tower, that he would release Gardiner and Bonner and "bring in again the old mass." While awaiting news from the council, he took the King to Windsor and, in a state of near hysteria, threatened on the 7th to carry the matter to "these extremities" (i.e. violence), if the councillors "will take no other way."[32]

The next two days were filled with an exchange of letters between the principals, who returned to a more reasonable position and renounced violence. Through Sir Philip Hoby, the council promised no harm to the duke and pledged not to take away his lands. They wanted "only to give order for the Protectorship, which has not been so well ordered as they think it should have been."[33] On October 8, Somerset wrote the most revealing letter he ever sent to Warwick:

> My lord, I cannot persuade myself that there is any ill conceived in your heart as of yourself against me; for that the same seemeth impossible that where there hath been from your youth and mine so great a friendship and amity betwixt us, as never for my part to no man was greater, now so suddenly there should be hatred; and that without just cause, whatsoever rumors and bruits, or

persuasion of others have moved you to conceive; in the sight
and judgment of almighty God, I protest and affirm this unto you,
I never meant worse to you than to myself; wherefore my lord,
for God's sake, for friendship, for the love that hath ever been
betwixt us or that hereafter may be, persuade yourself with truth,
and let this time declare to me and the world your just honor
and perseverance in friendship, the which God be my witness,
who seeth all hearts, was never diminished, nor ever shall be
whilst I live. . . .[34]

Gradually the few supporters of the Protector deserted him.
Smith conceded, "I cannot deny but I have misliked also some
things that you and the rest of my lords there did mislike" and
thanked Warwick, Petre, and Arundel for permitting his brother
to visit him.[35] Cranmer and Paget also negotiated separately for
the removal of Somerset's servants and finally, on October 10,
for his arrest by Sir Anthony Wingfield, the vice-chamberlain.
The anticipated help from Russell failed to materialize when
both he and Herbert announced their support for the council.
With little more than a loud whimper, the regime of the Protector collapsed. In the final act of the crisis, the fallen duke was
removed from Windsor and lodged in the Tower of London.[36]

From the moment the Privy Council first assembled, Warwick
was its foremost member. None could rival the prestige of the
conqueror of Kett. Yet the opposition to Somerset was by no
means a personal vendetta between two men, each bent on de-
stroying the other; nor is there any evidence to support Pollard's assumption that Warwick was the "subtlest intriguer in
English history." At each stage in the negotiations, the councillors acted as a body and repeatedly stressed the fact that they
were "almost the whole council." Having resisted the despotic
tendencies of the Protector, they would not quickly dance to another's tune. Somerset, fully aware that he was opposed by the
council and all the gentlemen of England, never directed his
propaganda against Warwick or any other individual. Instead,
he styled himself as one of the poor commons injured by the
nobles and gentry, an approach savoring of class warfare. Van

der Delft believed the leadership was composed of Warwick, Southampton, Arundel, and St. John, and was probably correct. Gilbert Burnet thought the mainspring of the opposition was not Warwick, but Southampton, who gained the former to his side.[37] This assumption, however, is as difficult to prove as the notion that Warwick was so subtle in his intrigues that he left not a trace of evidence.

Warwick now faced a political situation offering vast opportunities for distinguished statesmanship, but even greater pitfalls. The removal of Somerset was merely a first step in the restoration of the country's fortunes. Finances were on the verge of collapse, all advantage had been lost in Scotland, and France threatened Boulogne. Whether a council of equals could rule was an open question; the events of 1547 argued against the possibility. Nor could the state of religion offer much comfort. Then there was the fallen duke himself. For far less treasonous behavior, Warwick's father had lost his head, and all experience taught that fallen ministers were safer in the grave. Warwick could easily write, "The man that ruled all by his willfulness is restrained, and now things is [*sic*] like to pass otherwise than of long time it hath done, more for the King's honor and wealth and surety of his realm and subjects."[38] To show the country that he could do better than Somerset would be a more difficult task.

V / The Dudley
Ascendancy Established

The overthrow of the Protectorate in 1549 thrust Warwick into a position of leadership never equaled by a Dudley. For the second time in as many years, it became necessary to fill a void at the highest level, and Warwick was the only man to whom the country could turn. He had not resisted the regal pretensions of Protector Somerset in order to take the same powers for himself. He neither sought absolute authority nor enjoyed legal supremacy over his colleagues in the council. Yet, as leader of the government, Warwick wielded vast power and made the Dudley family first in the kingdom. From the establishment of the Dudley ascendancy until the death of Edward VI in 1553, England was buffeted by exigencies calling for extraordinary statesmanship. Although poorly prepared for these responsibilities and plagued with ill health, Warwick acted with courage and conviction. The challenges of the hour called for political genius of the highest order, but England had to make do with the talents of a man who was acutely aware of his limitations and a council that had been scarred by internal discord.

The Protectorate collapsed in October 1549 because its policies at home and abroad met with humiliating reversals and the willfulness of Somerset alienated councillors who believed their advice should be heard and acted upon. Warwick's decision to turn against his old friend must have been a painful one, for their comradeship had endured over a quarter century, indeed, for the entire mature life of each man. Both were soldiers who had fought valiantly against France and Scotland to extend the power of England. Both were inclined toward similar political programs, with the exception of Warwick's greater realism on the enclosures' question. After 1549 new policies were required. The resurgent power of France overwhelmed Scotland and threatened Boulogne, and Henry VIII's Imperial alliance proved as sterile as in the past. Without a reliable ally, England was at the mercy of the Continental powers. Finances were on the verge of collapse, and the religious question far from settled. If this situation was not menacing enough, domestic unrest made matters little short of catastrophic. To restore tranquility at home a Tudor government had only one remedy, the use of force, irrespective of its justice. Like the great Tudor sovereigns, Henry VII, Henry VIII, and Elizabeth, Warwick knew full well that resistance of the subject must be met with repression; yet he lacked their divine authority. Unfortunately, the popularity of Somerset among the lower orders made a return to established Tudor policy very difficult, especially when it was combined with an inglorious retreat in foreign affairs. Forced to carry out unpopular but necessary policies, Warwick could scarcely expect to win the hearts of his countrymen.

The first problem concerned the fate of Somerset and his followers. Here Warwick showed moderation and a willingness to give Somerset the second chance that the latter denied his own brother, Thomas Seymour. Imprisoned in the Tower on October 14, 1549, Somerset was charged in thirty-one articles submitted to him by the council with subverting the laws of the realm and usurping power. No charge of conspiracy or treason was made. Although many of the acts described as illegal were within the powers granted him as Protector, he subscribed to twenty-nine in an open admission of guilt. The office of Protector was revoked by letters-patent on October 13, and Parliament subse-

2. JOHN DUDLEY, DUKE OF NORTHUMBERLAND

quently approved a fine, which apparently was never collected. By February 1550, Somerset was released and fully pardoned.[1] Rarely in Tudor England did a man fall from exalted office and receive so mild a punishment. Judging from its actions, it is clear that the council wanted only to destroy Somerset's pre-eminence as Protector, not his property or person.

Although we do not have his word on it, Warwick's opposition to Somerset was apparently confined to an assault upon his political position. A faint hint of Warwick's attitude toward Somerset and his followers is contained in an undated letter to Sir John Thynne by an anonymous friend. The correspondent explained that he had been with Lady Warwick, "whose advice in any wise is that he should submit himself" and related that Somerset, Sir Ralph Vane, and all of his friends agreed. Thynne replied to the council's interrogations at the end of November, a fact suggesting that the letter was written at the same time. Warwick, through his wife, was thus attempting to assist in Thynne's rehabilitation with advice concurred in by Thynne's closest political allies. His answers to the council were nevertheless extraordinarily evasive and, assuming they were accepted, little more than a formality. By the following month any doubts about Warwick's attitude toward Somerset were dispelled. Dazzled and exasperated by the rapid turn of events, Ambassador Van der Delft decided Warwick was changeable and unstable when he learned favor was being shown to the fallen duke. The ambassador believed Warwick had been won over by the Duchess of Somerset, "who is always in his house; I believe he will not escape [*sic*]." It might well be asked precisely what the duchess was doing at the Dudleys and at what hours, but it would be most reasonable and charitable to assume the wives intervened jointly to restore amity between the two houses.[2]

Prior to Somerset's release, the Duchess of Somerset and the Countess of Warwick exchanged banquets and festivities daily in order to promote reconciliation between their husbands. Somerset's wife was not an altogether charming woman and has been used as a scapegoat for the duke's downfall. While he was still in the Tower, she was involved in a dispute with the wife of Sir John Cheke that would tend to support her unfavorable reputation.[3] Jane Dudley, in contrast to her husband and the duchess, enjoyed a faultless reputation as a devoted wife and mother. It is likely that both women worked toward the same end for different reasons; the duchess, jealous of her place at court, wished to save the duke for her own sake, while the Countess of Warwick simply desired the end of an unhappy quarrel.

When Somerset was released from the Tower on February 6, 1550, he went directly to the house of Sir John York, sheriff of London, in Walbrook where Warwick frequently stayed and met the council. After dining there with Warwick, Somerset, a free man, departed to his own residence at Sheen.[4] In April, he resumed his place in the Privy Council. Paget told the Imperial ambassador that while Somerset had governed badly, he would come back into authority "because there is no one else to take his place." The remark closely paralleled the one made by Chapuys in 1547 that Hertford and Lisle were the only men capable of governing after Henry VIII. Only conjectures may be advanced to explain why Paget believed Somerset to be the indispensable man in 1550. Certainly his kinship with the King made him a formidable power in the realm. Warwick, Northampton, Arundel, or Paget himself, might retire in disgrace to the country, but for Somerset this would be unthinkable. Paget may have assumed the fall from power would make Somerset wiser and enable him to recover his influence. He was also aware of Warwick's precarious health, which never allowed him to manage affairs with the vigor characteristic of the Protector. After speaking with Paget, Ambassador Van der Delft concluded that Somerset would regain power, not by resisting Warwick, but rather "by the hand of Warwick." Van der Delft held the same view a month later and wrote that Warwick and Somerset were in close communication and visited each other every day.[5]

Although Somerset had suffered a heavy reverse, he still remained a considerable political force. The mildness of his punishment was unique by Tudor standards and was distinctly foreshadowed in the agreement of October 1549 between the council and the Protector's adherents at Windsor. So untypical was this crisis that reliable observers were badly confused and misinformed in evaluating its significance. Consequently, the widespread notion of a "Catholic revival" in 1549 and 1550 has obscured the true nature of the political changes.[6] At the root of the confusion was the contemporary tendency to assume the inseparability of politics and religion. By this logic it was believed that changes in political leadership must bring corresponding religious changes. For most observers religion offered only two possibilities, either furtherance of Protestantism or a return to Rome. This mentality helps explain why the overthrow of the Protectorate was expected to preface a return to Catholicism. Somerset was a Protestant; his removal must be a defeat for his religious cause. So ran the logic. However, by the mid-sixteenth century times were changing, and it was more and more common for politics and religion to exist independent of one another.

In the particular case of Ambassador Van der Delft, wishful thinking of an advanced variety and a personal desire to ingratiate himself with Charles V must be added to an obsolescent political outlook. For example, Van der Delft flattered himself into believing that his advice to Warwick in September 1549 had been instrumental in bringing about the Protector's overthrow. During the succeeding months he found it increasingly difficult to gain first hand information about proceedings in the council. At one point he bewailed the fact that his old confidant, Paget, ignored him. Obviously with critical negotiations underway with the French, the good will of the Imperial ambassador did not receive a very high priority among the councillors. Denied reliable information, he was obliged to satiate the Emperor's appetite for news with confusing and contradictory rumors. Shortly before his departure from England, the ailing Van der Delft wrote in self-pity of his misfortunes, "I am not to blame, having exerted myself to the utmost to discover the sum to be paid by France and other details as well."[7] The total failure of the plot to remove Princess Mary from England, a scheme of his devising, undoubtedly hastened his death and discredited his record as ambassador to England.

Privy councillors and other English officials should have had few doubts about the significance of the October crisis. During negotiations with the mayor and aldermen of London, Warwick and his colleagues gave assurances that there would be no changes in religion. As early as October 17, even Van der Delft admitted reluctantly that Warwick was loyal to the Protestant cause, although he still believed a return to Catholicism was forthcoming. At the end of the next month, Warwick told him in unambiguous terms, "I am not as opinionated as you think, but we have a law here which was made not by the Duke of Somerset alone, but by all the members for the kingdom, and previously the matter of religion has been gone into by the bishops and learned men." The statement reveals a good deal about Warwick's own outlook. He fully accepted the religious settlement sanctioned by Parliament and in no way repudiated that part of the Protector's achievement. In the same breath he implied that theological subtleties were, in the first instance, the concern of experts among whom he did not include himself. A letter of the King and council (including Warwick) to the bishops repeated what Warwick had told Van der Delft earlier and should have dispelled any remaining doubts about the inclination of the new government. The signatures of the King and council were intended to demonstrate once again that the introduction of the prayer book was not a unilateral innovation of the deposed Protector.[8]

The usual arguments for a Catholic revival are based on the increased influence of conservative members in the council and their subsequent removal after the release of Somerset. Unfortunately, until more detailed studies of such figures as the Earls of Arundel and Southampton have been made, any statements must be tentative. Both men were supposed to be "Catholics," but the term is never adequately defined. Did it mean they denied the royal supremacy and worked for a papal restoration? Were they Henricians? Or were they merely more conservative than others? In the last instance the term becomes devoid of meaning and worthless in identifying a political faction or party. Since both Arundel and Southampton held office under Henry VIII, they were presumably not papalists.

Southampton (then Wriothesley), Henry's lord chancellor, was named a councillor and executor in the late King's will, while Arundel was an assistant executor. If the journals of the House of Lords are to be trusted, neither dissented during the passage of the first act of uniformity and the debates over the prayer book. John Ponet, writing six years later, regarded Southampton as the leading figure in the overthrow of the Protector rather than Warwick. Whatever role this man hoped to play was cut short by illness in January 1550 and death six months later. Arundel was charged with abusing the office of lord chamberlain. His crime appears rather dubious by twentieth-century standards, but in an age when the Duke of Buckingham, Cromwell, Surrey, and Thomas Seymour died for questionable offenses, his treatment by Warwick would seem mild in the extreme. By strange coincidence the three men, Warwick, Southampton, and Arundel, were all reported sick during the months following the Protector's fall. That all such rumors were not feigned or diplomatic illnesses is supported by Southampton's death. Even in death Thomas Wriothesley, Earl of Southampton, the alleged "conservative" and "Catholic," was an enigma, for the preacher at his funeral was none other than John Hooper, first of the Puritans.[9]

Continuity between the Protectorate and the concilliar rule under Warwick that followed is evident from the composition of the council. There is little evidence to support allegations of a Catholic revival or a packed council of sycophants to Warwick. The leading figures, with one exception, were all members of the Protector's council. The only new member of importance was Henry Grey, Marquess of Dorset, a councillor under Henry VIII, and hardly an unfamiliar face or upstart. The important offices and promotions went to men who had been prominent for nearly a decade. Russell and St. John became the Earls of Bedford and Wiltshire, and Paget received the barony promised him by Henry. Wiltshire then replaced Somerset as lord treasurer and was himself succeeded by Warwick as lord great master of the King's household. Northampton followed Warwick as lord great chamberlain, while Bedford and Rich retained their posts as lord privy seal and lord chancellor, respectively. Petre continued as senior secretary, but Smith yielded his secretaryship to Dr. Nicholas Wotton, a "conservative" and long-time diplomatist. Whatever were the sympathies of the smaller fry who were added, it was of small consequence when the men at the top were oldtimers in harness as Tudor councillors under both the King of beloved memory, Henry VIII, and the Protector.

The Parliament that convened in November 1549 was elected at the beginning of the Protectorate. Warwick was rarely present in a session primarily devoted to questions raised during the past year. Acts were passed against unlawful assemblies, breaking of hedges around enclosures, and seditious prophesies about the King and council. After a committee of lords visited the Protector in the Tower to assure themselves that his confession was freely given, an act of fine and ransom was passed against him. In ecclesiastical affairs the new service for ordination of priests was the most notable measure. Because of the altered function of the priesthood in the new English service and the movement toward Zwinglianism by Cranmer and other reformers, a new ordinal was required that de-emphasized the sacrificial powers of the clergy. A commission headed by Cranmer was given statutory authority to prepare the new service which was later incorporated in the second *Book of Common Prayer*.[10] In spite of the revolts and overthrow of the Protectorate, the mild treason act, originally urged by Somerset and praised so highly by Pollard as a symbol of freedom, remained in force.

The most serious question confronting England was the ruinous war with France and the danger it posed to Boulogne. The council wished to retain the fruit of Henry's victory until 1554, when it was to be restored to France by terms of the Treaty of Camp negotiated in 1546, and was reluctant to accept that its loss was inevitable. In keeping with this attitude, Antonio Guidotti, a Florentine merchant enjoying the confidence of both sides, undertook exploratory communications between France and England. After it became clear that formal negotiations would be necessary, Bedford, Paget, Petre, and Sir John Mason were instructed to meet French commissioners and negotiate the return of Boulogne on terms favorable to England. Their first position was to press the French to honor all treaties made by Henry VIII and Scotland and to deliver Mary, Queen of Scots to England, so the marriage with Edward could be performed. If these terms were not acceptable, tactical retreats were outlined.[11] Well aware of English weaknesses, the French drove a hard bargain and forced the negotiators to yield.

Paget explained the situation to Warwick in unequivocal terms. The French, he said, would have Boulogne by "fair means or foul." They refused to satisfy English demands for Scotland and acknowledge any debt to England beyond a reasonable sum for restoration of Boulogne. Knowing the superior strength of Henry II, Paget urged Warwick to accept peace on French terms as the lesser of two evils and advised him to convince the rest of the council to take the money offered. Paget and his colleagues might easily be accused of appeasement by chauvinists, longing for the good old days when Henry V brought France to her knees, but for realists there was no other choice. The council relented and rapidly sent new instructions that virtually accepted peace at any price. Nearly two months of negotiations came to an end on March 15, when Paget again wrote Warwick, "We have agreed upon a peace although not with so good conditions as we could have wished, yet within the limits of our instructions, and somewhat better in some things and might peradventure have been much better in many things if peace and war had been so indifferent to us."[12]

The treaty, dated March 24, 1550, provided for the evacuation of Boulogne within six weeks after signing. The French agreed to pay 400,000 crowns, of which half would be paid immediately and the remainder the following August. England agreed to raze the few small forts remaining north of the Scottish border. Peace with France may not have been the most popular foreign policy in an age that still thought in medieval terms about English claims in France; it was, however, a first step toward a policy consistent with England's declining power on the Continent. Within a decade all English pretensions for a European base collapsed with the loss of Calais and were never seriously revived again; this defeat was so ignominious that the surrender of Boulogne appeared in contrast almost a diplomatic triumph.

Much of the credit for a realistic foreign policy must go to Warwick, whose reputation with the public suffered heavily on its account. Yet, the treaty was no single-handed triumph. Far from being Warwick's tools, the commissioners sent to France were among the most astute and experienced men available for the task. Bedford and Paget had been privy councillors as long as Warwick and had repeatedly demonstrated their competence and integrity, while Petre and Mason were respected by men of all shades of opinion. Although England's old ally, the Emperor, was displeased with the treaty, he had refused any military assistance to help England defend Boulogne. The council harassed Van der Delft and referred him to Warwick, who, according to the ambassador, refused to see him by feigning illness. When the treaty was published, Van der Delft was unable to send any news of its terms and complained of his bad treatment.[13]

By the summer of 1550, Warwick and the council had successfully resolved two of the most pressing political questions facing the country. The Duke of Somerset was not only alive and free, but also readmitted to the Privy Council. Not one of his confederates had lost his life for resisting the council. The achievement of peace with France likewise augured well for the future, if no new storms appeared on the horizon. After Te Deums were sung in thanksgiving for peace, delegations from both countries formally accepted the treaty. Lord Cobham, Petre, and Mason were received by Henry II and the French court at Amiens early in May. When the King had taken the oath of acceptance, Mason remained behind as resident ambassador.

At the ceremonies welcoming the French delegation to England a few weeks later, Warwick's eldest son, Lord Lisle, received his first notice at court. The French dignitaries dined with Edward at Greenwich on May 25 and afterwards saw "a pastime of ten against ten at the ring" in which Lisle, the young Duke of Suffolk, and eight others appareled in yellow competed against Lord Strange, eldest son of the Earl of Derby, and others dressed in blue. Surprisingly, there is no record of the King, now in his thirteenth year, participating in the sport. Edward watched the competition with his older guests and did not join the hunting parties on the following days. Before leaving England, the ambassadors "had a fair supper made them by the Duke of Somerset, and afterward went into the Thames, and saw both the bear hunted in the river and also wild-fire cast out of boats and many pretty conceits."[14]

A few days later the marriage of Lord Lisle to Lady Anne Seymour affirmed the reconciliation between the houses of Dudley and Seymour. Warwick undoubtedly hoped this union would symbolize the end of the quarrels and discord that had caused a rupture in personal relations and had also done harm to the whole country. If he were already contemplating a grand design for killing the duke and gaining control of the throne, as his enemies have contended, he would scarcely have been fool enough to bind his own heir to the family scheduled for destruction and then been obliged to marry a younger son to Lady Jane Grey. In consenting to the marriage, Warwick and Somerset must have believed that the interests of each family would be served; otherwise, they would have been guilty of betraying their own offspring.

The celebrated wedding took place on June 3 at Somerset's residence of Sheen on the Thames with the guest list headed by the King himself. After a "fair" wedding feast and joyous dancing, the King and ladies went into two ante-chambers of boughs where Edward saw "six gentlemen of one side and six of another run the course of the field twice over."[15] Warwick did not attend the festivities and remained confined to his own house because of continuing ill health.[16] If rumors were correct that the mothers instigated the match, there is ample scope for assuming the wisdom of Tudor wives was greater than that of their husbands.[17]

A wedding of far less immediate significance took place only a day later. Warwick's younger son, Lord Robert, married Amy Robsart, daughter and heir of Sir John Robsart, a substantial Norfolk gentleman. Compared with the prize of the previous day, Warwick accepted an undistinguished match for what was to be his most gifted and able son. None of the provisions of the marriage settlement suggest Amy to have been an attractive wife from a financial standpoint. A better possibility was genuine love between the two young people, both about seventeen. This was the view of Cecil, who later referred to the marriage in most pessimistic terms, "Nuptiae carnales a laetitia incipiunt et in luctu terminantur." Even if his harsh indictment of love is questioned, Cecil was probably correctly informed about the motives behind the marriage. But in 1550 there was no more reason to doubt the happy union of Robert and Amy than that of Lisle and Anne Seymour.[18]

For a brief moment in 1550, peace and tranquility seemed assured by the French treaty and the marriage alliance joining the Dudleys and Seymours, but all too quickly the optimism proved illusory. Until his death, John Dudley—and, indeed, the whole country—passed through a tortuous succession of perils. Almost as if the King and his councillors had been destined to suffer vexation by an unseen hand of fate, trouble and misfortune began to appear. Perhaps only the sins of his father were visited upon the young Edward. The others, however, suffered in large measure because of their own folly and miscalculation.

Possibly the least serious of the year's problems was the growing estrangement between the King and council and the Emperor and Princess Mary. Improved relations with France automatically heralded increased tension with Charles V, and the Imperialists shamelessly exploited the Emperor's cousin as the instrument by which they could vent their rage against an England no longer dependent upon them. Matters were complicated by efforts of the Emperor to obtain written assurances from the English government permitting Mary's household to serve as a center for loyalists to Rome. Furthermore, a sense of psychological insecurity and fear threw Mary so completely into the arms of the Imperialists at several points that Charles himself was forced to restrain her. Van der Delft finally advised her to flee the country, and in June 1550 an abortive attempt was made.[19]

After the failure of the plot to remove the princess from England, a long and pointless series of charges and countercharges were made by the Imperial ambassador and the English concerning what promises had been made to Mary about her religious liberty. It would be hard to believe that Warwick and the Reformers in the council were naive enough to believe Mary could be converted to Protestantism. On the other hand, had they wished to stop her personal attendance at mass, it would have been a very simple matter to place her under close surveillance in the Tower or elsewhere. Warwick was not a bigot or persecutor by nature, but Mary's obstinacy placed him in a very difficult position. The council's policy was to give no written guarantees that would injure the cause of reform throughout the country and to attempt to limit the celebration of the illegal service to Mary herself.

The question of Mary's mass, as well as maritime disputes, quickly initiated the new Imperial ambassador, Jehan Scheyfve, into the mysteries of dealing with Englishmen. Scheyfve replaced Van der Delft, who was recalled before the plot to remove Mary occurred and died shortly afterwards. When Scheyfve protested to the council about two Dutch vessels seized in English waters by Scots pirates, the councillors told him the lord admiral was collecting information about the affair; and Warwick, who was greatly displeased about the whole business, stated bluntly that because the King was at peace with Scotland, their mariners could not be molested. Paget supported Warwick's views, and the new ambassador withdrew empty-handed.[20]

Darker shadows were cast by reports of a new breach between Warwick and Somerset. A most revealing letter concerning the duke passed between Richard Whalley and Cecil, two of Somerset's own followers, on June 26, 1550. While discussing "the estate and proceedings" of Somerset with Warwick, Whalley was convinced that Warwick was "a most dear and faithful friend unto my lord's grace." Warwick was "vehemently troubled" by Somerset's actions and showed "the inward grief of his heart with not a few tears." Particularly disturbing were Somerset's efforts to secure the release of Stephen Gardiner from the Tower and to assist the Arundells, who were implicated in the Western rebellion. Because of this, the whole council was displeased and fearful that Somerset had designs to regain the protectorship. "Why will he not see his own decay herein?" asked Warwick. "He will so far overthrow himself as shall pass the power of his friends to recover." Whalley advised Cecil to warn the duke of impending dangers and added that Warwick "will be very plain with him in the premises at his coming to court." The letter further showed that Cecil was already in correspondence with Warwick, possibly with a view toward smoothing out differences with Somerset. The greatest significance of the letter, however, was that it left no doubt that one of the duke's supporters was having second thoughts about the wisdom of his actions.[21]

Warwick's involvement in religious affairs increased as he concerned himself with the two conservative bishops, Stephen Gardiner and Cuthbert Tunstall, and the radical, John Hooper. Gardiner, imprisoned during the Protectorate, found to his surprise that his cause was championed by Somerset after his return to the council. Gardiner had so completely misjudged affairs the previous autumn that he believed Warwick would release him after delivering the country from the "tyrannous government of the Duke of Somerset." In truth, both Somerset and Warwick would have probably permitted his release if the wily Bishop of Winchester had given adequate assurances not to obstruct the cause of reform. After conferring with Somerset, Northampton, Wiltshire, Russell, and Petre in June, Gardiner showed a willingness to cooperate. To be certain that Gardiner was sincere, the council sent a list of articles for his subscription in an order signed by both Somerset and Warwick.[22] These were presented to him on July 9 by a delegation composed of Warwick, Wiltshire, Herbert, and Petre. "My Lord of Warwick entertained me very gently," said Gardiner, "and would needs, whiles I should write, have me sit down by him; and when he saw me make somewhat strange so to do, he pulled me nearer him, and said, we had or this sat together, and trusted we should do so again [*sic*]." Gardiner subscribed to the articles, but found the preface to them against his conscience. According to Warwick, the councillors then departed "being sorry they could do him [Gardiner] no more good."[23]

Whereas Warwick acted strictly within the orders of the council in interviewing Gardiner, he exerted his personal influence in behalf of Hooper, bishop elect of Gloucester. Fearful of Hooper's extremism, Cranmer raised questions about his refusal to wear the tonsure and prescribed vestments and to swear the oath of supremacy by the Saints and Evangelists. At this point Warwick intervened and sent Hooper to Cranmer with a personal message, requesting the archbishop not to charge "this said bearer with an oath burdenous to his conscience." Cranmer was unmoved by Warwick, and a few days later on August 5, the King and council (including Somerset) sent another letter promising pardon against praemunire and discharging him of all real or supposed dangers in consecrating Hooper. The words of Warwick, the King and council, notwithstanding, Cranmer remained recalcitrant and did not consecrate the new Bishop of Gloucester until the following March.[24]

Throughout the summer of 1550 the countryside seethed with discontent in anticipation of a poor harvest. A repetition of the violence of the previous year was prevented by firm action on the part of the council. Warwick was appointed lieutenant of Warwickshire with full judicial and military powers "to enquire of by oaths of good and lawful men of our country." It does not appear that Warwick actually went northward on account of ill health, but he probably supervised through the deputies he was empowered to appoint. Somerset likewise cooperated and personally visited Oxfordshire, Sussex, Wiltshire, and Hampshire. The effectiveness of the council's enforcement of law and order is confirmed by the extreme types who suffered punishment. Presumably the more intelligent potential agitators were obliged to keep their heads down. In August a miller's servant was pilloried in Cheap for speaking seditious words against Somerset. For alleging that Somerset proclaimed himself King of England in his country, the depraved fellow also suffered the loss of his ears by order of the council.[25] Stephen Caston, a clerk of Sutton, Essex, rashly proclaimed that Henry VIII was a papist and uttered "many opprobrius words of him as it was heard."[26] One Greg, a poulterer of Surrey, gained a following as a prophet able to cure "divers diseases by words and prayer." By commandment of Warwick and the council, this man was set on a scaffold in Croydon with a paper on his breast "wherein was written his deceitful and hypocritical dealings."[27]

Toward the end of the year, a flood of rumors obscured the political situation. There were reports of a quarrel between the two northern earls, Derby and Shrewsbury, and Warwick and Paget. The council allegedly ordered Derby to meet Warwick at Newcastle for talks about Derby's joining the government. Fearing a trick, he refused and said he desired no change in the government. Coinciding with this was a story that Warwick went to Newcastle to seize Derby and bring him to London by sea.[28]

In November Ambassador Scheyfve spoke of deep discord among the council and said Somerset was doing his utmost to acquire friends and "especially to win over the people, which he had not tried to do before." He also heard from "a safe source" that Warwick was about to cast off his wife and marry Princess Elizabeth, with whom he had had several secret and intimate personal communications. The motive behind this was seizure of the crown. An Imperial ambassador so uninformed about Somerset and gullible about Warwick was the ideal man for the post in 1550—from an English standpoint, that is. If there was any truth in the talk of factionalism, it was apparently smoothed over by December when Sir John Mason wrote Cecil from Blois that he had sent letters of thanks to Somerset and Warwick "of whose good agreement I do rejoice even at the bottom of my heart." He continued, "For in so doing consists their own healths and the upright administration of the commonwealth." Many abroad whispered to the contrary, "because they would gladly have it so." Mason closed with the quaint homily, "When all the horses draw one way, the cart sticketh not lightly in the mire."[29]

The life upon which the English Reformation depended was endangered in November 1550. Scheyfve's report of Edward's grave illness is supported by the paucity of entries in the King's *Journal* for November and by warrants issued by the Privy Council. "Eight elles of white holland cloth" were ordered on the 4th "to be employed for the King's majesty's use to a little bed for his own lying." The versatile Sir Andrew Dudley was directed at the same time to deliver "one yard of crimson taffeta to be employed about the said little bed" to a yeoman of the removing wardrobe. Two weeks later Sir Ralph Sadler received a warrant to deliver six pairs of sheets also for the King's use. Although the frail boy recovered, minds in all quarters must have been troubled with the thought of Edward's condition and the perils that would ensue were he to die before leaving a Protestant heir. Given a normal life—or even a brief one of thirty years—Edward could be expected to bar forever the succession of either of his sisters.[30]

Warwick was plagued with illness himself throughout the

year. The nature and seriousness of his indisposition is never precisely stated, but there are too many references to allow the assumption that sickness was feigned. When England cried out for leadership, a responsible and perhaps ambitious man like Warwick would never have lingered in bed. On the other hand, the council probably would have forced him into retirement if he showed signs of becoming a complete invalid. His spirits undoubtedly rose in September with the accession of the capable, young Cecil to the secretaryship. Reasons for Cecil's appointment unfortunately eluded even his biographer, Conyers Read. One of Warwick's first letters to his new colleague dwelt on an expected and time-worn subject: Again Warwick was away from court "purposely to take a bath" for his health. Like the King, Warwick also revived to face another year. But if his strength had been sapped during the past months, the new year would offer few opportunities for a tired and aging man to convalesce in peace.[31]

January 1551 found Warwick with the King at Greenwich assiduously attending to the details of government. He had been the leading councillor for over a year, but even his enemy, Ambassador Scheyfve, was forced to admit that England was ruled by an oligarchy, not by one man as under the Protectorate: "Warwick governs absolutely with Northampton and Herbert. Even Somerset bows his head and waits for a better time. Warwick is hated by the commons and more feared than loved by the rest." At his first meeting with Scheyfve on the 8th, Warwick was grieved by a certain rumor going around and gave assurance that he would always foster friendship with the Emperor. The ambassador returned the compliments and, by saying all sorts of things were being uttered, diplomatically dodged the question of rumors. Still he found no more satisfaction in his complaints about English shipping practices; Warwick and Somerset together told him that under English laws every man might enter and search ships as often as he desired. Among routine matters receiving Warwick's attention was the supplying of the new ambassador to France, Sir William Pickering, with suitable furniture including "two nest of gilt bowls" and "silver candlesticks." Sir Reginald Scott was directed to sell all wood and coal remaining in his custody upon the dissolution of the mint at Canterbury and "make payment of the money thereof growing" to the high treasurer of the King's mints "without any delay." On the last day of the month, Warwick, Somerset, and the rest of the council underwrote a letter of introduction for Sir Henry Dudley, who was journeying to France.[32]

The long trial of Stephen Gardiner concluded on February 14th with his deprivation from the see of Winchester. These proceedings were the logical result of measures taken against him at the beginning of the Protectorate. Much has been made of Somerset's efforts to assist Gardiner in 1550, but all too rarely noted is the fact that Somerset as well as Warwick testified against him at the trial. Somerset's treatment of Gardiner was unquestionably one of the most confusing and seemingly irrational aspects of the former Protector's policy. John Ponet, who succeeded Gardiner at Winchester, however, was unequivocal about his predecessor. "This doctor," he said, "hath a swart color." "He had a hanging look, frowning brows, eyes an inch within the head, a nose hooked like a buzzard, nostrils like a horse, ever snuffing in the wind, a sparrow mouth, and great paws, like the devil's talons on his feet." It was also the foul tongue of Ponet that termed John Dudley the English Alcibiades.[33]

The climax to the long and tedious dialogue between the council and the Imperial ambassador over Princess Mary's mass came with a threat of war from Charles V. Scheyfve, while talking with Warwick at the council in March 1550, argued that Henry VIII had promised that Mary's mass would never be denied. Warwick avoided giving a negative answer and replied diplomatically that Edward would have to be consulted. The impetuous Dutchman said further delay should not be necessary. His patience exhausted, Warwick, seconded by Paget and Northampton, demanded to know whether the pledge continually referred to had been given personally to Scheyfve since he was so sure of it. The war ultimatum followed a stormy meeting the same month between the royal brother and sister in which one proved as inflexible as the other on the question of the mass.[34]

This issue was also the occasion of a sharp argument between Warwick and Mary. To her assertion that Henry VIII cared more for the kingdom than all the councillors put together, Warwick retorted, "How now my Lady? It seems that your grace is trying to show us in a hateful light to the King, our master, without any cause whatsoever." Cranmer, along with Ridley and Ponet, attempted to salve the King's stout Protestant conscience with an argument that "to give licence to sin, was sin; to suffer and wink at it for a time might be borne"; but what was sound logic for learned doctors and experienced councillors ill-satisfied the son of Henry VIII. Exactly how Edward was dissuaded is not known. Hostilities were averted, however, on April 2, when Warwick and Somerset informed Scheyfve of the decision to send Dr. Wotton to the Emperor for talks replacing Morison, who had mishandled negotiations earlier.[35]

To maintain a firm posture against legalizing the mass for Mary, Sir Anthony Browne, one of the King's servants, and later, Dr. Mallet, Mary's own chaplain, were imprisoned for hearing the illegal service.[36] Although it became evident that Mary would never be compelled to listen to the service from the *Book of Common Prayer*, and that Charles V would never go to war over such a trifling issue, the controversy dragged on. In September Warwick asked Scheyfve if he had express orders from the Emperor to bring the question up again and again. Another argument of the Imperialists was that Paget had promised Charles V on the King's behalf that Mary should hear mass privately. Paget denied making any promises, and the council was "disposed to believe him." Nevertheless, Paget was secluded from the council and court in October and committed to his house where he was "prohibited to speak or confer with any but those of his own family."[37] This play-acting by the English and the Imperialists carried over into 1552 and did not become more edifying with the passage of time.

The continued courtship of France was a more positive policy of Warwick's government. After the return of Boulogne, the English and French negotiated a marriage treaty between Edward VI and Elizabeth, the daughter of Henry II. Throughout the elaborate ceremonies celebrating this match, Warwick charmed his French guests and won the admiration of the young King. These proceedings were anathematized by medievalists living in the never-never-land of the Black Prince and Henry V and later by nationalistic enthusiasts, but common sense dictated that an England no longer able to conquer France must live in peace with her. Moreover, Scotland was not to be won to a Greater Britain by force of arms, for that proud nation would turn to France rather than accept English conquest. And, like the English in Ireland, the French in Scotland would in time defeat themselves. It cannot, of course, be proved that Warwick foresaw the verdict of history; nor is it clear to what extent he was personally responsible for the French alliance. Warwick was an opportunist in foreign policy. He formulated no long-range plans and was generally concerned only with the problems of the hour. Before 1549 there is every reason to believe that he accepted and supported the totally different policies of Henry VIII and Somerset.

The English embassy to France in May 1551 was headed by the Marquess of Northampton and included Warwick's son, Lord Lisle, and Sir Thomas Smith, the former secretary and adherent of the Protector. Traveling in great style, the marquess was accompanied by an entourage of 62, while Lisle and Smith had only eight and seven servants respectively. Warwick explained to Mason, who in May was still in Paris, that the King had asked Henry II, "his good brother," to receive Lisle into his service. Besides sending best wishes to the Masons for himself and his wife, Warwick said, "As so poor a man may render thanks unto so noble a prince [Henry II], I pray you to execute the office for me because you have advertised me that it has pleased his grace to remember me." The ambassadors invested Henry II with the Order of the Garter and parleyed over the all-important financial arrangements surrounding the marriage treaty. Although war broke out between France and the Empire during the visit, making England a more attractive ally, the English were forced to lower their request from 1.4 million crowns to 200,000. Included within the treaty was an interesting provision that if the King died, the princess should not have the dowry. "They did that for friendship's sake without precedent," Edward recorded in his diary. In the midst of debate over an agreeable sum, Northampton wrote both to Warwick and the council for new instructions, a practice that suggested Warwick was only *primus inter pares*.[38]

In London Edward, Warwick, and Somerset wined and dined the French mission in grand style. In exchange for the Garter presented to Henry II, Edward was duly installed in the Order of St. Michael. The King, now in his fourteenth year, delighted in displaying his ample talents. He shot, rode, played the lute, and received the dignitaries in his study at Hampton Court. Yet, there was a feeling that England received the short end of the bargain. Northampton did accept a smaller dowry, and the gifts presented in behalf of the French were worth only about one-fifth those given by the English. The provision that neither party was bound in conscience or honor until the princess reached the age of twelve was perhaps a useful face-saving clause. Nevertheless, the marriage treaty had the anticipated effect on relations with the Emperor. When Scheyfve protested in September about the capture of an Imperial vessel off English shores, he was given short shrift. "Do you want the King to keep up a fleet especially to drive off French men of war," Warwick replied and added charges of his own against the Emperor.[39]

While improved relations with France strengthened the English position on the Continent in 1551, the problem of Somerset's role in the government reappeared once again. The thread of events leading to his second and final fall in October 1551 is slender and contains little proof of a plot on the part of Warwick. On the contrary, according to the best contemporary sources, he made sincere efforts to reconcile the duke with himself and the council and to allow him an active part in the government short of reviving one man rule. Somerset acquiesced to a large degree throughout 1550 and 1551 and was given the confidence of his colleagues. To speak of him as leader of the King's opposition, as Pollard did, is to gloss over wide areas of cooperation in depriving Gardiner and treating with the French ambassadors. It also ignores Somerset's participation in the council's repression of popular discontent. In December 1550 he was assigned one hundred horsemen, twice the number entrusted to Warwick. He was named lord lieutenant of Buckinghamshire and Berkshire the following May and was empowered "to enquire of all treasons, inspirations of treasons, insurrections, rebellions, . . . and other evil deeds."[40] As late as the end of August, the King recorded in his diary, "The Duke of Somerset, taking certain that began a new conspiracy for the destruction of the gentlemen at Wokingham two days past, executed them with death for their offence."

The whole idea of Somerset or anyone being in opposition confuses the substance of Tudor politics with a later era. To use modern terminology, the English constitution of the time resembled a one-party system in many respects. A politician could cooperate with the ruling faction, revolt, or on rare occasions retire from political life. To conduct a vigorous and concerted opposition was tantamount to treason. So long as Somerset was willing to abide by the political system, he could exert his own influence within the council; but the moment he pursued an independent policy his actions would be regarded as rebellious.

The recurrent references to friction within the council indicate uncertainty on the part of Somerset whether he could tolerate a position of equality with former subordinates. Certainly no man had more ample warning from his friends about the probable results of his ambition. Before the fall of the Protectorate, Paget spoke unequivocally of impending dangers, while Warwick and probably Cecil did likewise in June 1550. New rustlings of trouble were heard in January 1551, when Warwick wrote Paget imploring him "to be vigilant and circumspect in the matter which now you have in hand." Unfortunately, the letter does not state precisely about what Paget should be vigilant. Warwick, however, left no doubt that relations between Paget and him were strained.[41]

A month later the council examined the enigmatic Richard Whalley "for persuading divers nobles of the realm to make the Duke of Somerset Protector at the next parliament." Although Whalley "stood to the denial, the Earl of Rutland affirming it manifestly," he was briefly committed to the Fleet. An anonymous letter, dated February 17, 1551, sheds some light on the affair. The writer "by nature grounded in consanquinity and nearness of blood" to the addressee, a noble, disclaimed reports of practicing to undermine the friendship of Somerset and Warwick:

> My lord, if any person have made this report of me he had most untruly slandered and belied me; God defend that I, considering the trust that it has pleased the King's majesty to repose in me, should so long live to mind any dissension in this his highness's realm, and as concerning agreement between my said lords, albeit I have heard certain rumors in the country that they should not be in full and perfect amity, yet did I never give credit there to, but thought and said that I trusted my said lords were too wise to do considering the great inconvenience that might come thereof. . . .
>
> I never intended to take party with any noble man against others, but to my power to increase their friendships, and to serve the King. . . .[42]

Sir Ralph Vane, a veteran of the Scottish wars and a neighbor of Warwick, was another supporter of Somerset. A dispute between Warwick and Vane over land rights came to the attention of the council and resulted in the latter's commitment to the Tower in March. An adherent of Warwick, Sir Henry Isley, testified how he with servants of his own and of Warwick "repaired by his lordship's appointment to the park of Posterne" where they met Vane armed with sixty men. When Vane was ordered to remove his cattle, he said he had the "herbage and pannage thereof by the King's letters patent" and would not leave, but rather die in the quarrel. He bragged that he had over three hundred men at his commandment and was soon apprehended by Thomas Hale, sergeant at arms. Included among the councillors who sent him to the Tower was the Duke of Somerset. That Vane was a swaggering trouble-maker seems clear. Yet, Isley declared that he had taken the initiative on Warwick's orders; moreover, Vane was apparently within his rights in keeping cattle on Warwick's land. His summary treatment by the council underlines the power in Warwick's hands and the arbitrary way he would use it against a man who defied him.[43]

His ear always to the ground, the intrepid Ambassador Scheyfve heard rumors in April that Somerset might take up the old religion. But the ambassador's wisdom was increasing: "This gossip is not to be taken seriously for everyone is ready to say anything he imagines may work out to his advantage." Another rumor of a quarrel between Somerset and Warwick in "open council" is supported by Edward's *Journal*, which reported the councillors banqueting together on four successive days "to show agreement among them, whereas discord was bruited." The problem is a difference of dates; Scheyfve wrote on April 9, while Edward's entry is for April 24. There is a possibility of two different quarrels, but this is discounted by the ambassador's report that "the matter was calmed down" with Warwick and Somerset still "good friends and allies." News of discord must have reached Sir Richard Morison in Augsburg, for he wrote to Cecil advising him to regard the security of the King and kingdom as his chief object. Assuming Cecil still a friend to Somerset, Morison hoped the letter would influence both men. On April 17, Warwick became earl marshal of England, a position formerly held by the duke. Scheyfve, in two subsequent dispatches, referred to Warwick's suspicion of Somerset's relations with the Earls of Shrewsbury and Derby and what proved to be a false rumor of rebellion by Somerset.[44] From these reports and rumors, while not necessarily accurate, it must be assumed that trouble was brewing. Somerset **was** apparently taking the initiative and being checked at every point by Warwick.

Until October Warwick's known political maneuvers are little more than a collection of tales and suppositions. In May Scheyfve learned that Warwick had denied Somerset the separate table he enjoyed by way of salary on the grounds that the council board was sufficient, since the duke held no particular office. The alleged intrigues of Shrewsbury and Derby failed to materialize. Both arrived in London in June. Two months later Derby was admitted to the Privy Council, and Shrewsbury remained president of the council of the North. Once again Warwick suffered a relapse and underwent medical treatment. From Drayton Paget endured his rustication, constantly writing Cecil to learn how the political winds were blowing. In August there were rumors that the Duke of Norfolk and Edward Courtenay were to be released and that Arundel was returning to the council.[45]

The most plausible interpretation of the political situation is to recognize the ascendancy of Warwick. After 1549 none of the councillors could rival his reputation or authority. In high favor with the King, Warwick was content with a position of first among equals in the council. Under his leadership a large measure of domestic tranquility and political harmony had been restored during the past two years. Even if he was not beloved by his fellow councillors, Warwick was a man the nobility and gentry of England could accept. His role was a simple one; he needed only to maintain his ascendancy and crush with overwhelming strength anyone bold or foolish enough to raise his hand. Too proud a man to suffer eclipse in silence, Somerset made a last desperate gamble to regain power, but in 1551 he was more isolated than he had been in 1549. If he could have decreed manhood suffrage and called a general election, Somerset might have swept not only Warwick, but all men of property from office; what Somerset and most writers on the period forgot was that popular government was three centuries away. It is easy to label Somerset a blundering and visionary politi-

cian. This he was; nevertheless, it is difficult to imagine how anyone with his limited resources could have overthrown the government. A united council ruled out the possibility of a *coup* or
civil war, an entente with Mary was not only impossible, but
useless, and foreign intervention was equally unthinkable in
1551.

The promotion of Warwick to a dukedom was anticlimactic
and merely confirmed the obvious. On October 11, 1551, the son
of Edmund Dudley became Duke of Northumberland. It was
not a solitary honor, because Dorset became Duke of Suffolk
and Wiltshire and Herbert were advanced to Marquess of Winchester and Earl of Pembroke, respectively. In the King's presence and before Somerset and the nobility of England, Secretary Cecil read aloud the letters patent. John Dudley, K.G., Viscount Lisle, Earl of Warwick, lord great master of the King's
house, and earl marshal of England, now a duke, stood at the
King's left hand. When the ceremonies were completed, the
lords took off their robes and feasted. "First on the bench sat the
Duke of Suffolk, next to him the Duke of Northumberland, then
the Marquess of Winchester, and last the Earl of Pembroke. And
then on the other side a little lower, sat the Duke of Somerset"
with Russell, Northampton, Rutland, Cobham, Fitzwater, and
Lord Thomas Howard. After the lords departed, the King
knighted Cecil, and three of the privy chamber, John Cheke,
Henry Neville, and Henry Sidney, who had recently married
Mary Dudley.[46]

The arrest and trial of Somerset proceeded along lines not untypical of the sixteenth century. A great deal of scholarship has
been expended in determining the reliability and legality of the
charges against him, and the results have not been flattering to
Tudor justice. To utterly deny, however, that he intrigued to
overthrow Northumberland and others in the council is to fly in
the face of overwhelming evidence.[47] The indictments of the
grand juries of Middlesex and Kent as well as testimony by Sir
Thomas Palmer and William Crane all refer to machinations
taking place the previous April, a month in which political un-

rest was reported by a variety of sources.[48] The equilibrium in the council could only be upset by Somerset, for Northumberland (then Warwick) through word and deed had shown his willingness to permit—and indeed to encourage—Somerset's participation in the government. On October 18, two days after Somerset's arrest, Scheyfve reported that Northumberland could not imagine what drove Somerset to it, since he had great authority in the council and a fortune of £15,000–£20,000 per year.[49] Northumberland was asking the great question of Tudor politics: What moved men to grasp for supreme power when they already enjoyed both great influence and wealth?

Singularly impressive was the solidarity of those who opposed Somerset during the weeks between his arrest and the trial on December 1. As in 1549, the whole council was united against him. Neither Paget nor Cecil exerted themselves on his behalf; on the contrary, rumors had it that they gave him away. The overseas ambassadors likewise accepted his guilt. Peter Vannes, ambassador to Venice and formerly Latin secretary to the King, congratulated the council for their discretion and dexterity used "in putting toward, without any noise or tumult, the Duke of Somerset, whose evil disposed mind and forgetfulness of the great clemency received hitherto at the King's hands he understood greatly to his heaviness." Morison was sorry Somerset "bred new troubles to the country," but was glad Cecil was "as far from shoutings as void of fault." He observed cynically that "it were a way to make an end of amity, if when men fail, their friends should forthwith therefore be troubled." The duke had "years but too many; . . . let him bear his own burden, or cast it where he can." In another letter, Morison confessed to Sir Nicholas Throckmorton that he was mistaken about Somerset's nature, whereas Throckmorton "saw deeper and guessed more rightly of his doings." His dislike of Somerset notwithstanding, Morison was not one who would grovel before Northumberland. In December he wrote Northumberland that he would only send news if he were paid and asked brashly, "Is it possible that I can serve the King without wages?" Vannes complimented Northumberland personally and went on to warn him that some thought "your great clemency and earnest labor for to reduce the said duke to the King's majesty's favor has been much the occasion of your peril."[50]

Somerset was entitled to and received trial before his peers. No evidence has ever been produced to prove that the twenty-eight peers were selected for their prejudice against him, despite Pollard's suggestion to the contrary. Two surviving accounts of the trial, one in Edward's *Journal* and the other in manuscript, tell essentially the same story.[51] On the basis of flimsy evidence the duke was acquitted of treason, but convicted of felony.

Northumberland alone spoke out for the accused. According to Edward's account he "would not agree that any searching of his death should be treason." The other version, written after the journal, relates the same facts, but attributes base motives to Northumberland. "The Duke of Northumberland in countenance bearing show of sadness (but in truth stiffly obstinate) denied that he would ever consent that any practice against him, should be either imputed or reputed treason, yet this was not taken to proceed from modesty as he expected, but that he could not with his honor or reason so enforce it." A third report of the trial, highly favorable to Northumberland, is the least trustworthy. John ab Ulmis, a longtime admirer, wrote Bullinger attributing the following speech to Northumberland. "Duke of Somerset, you see yourself a man in peril of life and sentenced to die. Once before I saved you in a like danger, nor will I desist to serve you now, though you may not believe me. Appeal to the mercy of the King's majesty, which I doubt not he will extend to you. As for myself, I shall willingly forgive you everything and will use every exertion in my power that your life may be spared."[52]

Apart from the word of Peter Vannes, only the reports of the unsympathetic Ambassador Scheyfve suggest that Northumberland did anything to save Somerset's life. In December he related that Northumberland, frustrated by the outcome of the trial, promised to omit no good office in obtaining a pardon. A few weeks later Northumberland reportedly talked at length with Somerset on several different occasions and thereby aroused the ire of Pembroke, Northampton, and others. Although all was smoothed over, Northumberland seemed sorely puzzled how the whole affair would end. Following Somerset's execution in January, 1552, informants told the ambassador that he asked the King to grant pardon, but Edward refused.[53] In light of this it is unwise to assume, as many have, that Northumberland was the prime mover behind Somerset's execution.[54] Other councillors feared and hated him, and the King was beginning to acquire the traits characteristic of his dynasty.

Northumberland could salve his conscience with the knowledge that Somerset received mercy in 1549 and ample warnings afterward. Few men of high rank in the sixteenth century enjoyed the luxury of a second political disgrace; the other notable example was the Elizabethan Earl of Essex. Northumberland was nevertheless troubled until his own death about the fate of the man who had been his friend and colleague for half a lifetime. Considering the vast power wielded by Northumberland, there cannot be the slightest doubt that he could have saved Somerset had he thrown himself fully into the task. No member of the Privy Council was strong enough to resist Northumberland single-handedly. Consequently, from the moment Somerset's head fell, Northumberland was a man with blood on his hands. His responsibility was greater than that of any other councillor, but less than that of Henry VIII, Mary, or Elizabeth for the executions of their reigns. Northumberland, unlike the crowned heads of state, paid for his crime with both his life and reputation. By the standards of the age he deserved better. As Somerset's executioner, he was neither God's annointed, nor was he, like the man on the block, guilty of the sin of Cain.

Edward Seymour, Duke of Somerset, passed from the scene as a tragic figure devoured by the furies of Tudor political life. A good man, with ideas centuries in advance of his time, Somerset fell short of greatness chiefly because he misunderstood the limitations of political leadership and turned his back on reality. He had been a capable and faithful servant of Henry VIII and was the obvious choice to rule during the minority of Edward VI. But as Protector, Somerset lacked the absolute authority of a King and was pulled down by his peers when reverses at home and abroad dictated a change of policy. Under similar pressures in the 1530s, Henry VIII sacrificed Thomas Cromwell; in 1549 Somerset sacrificed himself. He understandably found it difficult to subordinate himself or retire from politics after he was driven from power. A more astute and ruthless tactician might have weathered the storms. Somerset, however, was virtually isolated after October 1549, for Paget shifted with the winds after fair warning, and Cranmer and Smith lacked the power required to overthrow a majority of the council.

In his personal life Somerset tried to do what he thought right, but was forced to do what was expedient. After the execution of his brother, any aura of sanctity was swept away: Richard III was accused of killing his brother's sons, while Elizabeth slew only her cousin, Mary, Queen of Scots. Surprisingly, those who admired Somerset most accused him of the sin of greed, a charge that is scarcely tenable. In an age of magnificence, respect and obedience depended on outward appearance and grandeur. A Lord Protector of the realm who lived like a squire or burgess would have been guilty of consummate folly. Somerset House was no more than the requisite symbol of office. Condemned to suffer death, the "good duke" drew strength from his God and perished in the best tradition of his age.[55] No one sought to dishonor his memory. Brother to a Queen and uncle to a King, Somerset was, like many, destroyed by his virtues as well as his vices.

VI / Northumberland
Plays the Good Physician

Throughout 1552 Northumberland sought to play the good physician and thereby restore England to health and stability. He held no legal supremacy over his colleagues but was unquestionably the first councillor of Edward VI. With his great power, he advanced the interests of his family and built up a substantial political following. Northumberland, in spite of recurrent illness, worked assiduously through the council and attended to an immense variety of problems. His government achieved greater quiet at home, an improved diplomatic position owing to the conflict between France and Charles V, further religious innovations, and the beginnings of administrative reform. Although many of these accomplishments were due to the work of others and some to fortuitous events on the Continent, all of them are part of the Northumberland regime.

The King, entering his fifteenth year, enthusiastically assumed greater responsibilities in government. According to Ambassador Scheyfve, Edward began attending council meetings before the death of Somerset. Scheyfve observed in January 1552 that Northumberland, whom the King seemed to "love and fear," was beginning to grant him more freedom and authority.[1] The King's *Journal*, Northumberland's letters, and ambassadorial reports all testify to Edward's increasing involvement in the affairs of state. Northumberland never forgot his duty to the crown and at times ostentatiously reaffirmed his devotion. "I cannot enough (most gracious sovereign lord) lament and sorrow the miserable estate of my wretched and sick body," he wrote Edward VI, "the which by occasion of many infirmities is so oft driven to the walls, and thereby drawn from the service of your highness, whereunto I acknowledge myself as much bound as any other your subjects."[2] The Dudleys never failed to endear themselves to the sovereign; the ruin of Northumberland came only with the death of the King whom he had served too well.

Although Edward's government was led by men of limited vision and originality, it included administrators of marked ability. If Northumberland, Suffolk, Northampton, Bedford, and Pembroke were not the most imaginative statesmen of the Tudor era, the deficiency was partially remedied by the likes of William Paulet, Marquess of Winchester, Secretaries Petre and Cecil, and Sir Thomas Gresham, the financial expert. After the resignation of Lord Rich because of ill health and disfavor, the great seal passed to Thomas Goodrich, Bishop of Ely, the last of three Edwardian chancellors. The King was also well served by humanists like Sir Richard Morison, who filled ambassadorial posts abroad.

Parliament met on January 23, 1552, one day after Somerset was executed on Tower Hill. This Parliament, originally elected at the beginning of the Protectorate, had not been convened for nearly two years. Arguments that Northumberland was directly responsible for this extended interval are based more upon supposition and coincidence than substantive evidence.[3] Nor is it likely that the management of bye-elections significantly altered its composition.[4] The second act of uniformity, authorizing use of the revised *Book of Common Prayer* and prescribing penalties for non-conformity, was the most important religious legislation. An act to deprive Cuthbert Tunstall, the conservative Bishop of Durham, passed the Lords over the opposition of

Archbishop Cranmer, but apparently failed to win assent from the Commons. According to Ambassador Scheyfve, an act giving all orders of the council the same force as acts of Parliament was also rejected by the Commons. The treasons act of 1552 was a mixed blessing. While it re-enacted many of the treasons created under Henry VIII and abolished by the act of 1547, it broke new ground by requiring that two witnesses be brought in person before a party so accused.[5]

Northumberland's position gave him vast powers of patronage, and offices and favors of all kinds were granted to those who won his favor. Sir John Raynsford of Colchester, Essex, a former protegé of Thomas Cromwell, obtained a letter in his behalf addressed to the commissioners of sales. "I could not honestly deny him," said Northumberland, "so considering his old service, I have thought good heartily to require you the rather at the contemplation hereof to show him such favor and friendship . . . as you conveniently may."[6] At times Northumberland did no more than expedite regular administrative affairs, as in the case of a servant of the Earl of Huntingdon, who received the duke's letter to the secretaries for a warrant to pay the semiannual wages of a band of fifty demilances. William Winter, a sea captain, petitioned "the right high and mighty prince, the Duke of Northumberland's grace" regarding ships and goods taken from him and his brother by the French. Northumberland intervened to the extent of requesting Cecil to send a letter to the French for reparation; whether Winter received financial satisfaction is unknown, but highly doubtful. Northumberland asked Secretary Cecil "to be a means to the rest of my lords" that Mr. Cowne might be "handled something to his comfort." Comfort in this case meant remission of £100 in debt, which Northumberland thought had already been granted.[7]

Offices and land grants were the most common products of patronage. On June 18, Northumberland recommended Sir Ralph Bagnal for the fee farm of the monastery of Dieulacres, Staffordshire, and Sir John Capwold, a clerk of "good learning and forwardance in setting forth God's glory," for a vacant bishopric in Ireland. Only eleven days later, Bagnal received his grant from the King; the godly clerk apparently waited somewhat longer. The privy councillors themselves aided one another in various suits to the King and, thus, formed a veritable mutual aid society. Accordingly, Northumberland continually heaped praise on Cecil for his labors and personally befriended men such as the Earl of Huntingdon, Lord Darcy, and Sir John Gates.[8]

Less renowned for his patronage of the arts than his son, Leicester, Northumberland nonetheless obtained the council's license for a group of players, including Edmund Strodwick, John Smyth, Hugh Barnesby, Thomas Hillie, and Miles Rolfe to rehearse "within all the King's dominions such matters, interludes, and plays as tend not to exceed in any wise the limits and bounds of honest meaning. . . ." That the duke's ear could be inclined toward a young scholar is evident from the patronage offered to the "handsomely learned" son of his servant, John Harforde, who wanted the King's license to "apply his time as well in Paris and Orleans, as at Padua" for two or three years.[9]

The Dudley ascendancy was a good deal more than the elevation of a single individual, for the sons, a son-in-law, and a brother of Northumberland all held positions of influence. English politics have always been something of a family affair, and at no time was this more true than during the last years of Edward VI. Northumberland's eldest son, the Earl of Warwick, grew up at court, and, along with his brothers, the Lords Ambrose and Robert, was a friend and companion to the King. Edward's *Journal* contains numerous references to the young men enjoying each other's company. In January 1552, the King described "a match run between six gentlemen of a side at tilt." The winning side included Warwick, Lord Robert, and their brother-in-law, Sir Henry Sidney, while the losers counted Lord Ambrose among their number. Warwick, who was a son-in-law to the Duke of Somerset, began to assume greater responsibilities in the government. On January 18, four days before Somerset's execution, Northumberland gave fifty of his men at arms to Warwick. Three months later, he succeeded the Earl of Pembroke as master of the horse, with a fee of 100 marks annually.[10] In recognition of his service, Warwick received the Garter taken from the disgraced Lord Paget.

Sir Henry Sidney was brought up from infancy with the King and was one of his closest friends. He was introduced at court not by Northumberland, but by his father, Sir William, chamberlain and steward to Prince Edward before the death of Henry VIII. Nonetheless, the Sidney and Dudley families were joined through the friendship of Northumberland and Sir William and, later, by the marriage of Henry to Mary Dudley, a union that enriched the English literary heritage with their son, Sir Philip Sidney. Sidney, as well as his Dudley brothers-in-law, was rewarded with land grants and an assortment of stewardships and other sinecures, which sustained his dignity at court. Lord Robert Dudley, for example, became master of the buckhounds in June, 1552, with an annual fee of £33 6s. 8d., upon the surrender of the position by his brother, Warwick.[11] A diplomat, as well as a courtier, Sir Henry Sidney served the King abroad and held the dying sovereign in his arms when the end came in 1553.

Unlike Somerset, Northumberland was never troubled with family jealousy and dissension. His devoted brother, Sir Andrew, served loyally in distinctly subordinate positions. After military action at sea and in Scotland, Dudley, together with Francis Everard, was granted the office of keeper of the royal household within the palace of Westminister; the post, formerly held by Sir Anthony Denny, included responsibilities for receiving and paying out of the King's money. Later, Dudley and Arthur Sturton were appointed keepers of "all the jewels of the robes and other things in the palace of Westminster" with a fee of 100 marks annually, payable at the exchequer.[12]

Early in 1552, when Sir Andrew Dudley was captain of Guisnes, a jurisdictional dispute developed between him and the deputy of Calais, Lord Willoughby. Northumberland intervened in his brother's behalf and wrote to Cecil, "Since the lord deputy of Calais has 'willfully proceeded in the matter between him and my brother,' contrary to the letters of the council and 'to the renewing of more unquietness between them and their retinues, which is to be eschewed and removed, lest further displeasure might rise and grow with them; me thinketh now my lords have good cause to look upon such indiscreet dealing, rather than to suffer the man's willfulness to be the occasion of greater inconvenience.' "[13]

This feud was resolved several months later in an extraordinarily unprejudiced manner, considering that Sir Andrew was the brother of the most powerful noble in the kingdom: Both were removed from office. Explaining his actions, the King wrote, "Because Sir Andrew Dudley . . . had indebted himself very much by his service at Guisnes; also because it should seem injurious to the Lord Willoughby, that for the contention between him and . . . Dudley, he should be put out of his office; therefore, it was agreed that the Lord William Howard should be deputy of Calais and the Lord Grey, captain of Guisnes." Dudley did not return to England in disgrace, however, for he was immediately named one of the four principal gentlemen of the King's privy chamber.[14]

The powerful Dudley family, holding sway in the council and flourishing at court, was no more immune from the tragedy of death than the most wretched man alive. During the last week in May 1552, Northumberland was staying at his house at Otford, Kent, presumably resting and attending to affairs of state. At ten in the evening on the 31st he wrote, "My lord marquess [Northampton] has been with me; I thank him, and some good fellows with him; we have been merry. Tomorrow he departs from me by five of the clock in the morning." Even before Northampton's early departure, the joyous atmosphere changed, as Anne, wife of Lord Ambrose was fatally stricken. "It has pleased God to call out of this life the wife of my son, Ambrose, and has left no child alive," said Northumberland. "Her next heir now is the son of one Whorwood, whose father was my servant and slain at Musselburgh Field." The night before she had joined in the festivities and "was as merry as any child could be," but about three in the morning she awakened in a sweat. A little later, she had "a desire to the stool, and the indiscreet woman" in attendance allowed her to rise, after which she "fell to swooning." In the forenoon Lady Anne revived slightly, but "began to alter again, and so in continual pangs and fits till six o'clock at which time she left this life." Northumberland observed that when the body was examined, it was "very black between the shoulders and on one side of the cheek," and he believed the cause of death was "the sweat or worse." He went on to explain how she had recovered from an attack of the measles a month before, except "for a certain hoarseness and a cough, which remained with her still."[15]

So great was the fear of infection at court, that the council, after consulting with physicians, ordered Northumberland to stay away until the "moon be at full, after which time, if in the meanwhile no further infection happen, his Grace is desired with my Lord of Warwick to make their repair hither." Fully aware of the danger to the King, who had himself only recently recovered from the measles, Northumberland accepted his quarantine without question and promised to be at court on the assigned date, "if none other commandments come to me in the meantime from your lordships to the contrary."[16] In the correspondence concerning his daughter-in-law's death, he showed no remorse or fear for the safety of the others. Men accepted their fate as the will of God in an age when death struck quickly and without warning. From boyhood, Northumberland had lived in the face of many perils, and his large and happy family of five sons and two daughters represented only half of the children born to him and his wife.

Northumberland soon returned to the affairs of state and began an important tour through the North of England. As he proceeded, he occupied himself with local problems along the way and managed also a purge of political enemies and corrupt officials. Four of Somerset's adherents, Sir Ralph Vane, Sir Miles Partridge, Sir Michael Stanhope, and Sir Thomas Arundell, were executed on February 26. Earlier the same month a commission was established to investigate the officials and accounts of the exchequer, duchy of Lancaster, court of wards, court of augmentations, and court of first fruits and tenths.[17] The net was thus cast wide to catch those who had abused their offices. Although Northumberland apparently did not take an active, personal part in this inquiry, he followed the proceedings closely and offered advice.

The greatest rogue ensnared was John Beaumont, a notorious forger and fiscal manipulator, who was receiver-general of the court of wards and master of the rolls. Lord Paget, "the master of practices," was accused of malversation as chancellor of the duchy. Both Beaumont and Paget gave written "submissions," which Northumberland urged the councillors to scrutinize very closely. Because the clever Paget had been evasive, Northumberland believed the examiners did "right honorably in the refusal of his first submission, which, indeed, was farsed with subtlety and dissimulation." He thought Beaumont's submission should also be put in better form by the King's learned counsel. Beaumont was unquestionably guilty of corruption; Paget, on the other hand, was also disgraced for political reasons. From Burghley, Northumberland, Cecil, Pembroke, and Huntingdon expressed their satisfaction with the investigations: "Your proceedings with the Lord Paget and Mr. Beaumont signified by your letters seem to us for our part very good and substantial." The councillors also lost no time in staking out the claims of friends for the lands and goods of the two culprits.[18]

Richard Whalley, Sir John Thynne, and Sir Thomas Holcroft were similarly examined and deprived of their offices. Whalley enjoyed the dubious distinction of being the most frequently imprisoned man of Edward's reign. His receivership in Yorkshire was given to John Fisher, who had the support of Northumberland. Thynne lost his lease of the Savoy and other offices, while Holcroft surrendered the receivership of the duchy of Lancaster.[19] Northumberland exerted his own influence in one instance to secure leniency for the accused. Of two former confederates of Somerset, Thomas Fisher and one Brett, he wrote to Lord Darcy, "I am of your lordship's opinion that for their offences they have been sufficiently punished. Marry, by the duke's own confession to me, he declared Brett to be a very evil nature. He sought all the ways he could to irritate the said duke against me; whereby it should seem he cared not to have had a ruffling world; nevertheless, I trust this punishment will be a warning to him for [ever]."[20] The exact motives behind the examinations of Paget, Whalley, Thynne, and the others are difficult to determine. *Corruption* is a term which almost defies definition in the sixteenth century. All of the victims, Professor Hurstfield has observed, "belonged to the entourage of the fallen Protector; and they paid at the same time for their political errors as for their official abuses."[21]

One of Northumberland's closest associates was Sir William Cecil, who achieved his greatest fame later during the reign of Elizabeth I. Although the alliance between the two has generally been played down by writers sympathetic to the great Elizabethan statesman, there cannot be the slightest doubt that Northumberland trusted and relied on Cecil as much as any man in the council. He was continually asked to further Northumberland's suits to the King and council and relay information. The problem is to determine Cecil's feelings about his master, a task frustrated by the paucity of letters written by Cecil to Northumberland. If we accept the judgment of Conyers Read, that Cecil burned his correspondence during those critical months in 1553 when his life and career were in jeopardy, it does not seem illogical to assume that Cecil had something to hide.[22] Since everyone knew his position and could see his signature on Edward's devise for changing the succession to Lady Jane for himself, the lost correspondence may have shown that Cecil was more than a reluctant associate. Perhaps he was Northumberland's most enthusiastic supporter and confidant to the very end—at least there is no contemporary evidence to disprove this conjecture. But what about the original letters that should have been in Northumberland's possession and, therefore, out of

Cecil's reach? Again, if we are to have letter burnings, it is quite possible Northumberland took steps to protect friends, who unlike himself, could live to fight another day.

Good documentation has fortunately survived for the hospitality Cecil extended to Northumberland at Burghley, Northamptonshire, as he proceeded on his tour of the North. Northumberland replied to Cecil's invitation in a genial and charming fashion. "And for your gentle and most friendly request to have me to your father's on my way northwards, I do even so 'semblaby' render my hearty thanks unto you, assuring you I will not omit to see him as I go by him, though I do but drink a cup of wine with him at the door; for I will not trouble no friend's house of mine otherwise in this journey. My train is so great and will be whether I will or not. And for your own being there, like as I think myself much beholden to you that would take so much pains, and to me a singular pleasure to have so much of your company. . . ."[23] Northumberland, who was never eloquent, and sometimes almost incoherent, left no doubt of his esteem for the junior secretary.

Northumberland did more than take a cup of wine with old Richard Cecil, for a small meeting of the council took place on June 8, at Burghley, with Cecil, Pembroke, and Huntingdon all in attendance. Had Cecil taken Northumberland at his word, the secretary could have remained at court and allowed a formal exchange of pleasantries at the door. Clinton, the lord admiral, was likewise eager for Northumberland's company and wrote to Cecil to learn the time of the duke's arrival. Since Clinton "would be loath to be disappointed," he proposed to meet the party between Burghley and Bourne.[24]

After Northumberland's entourage arrived at Clinton's house at Sempringham, talks were held concerning the Scottish Marches. An uneasy peace prevailed along the troubled Borders that separated England from Scotland. For years raiding parties from both kingdoms had been raising havoc and spoiling the countryside. Northumberland held the post of lord warden of the Marches, but had not been free to devote his personal attention to their supervision since his reappointment in September 1551. Even on this journey, he was obliged to turn one eye toward London and affairs abroad. He was, however, no fledgling in Border affairs having served an apprenticeship there under Henry VIII. The basic problem was unchanged; loyal officials had to be found who would maintain law and order while refraining from instituting a reign of terror that would provoke reprisals from the Scots and antagonize the populace. Before coming northward, Northumberland had charged Border officials with excessive cruelty and violation of the peace. As usual, wild rumors circulated in London about the nature of his mission. Some conjectured a purge of all officials in the county palatinate of Durham, while others speculated about preparations for a new conquest of Scotland.[25]

Northumberland was next heard from at Carlisle; only two days later he had crossed to York where he found "order and quietness." News arriving from the court at Greenwich prompted a puzzling reply. Thankful for the "joyful advertisements" of the "prosperous health" of the King, Northumberland said, "And so long as the almighty Lord will hold his hand there, though the other sickness, whereof your lordship do write to be much 'cresed,' were yet a great deal more fervent, we shall recover it well enough. . . . I do not but allow and commend your wise and politic orders for the shunning and avoiding the danger and peril of the said sickness. Which as it is not of one or two years infection and engendering, so must it have a time of purging." The Earl of Shrewsbury, who was with Northumberland at York, agreed that all measures should be taken to keep disease out of the court.[26] Anxiety about the King's health was understandable during a period of infection that had already claimed Northumberland's daughter-in-law, but there is a slight hint that he might have had something else in mind when he hoped the Lord would hold his hand. As was so frequently the case, Northumberland's remarks were vague and imprecise; yet we must wonder whether this letter was Northumberland's first acknowledgement that the days of Edward VI were numbered.

He returned to Carlisle by way of Alnwick at the end of July. In a letter to his son-in-law, Sir Henry Sidney, Northumberland foresaw the ruin and decay of the whole area unless a deputy warden for all three Marches was appointed. He believed the situation on the Borders was so serious that he hesitated to leave until proper measures were taken. Particularly disturbing were the large numbers of outlaws and murderers who submitted themselves to him in hope of pardon. Northumberland was determined to hold these men until hearing from the King and council, and he urged Sidney to recommend pardon. Furthermore, he said, "I pray you to show the King's majesty that my returning again to Newcastle will be to very good purpose for his highness's service and for the quietness of the country. I pray you keep this from my wife."[27] The devoted Sidney had, thus, the double responsibility of allaying the anxieties of the duchess and treating with the King and council.

The council responded almost immediately to Northumberland's request for a deputy. Only five days after the duke wrote from Carlisle, the council appointed Lord Wharton, who was to receive half of Northumberland's fee as lord warden. Fortification works that had been previously requested were also authorized. At Durham, after another five days, Northumberland wrote, "I am grateful for the King's letters and ashamed to receive his thanks, where, do what I may, I cannot discharge my duty." This particular incident shows dramatically how swiftly decisions could be taken when there was a powerful plea from the man on the scene and an energetic council to back him up.[28]

Northumberland concluded his tour of the North at the end of August, 1552. He then joined Edward VI's progress through Hampshire before returning to his residence at Knole.[29] According to Ambassador Scheyfve, Northumberland received a magnificent reception in the North, and, as far as Scheyfve could determine, was on the best possible terms with the people.[30] Once again the Imperial ambassador had defective intelligence reports, for Northumberland faced a number of agitators who were slandering him and contributing to general unrest. His detractors were in fact legion. During the past year he had been falsely accused of imprinting his insignia, the bear and ragged staff, on coins and of all manner of enormities.

No shroud of mystery need surround Northumberland's unpopularity. He lacked the divine authority of a King, and as Edward's first councillor, he became the scapegoat for unpopular policies. The Dudley ascendancy created envy among the older noble families, but more importantly the middle and lower classes believed their economic distress was due to Northumberland's rule. Rising prices and the heavy military expenditures of Henry VIII and Protector Somerset had encouraged debasement of the coinage and brought the country to the brink of bankruptcy. When Northumberland's government began reforms, which included deflationary measures, peasants and merchants alike experienced additional discomfort.

Like his father, Northumberland devoted himself fully to the King's affairs and had little or no regard for public opinion. Northumberland's own words clearly reveal his contempt for the man in the street: "If I should have past more upon the speech of the people than upon the service of my master, or gone about to seek favor of them without respect to his highness' surety, I needed not to have had so much obloquy of some kind of men. But the living God . . . shall be my judge at the last day with what zeal, faith, and truth I serve my master."[31] His mentality, to be sure, savored of selfrighteousness and was not that of a great statesman. It was at least free of the hypocrisy of those who played to the crowd, but did nothing to advance the prosperity of the commonwealth.

The case of Elizabeth Huggons, wife of William Huggons and a servant to the Duchess of Somerset, is typical of the opposition faced by Northumberland.[32] According to an informer, Sir William Stafford of Rochford, Essex, Mrs. Huggons imputed the death of Somerset "to no man but my Lord of Northumberland, who she thought was better worthy to die than he." She had previously said, with a stout gesture, "My Lord Guildford Dudley should marry my Lord of Cumberland's daughter and that the King's majesty should devise the marriage (have at the crown with your leave) [*sic*]." When examined by Sir Robert Bowes, master of the rolls, and Sir Arthur Darcy, lieutenant of the Tower, she changed her story. She categorically denied attributing Somerset's death to Northumberland. What she had said was, "Those, which were the procurers of the Duke of Somerset's death, his blood would be required at their hands even like as the lord admiral's blood was at the duke's hands; for . . . if the said duke had lived one hundred years, he would never have given any such occasion." Next to Somerset, her master, Mrs. Huggons bore "greatest favor and affection to the Duke of Northumberland's grace, of any other nobleman and specially since her husband was his grace's servant." She also denied connecting Lord Guildford's marriage with designs on the crown. At a later stage in the examination, Mrs. Huggons remembered more, possibly with the assistance of forceful persuasion, and admitted saying the world would condemn Northumberland for Somerset's death, even as Somerset himself was condemned for the death of his brother.

Northumberland's reaction to the Huggons affair is not recorded, but his views about other antagonists have survived. Hearing of the slanders of John Burgh, who accused him of "conveying [i.e. stealing] the King's majesty's coffers," Northumberland ordered the Earl of Westmoreland to deliver the culprit to the council. Burgh was duly bound over to the council and sentenced to be pilloried at Westminster. Before the penalty was imposed, Northumberland begged the council "to spare him from the pillory and other public punishment, for I trust with God's grace he will amend." Northumberland had learned that Burgh was of "a good house and not so much in default as others"; consequently, he believed him "sufficiently punished by this long imprisonment."[33]

Another slanderer named Ford was turned over to the council. "Because the matter as it seems touches none other of the council but my brother and me, I have refused to hear it, referring the order thereof to the rest of my lords," Northumberland explained to Cecil. Northumberland recalled that Ford was once punished in the porter's lodge "for such like matter, and yet I was then content freely to remit his offense towards me." "The man is not a little favored with some folks," he continued, "wherefore I pray you that the matter may be used indifferently." Northumberland undoubtedly despised people like Mrs. Huggons, Burgh, and Ford; yet from his lofty position, he deigned to be merciful. Both Mrs. Huggons and Burgh were exposed by private informers, who may have been loyal supporters of the duke, but were more likely angling for a generous reward. When the situation demanded, Northumberland took a harsher line. He was more annoyed by persons operating in public and, therefore, ordered fair means or foul used in discovering the accomplices of a man named Hawkins, who was accused of "casting of a bruit, . . . setting up of seditious bills done by himself, and the counterfeiting of the Archbishop of Canterbury's hand, with an intent to have stirred a rebellion and a commotion."[34]

Although Northumberland's government was unpopular at home, its position abroad improved by the end of 1552 mainly because of the military reversals of Charles V at the hands of the French. Nevertheless, England and France were briefly on the verge of war in September, and steps were taken to bolster the old Imperial connection. Northumberland and the council, angered by the high-handed dealings of Henry II and stunned by the revelations of the informer, Thomas Stukeley, about French designs on Calais, prepared for the worst.[35] Fortunately, the danger was entirely transitory. The French ambassador's secretary paid a personal visit to Northumberland, gave assurances of French affections, and entreated the duke to maintain good relations in spite of Stukeley. The secretary's sincerity deeply moved Northumberland, but he made overtures to the Imperial ambassador as insurance against his own deception.[36]

Northumberland stressed his own loyalty to the Imperial alliance and reminded Ambassador Scheyfve that Boulogne could have been retained with the favor of Charles V. Scheyfve denied that treaty obligations covered the conquests of Henry VIII. At this the duke laughed and took Scheyfve by the arm saying he would make him the judge of the question. Northumberland then told Cecil and Lord Cobham what argument had passed between them, and both agreed the duke was correct about Boulogne. Scheyfve also talked with Thomas Gresham, "a thorough-going partisan" of Northumberland, and came away with the distinct notion that the English were sincere in their protestations of friendship.[37]

In October Northumberland was once again stricken with illness and obliged to keep his bed at Chelsea until the end of the year. Though "as evil at ease" as he could be, he kept a steady eye on the delicate diplomatic equilibrium. Northumberland, writing from a sick bed in November, conceded that there was "more good will" from the Emperor than he had seen in a long time. About the same time the French ambassador's secretary came with a private message for Northumberland, who excused himself on grounds of illness and asked the secretary to deliver the message to the council. Northumberland explained in a letter to Lord Darcy, Cecil, and Petre that although he might be considered "affectionate" to France, he wanted to continue this amity only for a little while and never desired the alliance except "for the service of his master, as knoweth the Lord." Far from being the stooge of the King of France, Northumberland supported the alliance because it offered peace to England. "Our part is next," he believed, "if the Low Countries shall happen to fall into the hold of our ancient enemy."[38]

At the end of 1552, the council dispatched ambassadors to the Emperor and the King of France to secure peace between the warring powers and to improve England's position with both. Northumberland recommended the appointment of Sir Andrew Dudley for France and Sir Henry Sidney for the Empire, because the latter had "more means to express his mind in the Italian tongue than in the French." What advantage might accrue from speaking Italian to the French-speaking Emperor, Northumberland did not explain. Actually, this question was irrelevant, for the council ignored Northumberland's advice and sent the two men to the opposite courts. Dudley's instructions followed the time-honored lines; he was to express Edward's love for Charles V and concern for the public state of Christendom and suggest a Habsburg-Valois peace on the basis of an alliance against the Turk. If the Emperor mentioned the desirability of English assistance by the terms of existing treaties, Dudley was to answer that he did not know "what the treaty requires in that part, but he knows of our good affection. . . ." The two embassies were, in short, nothing more than posturing. England had no intention whatsoever of sending troops anywhere on the Continent except for the defense of Calais. When Sir Andrew bade his brother farewell at Chelsea, Northumberland advised the council to send a message from Princess Mary to the Emperor that would emphasize the good will of England toward the Empire.[39]

Until a preoccupation with the declining health of Edward forced Northumberland to lay aside all other interests, the diplomatic balance permitted the government to concentrate on the wide spectrum of domestic problems. If the efficient maintenance of law and order is the standard by which Tudor politicians are judged, Northumberland was remarkably successful. From 1549 until Edward's death, England was free from violent insurrections, and no open splits among the council occurred after the second fall of Somerset.[40] Sharing the outlook, if not the genius, of Henry VII, Wolsey, and Cromwell, Northumberland was primarily concerned with the welfare of the state, not its citizens. And if the false romanticism and self-glorification surrounding Tudor England is to be dispelled, we must admit that the political achievement of the age went little beyond ordering the affairs of the state and preserving law and order.

The country experienced as much reform in the last two years of Edward VI as in any comparable period in the sixteenth century, but none of these measures was popularly inspired or primarily conceived to promote the welfare of the majority of the commonwealth. Finanacial and administrative reforms were undertaken to prevent the catastrophe of bankruptcy, which threatened all governments; as Thomas Gresham wisely warned

Northumberland, the credit of England was in danger of falling "as low as the credit of the Emperor," who was offering "sixteen percent for money and could not obtain it."[41] While Northumberland lent his authority and gave encouragement to the experts, who stabilized the currency and investigated the operations of the financial courts, he personally supplied few of the ideas.[42] Nor did Northumberland have much in common with the zealous ecclesiastics, who flatteringly compared him with Moses. The religious reforms were stimulated and carried out by small groups of English and Continental divines. It was through the efforts of these men that the Church of England cast off the remnants of Roman Catholicism and took its place among the best reformed churches in Christendom.

The last great conservative bishop, Cuthbert Tunstall of Durham, was not deprived until October 1552, and the reorganization of the county palatine was not completed by the time of the King's death. Nonetheless, Northumberland had been at odds with Tunstall for the past two years. Accusations that Tunstall had consented to a conspiracy in the North prompted Warwick's examination of the bishop in September 1550. Tunstall was placed under house arrest in London and underwent further examinations before he was committed to the Tower in December 1551, as a result of the discovery of a letter in his own hand among the effects of Somerset. That the case against Tunstall was not the best was indicated by the Commons' refusal in 1552 to pass a deprivation bill from the Lords until they examined him and his confederates. Northumberland supported the bill and undoubtedly would have favored deprivation by the most popular means. However, what he could not achieve through Parliament was accomplished by a lay commission that deprived Tunstall of the see of Durham.[43]

Only a fortnight after Tunstall's deprivation, Northumberland wrote from his bed, "as ill at ease as I have been . . . in all my life," to Cecil and made recommendations for a new bishop and the reform of the diocese. He favored Robert Horne, the dean, for bishop at a reduced income and called for the removal of the suffragan, who, Northumberland believed, was hated in the country. Northumberland wanted the new bishop to receive full possession of the temporalities and then surrender these to the King. Horne would be regranted lands worth £1000 in addition to his deanery, and the balance of the property, worth at least £2000, would remain in the King's hands. It was here that Northumberland's scheme ran aground because Horne stubbornly refused the appointment on the terms offered. After learning the "truth" about Horne from Cecil, Northumberland admitted misjudging the man. "A sober man that did not stand so much in his own conceit were fit to have it," Northumberland wrote the secretary.[44]

His efforts to settle affairs at Durham were frustrated until the meeting of Parliament in 1553. Horne remained recalcitrant in spite of Northumberland's pressure, and apparently the other privy councillors gave little assistance to the duke. In January 1553, he complained to Cecil that a year had passed without a bishop in Durham. "What order was lately taken with the Dean of Durham [Horne] I neither yet did hear nor have been made privy to it." Vehemently he berated clergymen, who "be so besotted of their wives and children that they forget both their poor neighbors and all other things," and condemned their "great possessions." A few days later, he again wrote Cecil from Chelsea, "I have not had any answer from you whether there shall be a bishop of Durham or not. . . ." The entire proceedings over the diocese are totally out of tune with the alleged despotic power of Northumberland and serve to emphasize the degree to which the council continued to rule the country. By act of Parliament rather than by the fiat of Northumberland, the old see of Durham was dissolved and replaced by two smaller sees, which remained vacant at the death of Edward VI. Northumberland reaped temporary benefits from the lands bestowed on him by the King but never succeeded in establishing himself as prince of the North as charged by his detractors.[45]

It was during the proceedings against Tunstall that Northumberland had his famous encounter with that most intractable of men, John Knox. They met in June 1552 when Northumberland was at Newcastle. Knox preached a number of sermons before Northumberland and accompanied him as he traveled throughout the area. On October 28, the duke wrote Secretary Cecil, "I would to God it might please the King's majesty to appoint Mr. Knox to the office of Rochester bishopric;" he believed that Knox would be "a whetstone to quicken and sharp the Bishop of Canterbury," and that Knox's departure from Newcastle would cause his Scottish followers to return home. A month later Northumberland again stressed the latter point: "Some order must be taken for Knox; otherwise you shall not avoid the Scots from out of Newcastle, which, all things considered, me think should not be forgotten." Knox's refusal to accept the appointment angered the duke. After the two met at Chelsea in December, Northumberland sent Knox away, "because I love not men which be neither grateful nor pleasable." Knox had even the audacity to question his patron's religion, and Northumberland protested these accusations to Cecil saying, "But I have for twenty years stand [sic] to one kind of religion, in the same which I do now profess and have, I thank the Lord, past no small dangers in it." Nevertheless, Northumberland remained sympathetic toward "poor Knox" and seemed to understand "what perplexity the poor soul remains in. . . ." A year after Northumberland's execution, Knox wrote of him as a man of "stout courage and proudness of stomach" and was perhaps not altogether derogatory when he compared him to Achitophel, who was after all highly esteemed by both David and Absalom as the oracle of God.[46]

The administrative and financial reforms of the Northumberland regime were the products of necessity. The expensive wars of Henry VIII and Protector Somerset and the mid-century trade slump were chiefly responsible for the distress of the government. To finance the wars, debasement of the coinage was employed; in 1551 the first steps were taken for its restoration. Two proclamations, issued in May and August, brought down the value of the shilling to six-pence, and a new issue of silver was minted at a pure standard. In the very midst of reform, there was a final debasement in an attempt to gain the utmost financial benefit for the beleaguered government.[47] Investigations into the operations of financial courts begun in the autumn of 1552 resulted in a series of proposals for reorganization. The dissolution of the courts of augmentations and first fruits and tenths, and their annexation to the exchequer in January 1554 stemmed directly from an act of the Parliament of March 1553, empowering Edward to alter or abolish revenue courts by letters patent. As Professor Elton has remarked, "It was only the accident of death that made them the 'Marian' reforms; the Queen can claim no credit for them."[48]

Parliament passed acts in 1552 and 1553 against buying and selling offices and for more rigid requirements in bonding officials and auditing accounts. The court of wards, which betrayed "marked weaknesses" during the last years of Henry VIII, had a "chequered history" under Edward, but began to recover toward the end. At the same time the King and Secretary Petre joined forces to reorganize the work of the Privy Council. Time ran out before most of the reforms could be implemented, but this fact should not detract from the "heroic measures" of Northumberland and his associates to invigorate the Tudor administrative system.[49]

Northumberland correctly analyzed the financial ills of the country and outlined his attitude toward Parliament in letters to the council and Lord Thomas Darcy, the lord chamberlain. A new Parliament, wrote Northumberland, was the only remedy for the debts inherited by Edward VI from his father and

> augmented by the willful government of the late Duke of Somerset, who took upon him the protectorship and government of his own authority; and his highness being by the prudence of his said father left in peace with all princes, suddenly by that man['s] unskillful protectorship and less expert in government was plunged into wars, whereby his majesty's charges was suddenly increased unto the payment of six or seven score thousand pounds a year over and above the charges for the defense and

keeping of Boulogne, which charges were such as it almost
wearied his most noble father with the keeping of it. . . .

All remedies had been tried—sale of lands, calling in of debts,
and "the seeking of every man's doing in office"—Northumberland observed; "yet you perceive all this cannot help to salve
the sum it has so long been suffered to fester, for lack of looking
into in time." Contrasting the ills of the body politic with human ailments, he would "play the good physician" by calling
Parliament.[50]

The parliament of 1553, the last of the reign of Edward VI,
met in March of that year. Yet, as late as the previous December, Northumberland favored delaying the Parliament until "after the harvest time," because there would be less time to de-
fraud the winter collection of revenue and fewer opportunities
for "murmurings and grudgings."[51] His preference of an autumn
Parliament undermines conjectures that he foresaw the death of
the King and masterminded an elaborate plot months in advance; either the council persuaded him in favor of the earlier
date or else he changed his own mind. The question of the
King's attendance came up in January, and the following month
Lord Chancellor Goodrich reported that the legal officers of the
crown advised against holding Parliament without the King.[52]
Northumberland was under no delusions about the need for
money and was critical of Cecil's rather "ceremonious" list of
arguments for winning support from the Commons. It was
pointless to account to them for the King's "liberality and boun-
tifulness," Northumberland thought, "lest you might thereby
make them wanton and give them occasion to take hold of your
own arguments. . . ."[53] It is not known whether he understood
the inadequacy of traditional Tudor parliamentary taxes or
whether he was forced to accept a subsidy and two-tenths and
fifteenths; at least he was turning to the right body for financial
remedy.

The Dudley family and the minions of the duke were extraordinarily successful in finding seats in the parliament of 1553.

Northumberland promoted and secured the issuance of writs of summons for the young Earl of Warwick and other eldest sons to attend the House of Lords, but adhered to the traditional view that "no man's son . . . being not of the blood royal can claim any place to sit there but only to stand at the back of his majesty's cloth of estate. . . ."[54] In the House of Commons Robert Dudley sat for Norfolk, Sir Andrew for Oxfordshire, and Sir Henry Sidney for Kent. Northumberland and the council were anxious to secure a pliant House of Commons and sent directives to the sheriffs. The surviving letters are unsigned, and there is no evidence that Northumberland applied extreme pressure himself.[55] Cecil, on the other hand, was an active promoter of "the chiefest men of wisdom and good counsel" although he personally held no seat.[56] The total effect of management is yet an open question; until it has been resolved, we are on the safest ground in accepting the judgment of Professor Neale that "it would be absurd to speak of the government as either achieving or aiming at what has been called a 'nomination parliament.' "[57]

Northumberland and his followers labored to restore the health of the kingdom in an atmosphere of lurking nemesis, for the success of their efforts required time and depended on the life of Edward VI. Although Northumberland wished to play the good physician, he was ruined when the King's health began its fatal decline. The desperate attempt to transfer the crown to Lady Jane proved a colossal failure. In the end the mystique of the legitimate Tudor line exorcized the man who dared to alter the royal succession. Like an evil spirit, the Dudley ascendancy was struck down, and its achievements were forgotten.

VII / The Dudley
Ascendancy Exorcized

During the last four months of Edward VI's reign, the impending death of the King became Northumberland's prime concern, and his failure to meet this challenge destroyed the Dudley ascendancy. There is an almost complete lack of firsthand information about Northumberland's thoughts and intentions for this period, but it is nonetheless possible to make a sympathetic appraisal of his difficulties. In fact historians have rarely considered the alternatives that were available to him. The crisis of 1553 was not staged by Northumberland. He could only respond to events that were beyond his control. From Northumberland's point of view, the best of all worlds would have been one in which Edward attained his majority and fathered a healthy line of sons. With the future secure, the ailing duke could have entrusted the burdens of office to his sons and colleagues and enjoyed his last years in retirement, content that he had risen as high as was possible in the sixteenth century.

When it became clear that the King's days were numbered, Northumberland was confronted with the accession of Mary; but, contrary to the traditional view, this did not necessarily mean his ruin. While he would have lost all political authority, it does not necessarily follow that he would have suffered bodily harm or loss of estate. The best support for this assumption may be found by examining the fate of the others, who supported Lady Jane. Not a single nobleman was executed, except Northumberland; Suffolk and Lord Guildford Dudley suffered only after Wyatt's rebellion. Men like Pembroke, Bedford, and Winchester—all allies of Northumberland—even retained their seats in the council. Therefore, the safest course would have been to make peace with Mary. That Northumberland did not entirely rule this out is strongly suggested by his friendly relations with her until two days before the King's death.[1]

Nevertheless, good and sufficient reasons did exist for changing the succession. Dealing with Mary involved risk, and Northumberland could not ignore the possibility of being selected as the scapegoat for Edward's reign. As an unswerving Roman Catholic and an unquestioning adherent of Charles V, Mary also posed a threat to the whole commonwealth of England. Because the Reformation and, to a lesser extent, peace were issues most of the council and bishops supported, irrespective of their feelings toward the Dudleys, Northumberland was not alone in his desire to alter the succession. The best alternative candidate for the throne was unquestionably Mary's younger sister, Elizabeth. Little is known about Northumberland's relations with Elizabeth. Consequently, it must be assumed that Elizabeth placed loyalty to her sister and to her father's wishes above her own political ambitions; for, if Mary married and produced an heir, Elizabeth would have been virtually removed from the royal succession. As the daughter of Henry VIII and Anne Boleyn, Elizabeth would have been the most desirable successor to Edward in 1553.

Northumberland's choice of the Suffolk line was undoubtedly the worst and most dangerous alternative, unless he had been foolish enough to support the Stuart claim.[2] The Suffolk line is traced through the younger sister of Henry VIII, Mary, who married Charles Brandon, Duke of Suffolk. In 1553 the chief claimant was Frances, Duchess of Suffolk, wife of one of Northumberland's closest supporters. Her eldest daughter, Lady Jane, married Guildford Dudley. The main obstacle to the Suffolk claim was Henry VIII's Act of Succession which stated that the throne should pass first to Edward and then to his sisters, Mary and Elizabeth.

The dilemma of Northumberland has been all too little appreciated. Protestant writers have been more anxious to damn Bloody Mary and lament the burning of the martyrs than consider the only policy that might have prevented these horrors. By turning to the Suffolks, Northumberland risked everything, his life, his fortune, and his family. Blind ambition will explain all of his acts, and this cannot be ruled out as one possible motivation. But the plan to alter the succession was not carried out with Machiavellian thoroughness. Mary remained alive and at liberty to the very end. Edward's devise for disinheriting his sisters was itself a grotesque legal instrument, ill-conceived and ill-executed; and at the critical moment Northumberland lacked the vigor and enthusiasm of a true Renaissance despot. All of this suggests that Northumberland's choice may have been an act of futile desperation executed by a confused and sick man who had lost sight of his own interests.

If Northumberland had the slightest premonition of what the future held for him, we can easily understand his reluctance to accept the approaching death of the King. As early as February 17, Ambassador Scheyfve reported Edward's illness as "a visitation and sign from God."[3] Edward steadfastly refused to accept the sentence of death with all the mettle of a Tudor king. It is unlikely that he knew his affliction was acute pulmonary tuberculosis, a disease that was incurable in the sixteenth century. The strange concoctions and potions that passed for the best medicines of the day merely increased the King's suffering and prolonged the final agony. All Europe watched and waited as his strength ebbed. In April, when Northumberland was spreading news of the King's recovery, Sir Richard Morison wrote from Brussels, "There is a muttering in this court that the King, our master, . . . be very sick." Morison heard that Edward's stomach was swollen of a "post hume" and must be cut before he could be cured. Three new physicians, who were appointed early in May, took oaths in the presence of Northumberland, Suffolk, Northampton, Winchester, and Lord Darcy not to reveal the King's condition. One was Northumberland's own physician, the second, a professor from Oxford, and the third, a woman best described as a conjurer and a quack. As late as May 19, Sir Philip Hoby shrewdly used the example of Edward in assuring Imperial officials in Brussels of his disbelief in rumors about the death of Charles V: "As for example, I told him, the King, my master being but a little sick of a cough, the lewd people had devised and reported that he was dead."[4]

Northumberland apparently remained hopeful of the King's recovery until the latter part of May. The first draft of the devise for the succession, rather than an acknowledgment of the King's imminent death, was a declaration of the hope that he would live at least nine months. It cannot be dated.[5] What is significant about the first version is its failure to name a living person as heir to the throne. Unless a male child were born to the Duchess of Suffolk, one of her daughters, or her niece, the devise was unworkable. Lady Jane's male child would inherit the throne only if it were born before the child of her mother, two sisters, and a cousin. If the argument of Professor Bindoff that the second draft was not prepared until after May 28 is accepted, Northumberland had no assurance that his son, Guildford, was marrying the heir apparent on May 21.[6]

The succession by the terms of the first draft of the devise might best be described as a game of chance or lottery for the throne of England. The highest cards were in the hands of Henry Grey, Duke of Suffolk, not Northumberland. Suffolk had one chance to become father of the next king and three to be grandfather. Since the marriages of the Grey sisters were not consummated, the Duchess of Suffolk could reasonably expect the first son; and after his birth, the Dudley claim would be set aside. The Dudley family had two chances, one good, the other remote. Married to the eldest daughter of Suffolk, Guildford stood in good stead to father a king, while the projected mar-

3. KING EDWARD VI. EXCERPT FROM MY DEVISE FOR THE SUCCESSION

The Suffolk Succession

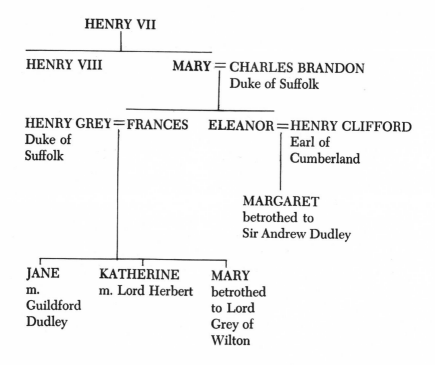

Figure 1

riage of Sir Andrew to Lady Margaret Clifford, daughter to the Earl of Cumberland, is hardly worth mentioning. Consequently, the Earl of Pembroke was almost as well off as Northumberland with his heir married to Lady Catherine Grey.

The whole arrangement is absurd when considered in detail. The crown of England was willed to an unborn son and no one else. The two sisters of Edward VI were removed from the royal succession, and three families were virtually competing against each other to prove their virility. Several explanations are possible. First, Professor Jordan has suggested that Edward composed the first draft as early as January or February when he, without the full knowledge of Northumberland, considered submitting the succession question to Parliament.[7] A second possibility is that the King and Northumberland never regarded the original draft as a workable solution to the succession question and agreed to the final version before the marriage of Guildford and Lady Jane. Or thirdly, Northumberland and his colleagues may have believed as late as the last week in May that Edward would live long enough to permit the required son to be born.

While these puzzling events were taking place, Secretary Cecil experienced the well-known illness that kept him away from court between about April 22 and June 11. It is unlikely that the illness was feigned because he recovered at the wrong time.[8] In his letter of May 7, Northumberland hoped the worst was past and praised the loyalty and efficiency of men like Cecil. Others, he remarked, were less diligent and neither "earnest zeal or consideration of time" could "awake them out of their wonted dreams, and smoothly wink all care from their hearts, how urgent or weighty soever our causes are."[9] A week later Cecil penned the only letter to Northumberland that has survived:

> My humblest commendations and duty remembered to your good grace. I trust your grace will be pleased with a little writing from me that could neither write nor read within these few days. I perceive by Mr. Petre's letters that your grace would know

for certifying of the King's majesty how I am likely to be there this Whitsuntide. True it is I have good desire to be there then, as at a place of my pilgrimage after my sickness and for a day or two with some foresight of same coming I am in hope to be able, if I grow from sickness but half so speedily as I fell into it. I send herewith to your grace the garland of the roses made in gold according to your grace's pattern to the intent your grace's allowance thereof may be had. . . .

I most humbly thank your grace for your comforting of me in my sickness. 14th May.

With a weary head of your grace's most bound,

W. Cecil[10]

A man, who himself longed for better health, Northumberland sympathized with his colleague; indeed on May 18, Petre wrote Cecil, "My Lord of Northumberland is not well at ease and mindeth to eat the diet for twelve or fourteen days."[11] Although Cecil's return helped matters not one whit, he was back at Northumberland's side during the closing days of the reign, lending support to every act.

The scheme to divert the succession to Lady Jane and her heirs male was completed on June 21, although Northumberland continued his courtship of Mary. The Marquess of Winchester, Bedford, and other councillors objected to the altered document, and their doubts were echoed by the judges, who questioned its legality. The chief justice, Sir Edward Montagu, argued that the terms of the devise embodied in letters patent would violate Henry VIII's Act of Succession. However, Edward's determination that his sisters should not succeed him and Northumberland's threat to "fight in his shirt with any man" withholding consent won the day. The command of a Tudor King, if only a dying boy in his sixteenth year, could not be lightly regarded, and the councillors and judges alike fell into line. On the 21st, the great officers of state, peers, eldest sons of peers, household officers, secretaries, and judges signed the letters patent that declared Mary and Elizabeth illegitimate and transferred the crown to Jane.[12]

The alliance between the Dudleys and Edward lasted to the

end. Northumberland was constantly in attendance at Greenwich, and in the late afternoon of July 6, the King died in the arms of Sir Henry Sidney. Elaborate plans had been made to secure the kingdom for Queen Jane against traitors. Northumberland, aided by his sons and brother, Northampton, Pembroke, and Suffolk held every conceivable advantage. He and his supporters had large numbers of retainers under their personal control. Furthermore, the fleet and all important fortifications were commanded by men believed to be loyal. His own military reputation was immense and was praised by foreign observers long after his death.[13] Between Northumberland and success stood only a frail woman and a handful of followers.

From the very beginning, however, Northumberland's plans began to fail. The King's death was not announced for three days so that the council would have adequate time to capture Mary and assure the orderly succession of Queen Jane. A small force commanded by Lord Robert Dudley rode to Mary's residence at Hunsdon, but when it arrived, she had already fled. Like all of the Tudor monarchs, Mary was at her best in times of crisis. Shrewdly husbanding her slender forces and executing her moves with great skill and bravery, she proved herself a worthy granddaughter of Henry VII. On July 9, Mary boldly wrote to the council in London and demanded that they acknowledge and publish her succession. Councillors, who had originally doubted the legality of Edward's devise and feared the ambition of Northumberland, quickly scrambled to save their lives and fortunes.

Queen Jane was herself the least important figure during the nine-day reign that bears her name. Although reputedly of brilliant mind and maturity beyond her years, she was easily manipulated by her father and Northumberland. After her marriage to Lord Guildford Dudley, Jane had continued to reside with her mother. On July 9, the same day that Mary issued her claim to the throne, Jane was brought to Syon House and informed of the death of Edward VI. She traveled by royal barge down the Thames the next day to the Tower of London where she was proclaimed Queen. London teemed with rumors during the succeeding days. Protestant preachers, loyal to the Northumberland regime, harangued the people, while increasing numbers murmured that Mary had the better title to the throne. News of Mary's growing strength throughout the countryside increased suspicion among the councillors and required immediate military action. Northumberland, the scourge of the Scots and the vanquisher of Kett, was the only man fit for the task, but the gloomy duke, who marched from London, was a mere shadow of his former self. If his famous comment, "The people press to see us, but not one saith God speed us," was actually uttered, it only underscored the despair and futility that had haunted him for days.[14] Without fighting a battle, Northumberland declared for Mary at Cambridge on July 20. The mystique of Tudor monarchy had exorcised the Duke of Northumberland, and the Dudley ascendancy collapsed, "not with a bang, but a whimper."

The defeated man, who threw his cap into the air at Cambridge and proclaimed the accession of Queen Mary, was a pathetic figure. With every resource of the kingdom at his disposal, Northumberland had failed to achieve the fundamental objective—the capture of Mary. A message, probably arriving in the late evening of July 19, ordered him to disarm and cause all his followers to do likewise. He was not to enter London "until the Queen's highness' pleasure be expressly declared unto him." The order hinted that mercy might be forthcoming, if he would "shew himself like a good quiet subject." Until the Earl of Arundel arrived to take Northumberland and his sons back to the Tower of London, they remained at liberty and declined the opportunity to escape.[15] Of even less fortitude were the councillors, whose treachery sealed Northumberland's doom. The same honorable men, who had signed the devise and declared for Queen Jane, now scurried for their lives and careers. At the center of this dismal spectacle was Jane herself, confused and bewildered by the rapid turn of events; only in death would she become an heroic legend. The sole figure who acted well her part was Mary Tudor. Her courage and determination won her the kingdom. Before the Queen ventured into London, the former citadel of Northumberland and his confederates, on August 3, all her enemies were safely under lock and key.

Mary was a woman of mild temperament and favored extending mercy to as many of the prisoners as possible. The council considered carefully how many persons should be indicted, arraigned, and executed. The decision that "such . . . would suffer as shall please her highness" suggests that the trials were only ceremonial and no acquittals were anticipated. Northumberland and his followers were examined by Norfolk, Arundel, Wentworth, Rich, Sir William Petre, Sir Richard Southwell, Sir Francis Inglefield, Sir John Baker, and Edward Waldegrave. In spite of the council's agreement that all prisoners in the Tower should be indicted and arraigned, the Duke of Suffolk was released at the end of July.[16]

On August 18, Northumberland, his eldest son, Warwick, and the Marquess of Northampton were tried before the Duke of Norfolk, sitting as high steward of England, and their peers. Northumberland came before the court "with a good and intrepid countenance, full of humility and gravity," and bowed three times before taking his place. Norfolk and the other peers "beheld him with a severe aspect, and the greatest courtesy shown him of any was a slight touch of the cap." Northumberland based his defense on two points; namely, that his acts were performed under the great seal of England, and that he was being judged by men guilty of the same crimes as himself. He then confessed to the indictment and was followed by the others. After hearing the sentence of death by hanging, Northumberland made four requests to the court. He asked to be executed as "a nobleman and not the other"; by this he meant beheading rather than the barbaric process of hanging and disemboweling. His second request was that "a favorable regard might be had of his children in respect of their age"; thirdly, "that he might confess to a learned divine"; and finally, "that the Queen might send to him four of the council to learn state secrets." The young Earl of Warwick, "finding that the judges in so great a case admitted no excuse of age," craved only one favor. It was merely that his debts be paid before his goods were confiscated for treason.[17]

The four days between Northumberland's trial and execution were the most crucial in his life. At eight o'clock in the morning, August 21, about ten thousand persons assembled at the Tower to witness the execution. The hangman was ready to perform his deadly office when the multitude of onlookers was suddenly commanded to disperse. Later the same day fifty prominent citizens of London, including the mayor, aldermen, and the "chiefest of the crafts," were ordered by the Queen and council to attend upon Northumberland in the Tower chapel. It was here that the famous conversion to Catholicism took place in the presence of the sons of the Duke of Somerset.[18] Surviving evidence gives an extraordinarily clear picture of what Northumberland did but no explanation for why he did it. Since his departure from London over a month before, Northumberland had lost the determination and courage that characterized his earlier behavior. While he waited in the Tower, he may very well have come to see the failure of his exertions as the judgment of God upon him. A sick and aging man who had faced mortal danger many times on the field of battle should have had little fear of death itself, but the prospect of eternal damnation may have been far more terrifying. Although Northumberland had been one of the staunchest advocates of Protestant reform under Edward VI, he was neither a theologian nor Biblical scholar. After the trial, he spoke with Stephen Gardiner, the Henrician Bishop of Winchester, soon to become lord chancellor of England.[19] He probably also received the tuition of Nicholas Heath, Bishop of Worcester, who confirmed his confession on the scaffold. Under the guidance of the bishops, Northumberland's anguish and despair may have been allayed as he was won over to their beliefs. His political philosophy offers a possible alternative explanation for his actions. Northumberland, like his father, believed in complete and unswerving obedience to the crown and may have submitted to Mary's wishes because she was the anointed of God.

Considering the prearranged gathering of notables at the Tower, it is obvious that the Queen and her councillors did not regard the repose of Northumberland's soul as a private, spiritual matter. His conversion would be a valuable asset in restoring England to the Papal fold. Both Mary and Gardiner preferred persuasion to persecution, and the spectacle of the ruined duke offered an attractive opportunity. John Foxe believed Northumberland was offered his life in return for renouncing Protestantism;[20] while this contention is open to serious doubt, we do know that the sentence of hanging was commuted to beheading. There is, therefore, a strong possibility that concerted efforts were made to achieve Northumberland's conversion. Because the Queen undoubtedly had genuine pity for him, a pious end would be both a spiritual and political victory for her. Gardiner, on the other hand, was probably more interested in the enormous political benefits that might be derived from using Northumberland as a public example before men closely identified with him and the Protestant cause.

In the presence of the lord mayor and distinguished citizens of London, Northumberland, Northampton, Sir Andrew Dudley, Sir Henry Gates, and Sir Thomas Palmer heard mass and received the sacrament "in form of bread." When the service was completed, "they turned to the people, everyone of them, the duke saying, 'Truly, I profess here before you all that I have received the sacrament according to the true Catholic faith; and the plagues that is upon the realm and upon us now is that we have erred from the faith these sixteen years. And this I protest unto you all from the bottom of my heart.'" Similar statements were made by the other four men.[21]

Probably during the evening of the same day, August 21, Northumberland wrote to the Earl of Arundel one of the most pathetic letters of the sixteenth century. It contained his last written words.

Honorable lord, and in this my distress, my especial refuge; most woeful was the news I received this evening by Mr. Lieutenant that I must prepare myself against tomorrow to receive my deadly stroke. Alas, my good lord, is my crime so heinous as no redemption but my blood can wash away the spots thereof? An old proverb there is and that most true that a lying dog is better than dead lion. Oh, that it would please her good grace to give one life, yea, the life of a dog, that I might but live and kiss her feet, and spend both life and all in her honorable services, as I have the best part already under her worthy brother and her most glorious father. Oh, that her mercy were such as she would consider how little profit my dead and dismembered body can bring her, but how great and glorious an honor it will be in all posterity when the report shall be that so gracious a queen had granted life to so miserable and penitant an object.

Your honorable usage and promises to me since these my troubles have made me bold to challenge this kindness at your hands. Pardon me if I have done amiss therein and spare not, I pray, your bended knees for me in this distress. The God of heaven it may be will require it one day on you or yours. And if my life be lengthened by your mediation and my good lord chancellor (to whom I have also sent my blurred letter), I will ever vow it to be spent at your honorable feet.

Oh, good my lord, remember how sweet life is, and how bitter the contrary. Spare not your speech and pains, for God, I hope has not shut out all hopes of comfort from me in that gracious, princely, and woman-like heart. But that as the doleful news of death has wounded to death both my soul and body, so the comfortable news of life shall be as a new resurrection to my woeful heart.

But if no remedy can be found either by imprisonment, confiscation, banishment and the like, I can say no more but God grant me patience to endure and a heart to forgive the whole world.

Once your fellow and loving companion, but now worthy of no name by wretchedness and misery.

J.D. [sic]²²

About eight o'clock the next morning, Northumberland, Palmer, and Gates were delivered to the sheriffs of London by Sir John Gage, lieutenant of the Tower. When the duke and Gates met, the latter said to Northumberland, "God have mercy on us, for this day shall end both lives; and I pray you forgive me whatsoever I have offended, and I forgive you with all my heart. Although you and your council was a great occasion thereof, well, my lord, I forgive you as I would be forgiven; and yet you and your authority was the original cause of it altogether, but the Lord pardon you; and I pray you forgive me." Each man made obeisance to the other, and Northumberland proceeded to the scaffold, took off his gown, leaned upon the east rail, and spoke to the people.[23]

Northumberland's final speech has survived in a variety of manuscript and printed versions. John Cawood, the Queen's printer, prepared an official edition that was widely circulated, and there were Latin and German translations.[24] Northumberland confessed that he had been "an evil liver" and had "done wickedly all the days" of his life. He reiterated his offenses against the Queen and begged her forgiveness. His one reservation concerned the scheme to alter the royal succession; Northumberland maintained that he alone was not the "original doer thereof . . . , for there were some other which procureth the same, but I will not name them, for I will hurt now no man." He stated that he had erred "from the Catholic faith and true doctrine of Christ"; the "true doctrine" was defined as that "which has continued throughout all Christendom since Christ." The people were exhorted to see what evils had befallen the country since the death of Henry VIII.[25] Northumberland then professed himself a "true Catholic Christian" and denied that "any have persuaded me in this." Standing witness to the duke was Bishop Heath, who affirmed the conversion. After asking and giving forgiveness of all, he knelt in the middle of the scaffold, read a prayer, repeated the creed in Latin, and made the sign of the cross.[26]

When about to stretch himself on the beam, Northumberland rose again upon his knees to adjust the bandage covering his eyes. The Spaniard, Antonio di Guaras, who stood very near the duke, recorded the final minutes. "At the moment when he again stretched himself out, as one who constrained himself and willed to consent patiently without saying anything, in the act of laying himself out inactively and afraid, he smote his hands together, as who should say, this must be, and cast himself upon the said beam."[27] The axe fell.

Guaras was convinced that Northumberland's "end was that of a true and Catholic Christian," and most historians have accepted his opinion. For a Spaniard, Catholic and Roman Catholic were synonymous,[28] but Englishmen appreciated the difference between a Catholic and a Papist. A close examination of the various versions of Northumberland's confession reveals that he made not a single statement that would qualify him as a Papist. The Catholicism of which the duke spoke was that of the Church Universal. He renounced Protestant doctrines but was characteristically vague and imprecise. Most significantly, Northumberland did not refer to the mass, and, therefore, made a less Catholic confession on the scaffold than he had made the previous day in the Tower chapel. John Foxe apparently recognized this fact when he wrote that Northumberland "denied in word that true religion, which before time, as well in King Henry the Eighth's days, as in King Edward's, he had oft evidently declared himself both to favor and further; exhorting also the people to return to the *Catholic* faith, as he termed it; whose recantations the *Papists* did forthwith publish and set abroad rejoicing not a little at his conversion, or rather subversion, as then appeared."[29]

If Northumberland actually had wished absolution by the Church of Rome in August, 1553, he would have found it difficult considering the state of religion in England. Both Gardiner and Heath were schismatics, if not outright heretics themselves, and the doctrinal reforms of the previous reign remained in force. What Northumberland had done was profess his adherence to the Catholic faith as it existed at the death of Henry VIII. He died believing himself part of the same "Holy Church" that Thomas Cromwell perished in thirteen years earlier[30] and may have carried to the grave strong doubts about the sacrament of the mass.

Men have always been judged by the way they die, and in an age of heroes and martyrs, Northumberland, indeed, made a poor showing. Historians seeking a figure to damn and ridicule found him an easy target. We are today perhaps better able to understand the unheroic figure than earlier writers, who painted their characters with bold strokes in sharply contrasting colors. The experience of recent wars and ideological conflicts has provided abundant examples of brave men turning coward on the field of battle or under the stress of persecution or intensive persuasion. Moreover, modern psychology helps explain the fears and inner motivations that determine human behavior. Even in the sixteenth century few were required to declare themselves for posterity as was Northumberland. The faith of Sir Thomas More, Hugh Latimer, and Nicholas Ridley never flagged, but Thomas Cranmer, who was infinitely more committed to Protestantism than Northumberland and both a scholar and theologian, had his moments of doubt and indecision. William Paulet, Marquess of Winchester, the Earl of Bedford, Cecil, and Cheke recanted and lived. Were they better men than Northumberland? What about the conservative Henrician bishops? Never put to the final test, Gardiner and Heath were offered the luxury of imprisonment denied Northumberland.

If men must judge their fellows, the fairest and most charitable method must be an examination and evaluation of a whole life. Northumberland faced the world with many disadvantages. The legacy of his ruined father overshadowed his career until the end. Living among humanists in a society dominated by men of sophisticated secular and ecclesiastical learning, he was ill-prepared for greatness. Little is known about Northumberland's education, but by his own admission, his formal training was limited, probably to the rudiments of law. His letters lack the wit, cleverness, and polish of men like Cecil and Sir Richard Morison. He knew little or nothing of the Latin and Italian languages,[31] and his understanding of French was probably superficial. Nor did Northumberland's political apprenticeship prepare him for the responsibilities of leadership. While his experience under Henry VIII provided some background in administration and diplomacy, he was primarily a soldier until 1547.

If Northumberland and Somerset were the only men fit to rule in the place of Henry VIII, the fault lay more with the country as a whole and with the old King. Henry should have been wise enough to know that he could not live forever; yet he willed his son a difficult political and religious legacy. After the failure of Somerset's policies in the summer of 1549, the path was open for new leadership. Northumberland courageously filled the void and set himself to the tasks of pacification and reform.[32] The Dudley ascendancy came closer to rule by a council of equals than the Protectorate. Northumberland enjoyed no legal supremacy over his colleagues, never employed the royal "we" in his correspondence as Somerset had done, and willingly accepted counsel and advice. When it became apparent that Edward would die, Northumberland committed himself to the only course possible that would assure the continuance of Protestantism. Those among the council who wavered did so out of indecision and intellectual bankruptcy; they had nothing better to offer.

Northumberland's character, if not heroic and inspiring, was at least free from glaring defects. His financial machinations as a young man on the make were scarcely out of tune with contemporary practices, and his acquisition of wealth was no crime in an age of grandeur and ostentation. Having succeeded in spite of severe handicaps, he was not wholly ignorant of the downtrodden. On one occasion he chided a servant after hearing "that the work folks at Dudley as well masons as all others are behind three weeks or more of their wages." He demanded that the wages be paid immediately. "I perceive that both I have been deceived and the poor men disappointed without knowledge to me," said Northumberland, "but as you mind my favor look that you endeavor to be more privy to all my affairs."[33] The frustrations and anxieties of politics never disturbed the harmony of the Dudley family; throughout his career, Northumberland enjoyed the full support of his wife, brother, and sons. He was aware of his own educational deficiencies, and consequently provided his children with excellent educations. Failing health hindered his effectiveness especially during the last year of his life, but he remained resolutely at the helm, often conducting affairs of state from a sick bed.[34]

Northumberland, who was often gloomy and pessimistic about his ability to serve the King, suffered from self-pity and hypersensitivity. He applied to himself the wisdom of the Italian proverb, a faithful servant shall become a perpetual ass, "which, though it become me not to say of myself, yet the saying is true." "When others went to their sups and pastimes after their travail," Northumberland said in January 1553, "I went to bed with a careful heart and a weary body, and yet abroad no man scarcely had any good opinion of me." At the very height of his power, he longed for the tranquility of retirement. "What should I wish any longer this life, that seeth such frailty in it?" he asked. "Surely, but for a few children, which God has sent me, which also helps to pluck me on my knees, I have no great cause to desire to tarry much longer here."[35] Northumberland had risen too high to withdraw unnoticed and after failing in his boldest enterprise surrendered to despair and humiliation.

Northumberland's wife, brother, and three sons did not long survive the ruin of the family. Guildford and Lady Jane were executed in February 1554, after Wyatt's rebellion shook the very foundations of Mary's regime. The Duchess of Northumberland died on January 22, 1555, at age forty-six and was buried at Chelsea. Hailed as "the greatest example of fortitude of mind in adversity," the duchess labored during her last years to win pardons for her sons and four days before her death had the satisfaction of knowing that Warwick, Ambrose, Robert, Henry, and her brother-in-law, Andrew, were set at liberty by the Queen. In her will Jane Dudley thanked the Queen and the Spaniards, who had shown favor to her sons, and remembered the ruined duke, "my lord, my dear husband." Bequests were made to each of the children, her brothers-in-law, Andrew and

Jerome, Lord and Lady Paget, and her little grandson, Philip Sidney. The young Earl of Warwick died shortly after his release. Henry Dudley was slain fighting for Mary at Gravelines two years later, and Northumberland's devoted brother, Andrew, died in 1559.[36]

The last vestiges of the Dudley ascendancy were removed in May 1554 when Queen Mary issued a warrant "for the throwing down the hatchments" of Northumberland from the Order of the Garter at St. George's chapel, Windsor. It was the Queen's pleasure that "in respect of his said offense," the hatchment of Northumberland did not deserve "to lie in so honorable a place amongst the rest of the knights of our order." For performing this duty Sir Gilbert Dethick received two pounds and twenty pence.[37]

Appendix:
The Family Fortune

The end of the Dudley political ascendancy led inevitably to the economic ruin of the family. Northumberland brought on not only his own destruction, but also the loss of the family fortune that he had built up with great effort over more than two decades. Because they had far more to lose, the Dudleys were much worse off in 1553 than in 1510 after Edmund's execution. Whereas Edmund left a marriageable wife and children who in no way participated in his alleged crimes, Northumberland was supported by an active family political machine. His sons and brother faced a future more bleak and hopeless than he had encountered forty-three years earlier. While Henry VIII could easily overlook the sins of the father in advancing young John Dudley, Queen Mary and all of England knew that Sir Andrew Dudley and Northumberland's sons, Warwick, Ambrose, Robert, Guildford, and Henry had been active parties in the scheme to exclude her from the throne. From the Queen's point of view, the country was well-rid of the Dudleys; moreover, the vast estates and princely personal possessions of Northumberland enriched the crown and the new crowd of favorites. With meticulous care and precision, the Queen's commissioners solved, in the best Tudor tradition, the administrative problem of surveying and distributing the rich harvest that had constituted the family wealth.

The commissioners' inventories reveal dramatically the rich and elegant surroundings in which Northumberland and his family lived.[1] At the time of his fall, he maintained elaborate establishments at Durham Place in London and at Syon on the Thames, formerly held by the Duke of Somerset. With Norfolk in the Tower and Somerset in the grave, Northumberland at the height of his power was easily the wealthiest man in England. Gorgeous tapestries ornamented his exquisitely furnished chambers. The wardrobe overflowed with fine gowns, doublets, and shirts, while the duke's table glistened with vessels of gilt. To treat his many ailments there was a whole carriage chest containing nothing but "apothecary and surgery ware." For happier hours "a perfume pan of alabaster finely wrought" held the scent that made Tudor social intercourse bearable. A well-supplied armory and maps describing "the Scottish field" and the "voyage" to Norwich recalled heroic military feats of the past. Seemingly endless lists of bedding stand in silent witness to the magnificence of Northumberland's household and the lavish hospitality offered to guests. On occasions both great and small, diners at finely covered tables displaying silver candlesticks could toast the duke's health with German, French, and Gascon wines from the cellar. During quieter moments, when the affairs of state were not pressing, Northumberland undoubtedly entertained his young sons with tales of his exploits at sea and explained to them the operation of his astrolabe. To make life as graceful and effortless as possible household servants numbering over 240 performed every imaginable function.

Although a man of modest means compared to his brother, Sir Andrew Dudley had an impressive collection of jewelry containing diamonds, rubies, and pearls, which he, as one of the most eligible bachelors in England, may have used to charm the beauties and tempting heiresses of the Edwardian court. The eldest son, Warwick, possessed besides sumptuous garments a fine library including works in Latin, French, and Italian, collections of plays, a Greek grammar, "a book to write the Roman hand," and a study of cosmography.[2] Such were the textbooks of a young gentleman schooled in the new learning of the English Renaissance. But as the son of his father, Warwick was more than a humanistic scholar; he was captured at Cambridge with Northumberland equipped with a full suit of armor. Another suit of armor was found at Greenwich that originally belonged to Henry VIII, presumably in the King's youthful days, before his figure assumed massive proportions.[3] All of this and more constituted the worldly possessions of the Dudleys. With so much to lose, their commitment to the altered succession was obviously not the result of lightly considered whims, and the psychological impact of the fall must have scarred the survivors for the rest of their lives.

TABLE I

INVENTORIES OF FAMILY WEALTH

Public Record Office

L.R.2/119	Inventories of goods of Northumberland at Durham Place, Syon, and goods brought from Kenilworth.
	Goods of Sir Andrew Dudley.
	Goods of the Earl of Warwick.
	Goods of Lord Robert Dudley.
E.154/2/39	Paper books containing inventories of goods of attainted persons. A later version of L.R.2/119. Includes goods of Northumberland, Sir Andrew Dudley, and also the Marquess of Northampton, Cranmer, Sir John Gates, and Sir Thomas Palmer.
E.154/6/42	Inventory of the possessions of the Earl of Warwick. Surveys goods, lands, and offices.

Bodleian
MS Add. C94   "The Lisle Inventory." Personal possessions of Lord

Lisle (afterwards the Earl of Warwick), eldest son of Northumberland. Prepared by a servant, J. Hough, and not part of inventories made by order of Queen Mary in 1553.

L.R.2/120   Goods of Northumberland at Syon and Durham Place. Similar to L.R.2/119 and E.154/2/39.

E.154/6/41   Inventories of goods of Northumberland, Warwick, Palmer, and Mrs. Cranmer. 1 packet.

E.154/6/40   Part of an inventory of goods in Warwick Castle and cattle in "Wedgnock" park. Fragmentary. Undated.

E.36/167   Survey of the possessions of Northumberland and others attainted. Accounts prepared by Clement Throckmorton August 20, 1553, of lands in Birmingham and Berkswell, Warwickshire.

E.36/168   Accounts of manors in Surrey. 2 Edward VI. Includes manor of Esher.

L.R.2/118   Accounts and vouchers relative to the goods, chattels, and other effects of Northumberland, Sir Andrew Dudley, Gates, Palmer, and Cranmer. Collected and arranged in 1793 by Richard Gray. A summary of earlier accounts and inventories. Warrants to commissioners.

E.101/631/44   Accounts of commissioners for taking over properties of Northumberland. 1 bundle.

Surviving evidence, however, leaves but an imperfect record of the family fortune. While the inventories detail everything from goblets of gold plate to chamber pots and broken dishes, they do not indicate that the Dudleys' standard of living differed in kind from the rest of the Tudor nobility. If a final report was ever made by the commissioners, it has not survived.

A declaration made by Lord Rich and the other commissioners on September 13, 1553, is qualified by the statement, "the said commission then not being fully executed."[4] According to this, the value of Northumberland's personal possessions was £5,900, of which £2000 was ready money taken from the duke at the time of his apprehension at Cambridge. Plate was valued at £2,700, excluding 651 ounces delivered to the duchess and other quantities found at Cambridge. Debts owed to Northumberland amounted to £867, while receipts from the sale of his goods were £335.[5] The various inventories suggest that the totals in Rich's declaration are too low, except for the ready money and plate. Moreover, no estimate was made of the total value of his goods that were given to the duchess, or other persons, or that remained unsold. Debts owed to Northumberland were about twice the total given in the declaration,[6] and the sale of goods brought at least £598. The highest total given for unsold goods and chattels was £1,912.[7] Therefore, the best estimate that can be made of Northumberland's personal wealth based upon the inventories would be approximately £9,000.

The personal possessions of the others attainted after Edward's death were small in contrast to the wealth of Northumberland. A rough estimate based upon the inventories, using methods consistent with those used in arriving at £9,000 for the duke, would place the Marquess of Northampton in second position with £2200 followed by Archbishop Cranmer and Sir Andrew Dudley with £1600 each. Sir Thomas Palmer's possessions were worth less than £800 and the others much less.

Efforts to determine the total wealth of Northumberland are frustrated by a lack of records. The pitfalls and dangers encountered in the use of family accounts have become common knowledge as a result of the protracted controversies arising from Tawney's theories about the rise of the gentry. Economic biographers such as Professors Bean and Simpson,[8] who concentrated on individual families and avoided bold generalizations, have stressed the limitations and ambiguities of relatively extensive accounts and manorial records. The Dudleys offer no problem in regard to the issue of rising and declining social classes or groups. Born into a prosperous Sussex gentry family of noble descent, Edmund rose by his own wits, first in the law and then in politics. John Dudley's elevation to the peerage under Henry VIII came as a result of royal favor, not through capitalistic estate management or business enterprise. As a prominent councillor to Edward VI after 1547, he had a legitimate claim to financial remuneration for services rendered, and his position assured the family of affluence. Similarly, the disasters of 1510 and 1553 have nothing to do with the disputes of declining gentry and decayed aristocracy. At any point in English history until fairly recent times, those who held the highest offices and assumed greatest risk and responsibility could expect lavish rewards and alternatively utter ruin when their fortunes passed into eclipse. What is required for the Dudleys then is not an elaborate theoretical argument, but rather an analysis of the means by which the fruits of political service were transformed into economic wealth; and it is here that we are hindered by the documentation.

An economic biography must rely heavily upon a set of family accounts. For Northumberland there are none extant. The disappointing collection of Dudley papers at Longleat, Wiltshire, contains for the most part bound volumes of correspondence relating to the Earl of Leicester. The miscellaneous pieces include the marriage settlement of Robert Dudley and Amy Robsart, the will and personal property inventory of Sir Andrew Dudley, a number of deeds, and other items. The inventories refer to chests of writings confiscated by the Queen's commissioners; these may have contained the accounts of Owen Whorwood, John Combes, and William Kenyatt,[9] general surveyors of the lands of Northumberland, and Henry Broke,[10] steward of the household. No valor has survived which gives a complete and detailed survey of the Dudley lands at the height of the family's power. The few extant manorial records provide only fragmentary information about widely scattered holdings. Thus without the all-important sources, which alone would permit us to see the over-all family fiscal operations from the inside, the problem becomes one of synthesizing diverse bits of evidence into an intelligible whole.

Although many of the most important questions cannot be answered, it does not follow that the difficulties are entirely insurmountable. It is possible to study the growth of Northumberland's estates and examine their geographical distribution. In some instances the values of significant holdings are known as well as former and future tenants. The register of all gifts, exchanges, and purchases during the reign of Edward VI reveals the degree to which Northumberland used his political influence to line his own pockets and those of his friends and relatives.[11] We also know the Dudleys' economic interests were not limited to landholding. Northumberland was connected with a variety of commercial and exploration schemes, most importantly the quest for the Northeast Passage. The profits of wardship as well as mines and fairs filled his coffers, and Northumberland was one of many nobles who invested in lead. Frequent references to projected purchases and anticipated rewards in Northumberland's letters give invaluable clues to his attitudes toward the accumulation of wealth. Northumberland left no will, but those of his wife and brother provide interesting insights into the condition of the family after the debacle of 1553. Moreover, enough statistical evidence exists at certain points to allow comparison of his income with that of others. The means by which Northumberland managed his widely dispersed estates and the methods used in arranging sales and exchanges, however are unrecorded.

The earliest picture of John Dudley is that of a young man attempting to redeem himself in the eye of Henry VIII. Service at court and on the battlefield quickly removed the stigma of treason and brought monetary rewards. That Dudley was not content to depend only on the King's favor can be seen from the host of legal actions in which he was involved in the 1530s. Blunderers like his cousin, Lord Dudley, offered easy pickings to a shrewd young man determined on success. Nor was Dudley's stepfather, Sir Arthur Plantagenet, any more than able to defend his own financial interest. He also had the good fortune of marrying Jane Guildford and securing her family's estates. With the assistance of well-chosen friends like Thomas Cromwell and Edward Seymour, Dudley entered the peerage as Viscount Lisle in 1542 no longer an upstart, but a well-to-do man. An income of at least £1000 per year flowed in from an assortment of manors scattered throughout the Southeast and the Midlands.[12] Nevertheless, the demands of a political and military career required him to seek further emolument to provide for himself and a growing family.

In a letter written in September 1545, Lisle explained to Paget the trials and tribulations of serving Henry VIII.

> Pray remember my suit to the King whereof I spake unto you yesterday. It was commenced before my going to the sea, at his grace's being at Greenwich, first for a college worth £400 a year, I offering 1000 marks in money and to found a free school in his majesty's name, which would ask £60 a year, besides that pensions for terms of lives would amount to £140 or £160 a year. The King, thinking it a great matter for me to pay so much ready money and so great pensions, answered my friend that it were better for me to have a portion of land; and so my suit has ever since remained unmentioned.
>
> Herewith, I send the names of certain parcels of land worth £193 a year. One £100 of them I must sell to pay my debts, the other £100 I am ready to sell when commanded to serve again, with all I have besides.

Lisle listed the site and demesnes of Hailes Abbey, Gloucestershire, "being leased for many years" at £99; the lordships of Birmingham, Warwickshire, £50; and Gannow, £13 and Kidderminster, £30, both in Worcestershire. Lisle's difficulties are strong evidence that even those in high favor had to accommodate themselves to the wishes and whims of the King, and that to receive land grants more was required than a polite request. As Lisle made very clear, royal service could be expensive and financially burdensome—at least until the rewards were passed around.[13]

The most explicit statement of Lisle's attitude toward office-holding and political activity is found in another letter to Paget in September 1545. He wrote expressing his interest in the office of great master of the household, vacated on the death of Charles Brandon, Duke of Suffolk, and then held by William Paulet, Lord St. John, who was currently ailing. "Whether to move it or omit it I leave to your discretion," he told Paget. "Albeit the thing is no higher than what I have, its being before occupied by such a personage would give it more estimation to the world. Take this not for ambition, for were it not my duty to offer continual service, I had rather seek no promotion." Appended to the letter was the postscript, "All places in the realm are indifferent to me, I must be holpen or sink."[14] Willing as Paget may have been to assist, the suit was doomed. St. John did not die. In fact, he outlived both Lisle and Paget and passed away at the ripe old age of eighty-seven in 1572. The key to Lisle's political motivation was a keen sense of "duty" that could easily be misinterpreted as "ambition." Duty led to ever-increasing involvement in politics and required Lisle to seek offices and land grants. Once caught in the treadmill of politics, there was no escaping. Today sociologists describe the same phenomenon as status-seeking. For Lisle, land and offices were the status symbols that provided tangible evidence of success.

The salaries received from office-holding were ordinarily small and in no way indicative of the position's real value or importance. Lisle was, nevertheless, well-compensated while lord high admiral. His monthly wage was listed at £93 6s. 8d., a sum that would amount to the substantial total of £1120 per year if paid regularly. In 1543 he was receiving an annuity of 200 marks paid quarterly at the court of augmentations; a year later what appears to be the same annuity was being paid semiannually. In addition to wages and annuities, Lisle received special allowances for diets and other expenses that further enlarged the profits of the post of lord high admiral.[15]

During the last years of Henry VIII, Lisle as well as other councillors of the King received generous land grants. In Middlesex his holdings were augmented by the hospitals of St. Giles in the Fields without the Bars of London and St. John of Jerusalem, Clerkenwell. The formal request for the latter property, prepared by Goodman, deputy to Lisle, has survived. Although he asked for St. John of Jerusalem "by way of gift," the hospital, valued at £30 annually, was granted for £1000 paid to the King plus £6 13s. 4d. paid to the treasurer of the court of augmentations. In Bristol and Gloucestershire, however, Lisle sold lands to the King worth £1,189 and alienated the manor of Preston upon Stour to Thomas Hunckys of Radbroke. Another hospital, Burton Lazars, Leicestershire, included a diverse assortment of lands scattered throughout Derbyshire, Norfolk, Suffolk, Lincoln, Rutland, Huntingdonshire, Northamptonshire, Yorkshire, and Northumberland.[16] A grant of such scope as this extended the Dudley influence into corners of England never before penetrated.

In contrast, acquisitions in Staffordshire, Warwickshire, Herefordshire, and Worcestershire were at the core of Lisle's territorial power in the Midlands. The priory of Dudley, the manor of Walsall, and other lands in Staffordshire were purchased in 1541 at the standard rate of twenty years purchase. Dudley was valued at £647 in the particulars prepared by the court of augmentations, while Walsall was listed at £952. Payment was to be made in five installments. As a reward for his services and for £69, Lisle received in 1545 lands worth over £200 annually. This grant included the manors of Birmingham, Warwickshire; Richards Castle, Herefordshire; and Kidderminster and Gannow, Worcestershire. These lands, which were requested by Lisle, constituted a gift of nearly £4000 from the King to his devoted lord admiral.[17] The carefully prepared particulars suggest that this grant was part of an efficiently administered program for rewarding devoted servants of the Crown. Certainly there is no evidence here of reckless plunder of royal wealth.

Because extant sources render an evaluation of Lisle's landed wealth in 1547 impossible, the most satisfactory alternative is found in the subsidy assessments of 1545. In her study of subsidy assessments for the reign of Henry VIII, Helen Miller found genuine efforts made to reach an accurate estimate of landed income. Lisle's income was listed at £1,360 and £1200 respectively for the two payments of the subsidy of 1545, the last surviving subsidy assessment of the peerage until the reign of Elizabeth. The wealthiest men in England were the Duke of Norfolk and the Earl of Derby with incomes of about £3000 each. Hertford, Russell, Wriothesley, and Arundel, all had incomes of less than £2000, but more than Lisle. The accuracy of these assessments is not supported, however, by a statement made by the son of Somerset in 1580 that the value of his father's land in 1547 was £4500.[18] Nevertheless, the figures are useful from a comparative point of view, if one is to assume that all nobles employed similar subterfuges in reporting their income. These assessments show that Lisle's wealth was far below that of the most affluent peers and slightly less than that of the men with whom he would share the governance of England during the reign of Edward VI. To reach merely parity with his colleagues in the council, Lisle would have to acquire more lands than they; to support the added dignity of a dukedom and enjoy the status of the richest ancient families of England, he would be required to exert herculean energies and risk denunciation for greed and ambition.

John Dudley, Viscount Lisle, became the Earl of Warwick by letters patent on February 16, 1547, but it was not until four months later that he received lands to maintain his new estate. The creation itself brought only an annuity of £20 from the petty custom within the port of London.[19] Judging from a letter to Paget, the grant of Warwick Castle was not a foregone conclusion. In March, Warwick wrote:

Perchance some folks will allege considerations concerning the not assignment of the lordship of Warwick, saying it is a stately castle, and a goodly park, and a great royalty. To that it may be answered, the castle of itself is not able to lodge a good baron with his train, for all the one side of the said castle, with also the dungeon tower, is clearly ruinated and down to the ground, and that of late the King's majesty that dead is, has sold all the chief

and principal manors that belonged to the said earldom and
castle. . . .
Of the which castle with the park and also of the town, I am con-
stable, high steward, and master of the game, with also the herbage of the park during my life, and because of the name, I am the
more desirous to have the thing, and also I come of one of the
daughters and heirs of the right and not defiled line.[20]

In the event the council would not favor him for this lordship,
Warwick was willing to accept Tunbridge and Penshurst in
Kent. A grant of lands worth £300 annually, originally intended
by Henry VIII "to strengthen his nobility and reward certain of
his councillors and servants," ended his anxiety—whether real or
feigned. In addition to Warwick Castle, he received Canonbury,
Middlesex; Melton, Leicestershire; Snowshill, Gloucestershire;
and many other manors scattered from Essex to Cheshire.[21]

In July Warwick was again complaining to Paget about financial difficulties and requesting favors of Protector Somerset
that Paget believed were "not unreasonable." Somerset's victory
at Pinkie, where Warwick "fought in the first rank and greatly
distinguished himself," provided rewards that should have
eased his distress. Lands worth £100 included former holdings
of Thomas Cromwell, Archbishop Cranmer, and the Duke of
Norfolk. The following year Warwick paid the augmentations
£1,286 for property worth about £56 annually. Since the cus-
tomary price for land was twenty-years purchase, Warwick's
bargain was not unfair to the crown, assuming the officials of
the court of augmentations did their work honestly and accu-
rately.[22]

Two subsequent transactions, however, appear more favorable to Warwick. An exchange took place in July 1549 between
him and Nicholas Heath, Bishop of Worcester, in which Warwick probably fared the better. Eighteen months earlier, he had
written to Somerset asking him to further the exchange. Warwick was especially interested in acquiring properties the bishop
held in Stratford, Warwickshire, to consolidate other holdings in the immediate vicinity. Warwick pleaded for the fair-

ness of the terms to Somerset and hoped he would be "nothing offended with my offer." The second, an exchange between Warwick and the King, was the result of laborious negotiation with Sir John Thynne for the Protector's favor. Warwick offered manors in Kent for Feckenham, Worcestershire, located between Warwick and Dudley. He wrote to Thynne in March 1549, "Whereas his grace has been informed that Feckenham is so stately a thing that it is not to be departed withall, I assure you that there is neither castle, manor, borough, nor market town belonging nor appurtenances unto the lordship."[23] Warwick believed it was worth above £34 plus £19 more for Oddingley, which was joined with Feckenham; a few days later he raised his estimate to £42 and insisted that Feckenham was "no such thing as my lord's grace did take it for."

The matter dragged into June when Warwick sent Thynne a list of his own manors that he would exchange for Feckenham and other property with the warning, "I pray you let not every man see these names of these manors." "The clear yearly value of £160 a year without any park disparked or any rent raised" was given for Westenhanger, Saltwood, Aldington, and Hythe, all in Kent. When the exchange was completed and entered on the patent roll, Warwick received property worth £210 including Feckenham, Oddingley, Worcestershire; Cheylesmore and Kenilworth monastery, Warwickshire; and Polsloe priory in Exeter.[24] Although Warwick expressed displeasure about Somerset's hesitancy in completing the exchange, the fact he did so to Thynne coupled with assurances of loyalty to the Protector suggests this issue was not the primary cause of the split between the two long-time friends. The transaction was, nevertheless, Warwick's last acquisition of land before the overthrow of the Protectorate.

It is possible to trace the later history of select portions of the preceding exchange. Two days after the transaction was completed, Warwick sold Polsloe priory to Sir Richard Sackville, chancellor of the court of augmentations, who in his turn resold the property to Sir Arthur Champernon of Modbury, Devon. Dr.

Joyce Youings, who calendared the particulars for Devon monastic grants, believes "either Warwick or Sir Richard Sakeville, or both together, made nearly 100% profit out of the Polsloe priory estate due, no doubt, to the early death of one of the life tenants."[25] On the following day the site of Kenilworth monastery was sold to Sir Andrew Flammock, a minion of Warwick. Years later in 1573, a dispute developed regarding the ownership of Kenilworth, wherein it was alleged that because Warwick had not sealed the deed of sale, the transaction was invalid. A witness before George Frenyle, Esq., baron of the exchequer, William Russell, Yeoman, formerly a servant to Sir Andrew Flammock, stated that Warwick told his master, "He could not spare the same because it lay so necessary for the castle of Kenilworth which he trusted shortly after to get into his own hands." Russell did not know whether the deed was ever sealed. The outcome of this action of the crown against Katherine Flammock has not survived in the muniments at Longleat. However, there is another deed of sale dated 1582 between Katherine and her husband, William Colburne and Robert Dudley, Earl of Leicester.[26]

Warwick's lease of a third parcel of the exchange, Cheylesmore manor, Warwickshire, to the city of Coventry furnished the inspiration for a local bard to write the memorable lines:

When flourishing state 'gan once to fade and common wealth decay,
No wonder that in cities great (for what endureth ay?)
John, late Duke of Northumberland, a prince of high degree,
Did grant fair lands for commons weale, as here in brass you see.[27]

In order to relieve the poor of Coventry, Warwick stipulated in the 99-year lease that the mayor, bailiffs, and commonalty "should yearly take to pasture in the said park, the number of 80 kyne or heyfers, and 20 geldings of such poor inhabitants of the said city and suburbs, as should not have elsewhere nigh thereto sufficient pasture; paying yearly for every cow or heyfer 1d. and for every gelding 2d."[28]

Beginning in 1550, Warwick's territorial power was extended into the North of England. Generous land grants accompanied appointment to office. In May he became "governor of the county of Northumberland and keeper or warden general of the marches against Scotland" for life, with a yearly fee of £1000 payable by the general receiver of the augmentations for the county of York. On October 20 the following year, he received what appears to be reappointment as "warden general of the marches against Scotland, namely the east march, west march, and middle march, and in the King's lordship of Scotland," with a yearly fee of 2000 marks during the King's pleasure, payable by the treasurer of Berwick and the treasurer of the augmentations. Prominent among his lesser positions was a grant for life of the office of chief steward of the East Riding in April 1552.[29]

The profusion of land grants in Northumberland and Yorkshire and a complicated series of exchanges defies logical analysis. Early in 1550, the castle and lordship of Warwick were exchanged with the King for an assortment of lands in Oxfordshire, Nottinghamshire, and Yorkshire worth £470. The Privy Council requested the chancellor of augmentations in April 1550 to grant Warwick, as a gift, lands in Northumberland, Yorkshire, and Worcestershire worth £660. The actual grant contained a slightly different assortment of lands, but was more valuable than the council's original request. Three justifications were given for this gift: First, the King endowed Warwick with "authority and possessions" for his duties there; second, Warwick's claim through his mother to "the fourth part" of the lands of Richard Beauchamp, Earl of Warwick (d. 1439) was acknowledged; and finally the King wished to encourage the earl's children in the hope that they "will follow in his steps and exhibit a like example of the virtues of true nobility." Many of these lands were returned to the King in July by terms of an exchange which returned Warwick Castle and granted other property in the Midlands and the South.[30]

After Warwick became Duke of Northumberland, he received more lands in the North including property formerly belonging to the Percy earls of Northumberland. The barony and castle of Alnwick, and the lordships of Warkworth and Ackling-ton, all former Percy lands, were granted to Northumberland in January 1552 for his surrender of a life annuity of 500 marks. At the same time he further strengthened his power in the North by exchanging manors in Oxfordshire, Worcestershire, Glou-cestershire, and Middlesex for property in Northumberland and Yorkshire worth approximately £500 annually.[31]

The dissolution of the bishopric of Durham in the last year of Edward's reign followed the profusion of grants to Northum-berland in the North of England. He received a life grant of the office of chief steward of all crown lands in Cumberland, Northumberland, Westmoreland, Yorkshire, and elsewhere in England, which formerly belonged to the Bishop of Durham with the power to appoint all officials. He was appointed con-stable and keeper of Durham Castle, and master forester gen-eral and master of the hunt of game of the forests formerly of the bishopric.[32] These offices and the vast landholdings gave Northumberland unquestioned supremacy in the North. How-ever, Northumberland was never granted the palatine jurisdic-tion; nor does it appear that he ever requested such powers.[33]

Although the rapid accumulation of estates in the North was the most apparent characteristic of Northumberland's acquisi-tions between 1550 and 1553, his interests were by no means re-stricted to this area. After the execution of Somerset, he received parcels of the late Protector's estates in Wiltshire. In Gloucester-shire, Herefordshire, Oxfordshire, and Nottinghamshire, he re-granted his lands to others or exchanged them with the King, in some cases within a few days of the original grant. Those who purchased land from Northumberland were frequently close as-sociates like Henry Broke, his steward, Sir Andrew Flammock, Sir Francis Jobson, Sir John York, Owen Whorwood, Sir Henry Sidney, and Sir Andrew Dudley. It was no coincidence that many of Northumberland's friends and grantees were also offi-cials of the court of augmentations; men like Jobson, Sir Rich-ard Sackville, Sir Edward North, Thomas Mildmay, John Horn-yold, and Richard Tavener could serve the augmentations and

Northumberland and at the same time increase their own fortunes.[34] Other administrators and courtiers such as Sir John York, John Beaumont, Sir Anthony Denny, and Sir William Cawarden were similarly well-placed to benefit from deals with Northumberland.

In spite of the vast wealth passing into his hands, there is evidence that Northumberland experienced financial difficulties as late as 1552. On June 4, he asked Cecil to obtain from the council a warrant to Sir John Williams, treasurer of the augmentations, for payment of £1000 as part of his fee for the marches. Northumberland went on to explain that he was "constrained of necessity" to send letters to the lord chamberlain and vice-chamberlain, his "special friends," to obtain his fee; if he had been able to sell land in London, he would not have required the payment. From the letter it is not clear whether he was asking for advance payment, or whether his fees were in arrears, and he was apologizing for demanding what was rightfully his. That Northumberland was pressing for financial relief is supported by the cancellation of a debt of over £2000 a few days later. This included unpaid rents and subsidy payments dating back to the reign of Henry VIII.[35]

The value of landed wealth obtained by Northumberland during the reign of Edward VI can be calculated from the register of gifts, exchanges, and purchases. Table II shows that he

TABLE II

GIFTS, PURCHASES, AND EXCHANGES OF LAND DURING THE REIGN OF EDWARD VI: JOHN DUDLEY

A. *Gifts* Date	*Annual value*	*Rent reserved*	*Consideration*
June 22, 1547	£ 498-18- 8	£63-16- 1	For service, and better maintenance of his es-

A. Gifts (cont.)

Date	Annual value	Rent reserved	Consideration
			tate, and fulfilling a "determination" made by Henry VIII.
December 22, 1547	£ 108- 5- 9	£ 8- 5- 9	Service against Scots.
May 20, 1550	£ 693- 6-10	£60-16- 7	Service.
May 19, 1551	£ 49- 3- 8	nil	Service.
January 5, 1552	£ 233- 6- 8	£ 2-15- 4	For the better maintenance of his honor and for the surrender of an annuity of 500 marks.
June 26, 1553	£ 400- 0- 0[a]	£46-13- 8	
Total	£1983- 1- 7[b]		

B. Purchase

Date	Sum	Annual value	Rent reserved	
August 17, 1548	£1286- 5- 7	£56- 2- 0	nil	Part to George Blunt, Hugh Ellys and Warwick.[c]

C. Exchanges

Date	Annual value	Rent reserved	Consideration of exchange
July 19, 1549	£210- 6- 3	£21- 8- 0	Chiefly manors in Kent.

C. *Exchanges* (*cont.*)

Date	Annual value	Rent reserved	Consideration of exchange
January 6, 1550	£470- 9- 7	£25-12- 2	Castle, lordship, and borough of Warwick and other lands.
July 25, 1550	£473- 5- 7	£50- 9- 0	Lands in Northld., Yorks., Middx., & Herts.
September 10, 1550	£105- 5- 6	£12-19- 4	Lands in Yorks., Kent, & Sussex.
March 14, 1551	£ 30- 3- 2	nil	Esher, Surrey, and other lands. Received Chelsea, Middx.
January 5, 1552	£695- 9- 9	£73- 2- 5	Lands in Oxon., Middx., Worcs., & Glos.
November 21, 1552[d]	£398-15- 7	£28- 0- 0	Lands in Northld. and £1,252-6-3.
March 2, 1553	£104-15- 5	nil	Otford and Knole, Kent.[e]
March 2, 1553	1000 marks (£666-13- 4)	£101- 0- 1	Castle of Tunbridge and other lands in Kent.
Total	£3155- 4- 2		

D. *Fee Farm*[f]

Date	Annual value	Rent reserved	Consideration
May 3, 1553	£ 229- 6- 3	£229- 6- 3	King's special favor.

SOURCE: P.R.O. S.P. 10/19.

ᵃ Cf. *Calendar of Patent Rolls, Edward VI,* ed. R. H. Brodie (London, 1924-29), V, 171ff. and British Museum Royal MS 18C 24, fo. 366. Yearly value of lands given as £300. Rents reserved, £24 4s. 7d. and £28 14s. 7d.

ᵇ Does not include gift of 1000 marks annually (lordship, manor and borough of Stratford, and Old Stratford, Warwickshire). Royal MS 18C, 24, fo. 303v. Not in *Calendar of Patent Rolls*. Does not include gift of lordship, manor, and castle of Kenilworth, Warwickshire, annual value £40 13s. 1d.

ᶜ *C.P.R.,* II, 29ff.

ᵈ B.M. Royal MS 18C, 24, fo. 272. Described as a "gift." Northumberland exchanged Tynemouth monastery and £1,252 6s. 3d. for the manors of Brokenborough, Burton, and Hankerton, Wiltshire; yearly value £398 15s. 7d.

ᵉ *C.P.R.,* V, 173, Knole not listed.

ᶠ Landholding in fee farm should not have existed in the sixteenth century. According to A.W.B. Simpson, *An Introduction to the History of Land Law* (London, 1961), 73–74, it did survive, although the distinction between fee farm and socage is far from clear. Barnard Castle in Durham, listed as a fee farm in the register, is described as a gift in socage in the *Calendar of Patent Rolls* and the Docquet Book of the Privy Council. *C.P.R.* V, 174-75. British Museum Royal MS 18C 24, fo. 339v.

received gifts of land worth nearly £2000 annually, a sum considerably larger than his entire income in 1547. In theory, the exchanges involved land parcels of equal value; in some instances this was, in fact, true. However, I cannot explain why certain lands changed hands so frequently. Northumberland's letters offer no clue to his logic, nor do the Dudley papers provide any help. Table III indicates the relative insignificance of

TABLE III

GIFTS, PURCHASES, AND EXCHANGES OF LAND DURING THE REIGN OF EDWARD VI: THE DUDLEY FAMILY

A. *Gifts* Dates	*Annual value*	*Rent reserved*	
Sir Andrew Dudley			
September 25, 1551	£180- 0- 7	nil	For Service.
February 3, 1553	£ 54-16- 2	£10- 6- 2	For Service.

A. *Gifts* (*cont.*)

Date	Annual value	Rent reserved	
Lord Robert Dudley (and William Glasner)[a] June 27, 1553	£149-10- 4	nil	For service and £400.
Earl of Warwick (and Sir Henry Sidney) July 4, 1553	£158- 0-10	£13- 1- 9	For service.

B. Purchases: None
C. Exchanges: None
D. Fee Farms: None

SOURCE: P.R.O. S.P. 10/19.
[a] B.M. Royal MS 18C, 24, fo. 365v. Glasner not listed.

gifts to other members of the Dudley family. Northumberland's sons were, of course, young, and Sir Andrew was always content to remain in the background.

At the time of his death, Northumberland held estates located in three main geographical areas, the North, the Southeast, and the Midlands. As we have seen, his holdings in the North were acquired only in the last three years of his career, but elsewhere his interests were continuous. In the Southeast, he built upon the Guildford inheritance in Kent and the lands of his father that were regranted by Henry VIII.[36] Monastic property was the basis of Northumberland's wealth in London and Middlesex and included the hospital of St. Giles-in-the-Fields without London, the hospital of St. John of Jerusalem, Clerkenwell, and Syon abbey. Formerly held by Protector Somerset, Syon was described by an official of the court of augmentations as a "capital mansion, lately built, but not thoroughly finished" and valued at £28. Syon was granted to Northumberland in June 1553 and became one of his principal residences.[37] Chelsea also served as a residence and remained in the possession of the duchess after her husband's execution.

Northumberland increased his holdings in Hampshire, Surrey, and Sussex very little during the reign of Edward VI. Greater activity can be seen in Essex and Kent where a host of exchanges and sales took place. The site of the abbey of St. John, Colchester, and Haroldspark in Essex were sold to Sir Francis Jobson and Sir Anthony Denny, respectively, almost immediately after they were granted in 1547. Halden, Kent, formerly of the Guildfords, passed to Cromwell, then to the Crown and back to Northumberland, who sold it to George Harper, Thomas Culpepper, and William Isley, and finally bought it back again. With such a rapid succession of transfers, the bailiffs of Halden must have been hard pressed to remember to which master they should account.

After receiving the manor of Otford, Kent, from the King in May 1551, Northumberland wrote that it had been given "as well for the better maintenance of my living as also for that I have no inhabitation in these parts to place me and my family upon, whereby I may the better give my daily attendance upon his majesty's service." He explained that he "besought the King's majesty to take again of me in recompense of the said manor of Otford, the manors of Langley and Burford with the parks and the forest of Wychwood in the county of Oxford." Because of his "liberality and bountiful goodness in respect of my continual charge," the King with the advice of the council refused and commanded Warwick to accept Otford as a free gift. The manor was valued at £49, but when the same property was exchanged with the King in December 1552, its annual value had more than doubled.[38] Assuming no elaborate improvements were made, it would appear that Northumberland had profited handsomely at the Crown's expense.

Other manors of Northumberland in Kent included Knole, Sevenoaks, Tunbridge, and Hadlow. In May 1552, Northumberland secured a license to place these properties in trust for his wife, in augmentation of her jointure. Nevertheless Sevenoaks, Tunbridge, and Hadlow were exchanged with the King the following year for a parcel of lands scattered from Somerset to Northumberland. If the trust was dissolved by the exchange, Northumberland had liquidated the bulk of his holdings in the county.[39]

What has become the vast Birmingham conurbation, spreading into three counties, was once the center of Northumberland's Midland estates. But it was long after the fall of Dudley that the manors of Birmingham, Wednesbury, West Bromwich, Walsall, and the college of Wolverhampton were transformed into the heart of industrial England. The area also contained the castles of Dudley and Warwick, the basis of Northumberland's claim to noble ancestry. A few years after Sir John Dudley received the prophetic appointment as joint constable of the castle and borough of Warwick in 1532, he managed to wrest control of the ancestral estates of the baronage of Dudley from his inept cousin.[40] Dudley Castle, languishing in decay under the impoverished barons, was repaired and remodeled by its new master. New buildings on the north side of the castle called the "new-work" were erected, and the gatehouse tower was adorned with the arms of Malpas, Somery, and the lion rampant, the coat of Sutton, which was assumed by Dudley.[41] Henry VIII proceeded to reward his ambitious young servant with a generous parcel of manors that made him one of the largest landowners in south Staffordshire by 1547.

A large portion of Northumberland's property in Shropshire, Worcestershire, and Leicestershire comprised former monastic and church lands. The hospital of St. John the Baptist in Ludlow was alienated to William and Edmund Foxe of that city in June 1547, just one day after it was granted. The following year Northumberland received the fraternity and guild of St. Winifred in Shrewsbury and the property of the chantry of the Holy Trinity in the church of St. Lawrence, Evesham, Worcestershire. The abbey of Halesowen, Worcestershire, with the site and demesne lands valued at £99 annually, was acquired in 1538 and included the priory of Dodford.[42] An exchange with Nicholas Heath, Bishop of Worcester, in 1549 and receipt of Hartlebury Castle four years later brought lands of the bishopric into his possession. The most important holding of Northumberland in Leicestershire was the hospital of Burton Lazars, granted by Henry VIII for services rendered in 1544.

All of the Dudley wealth in the Midlands did not come from the spoliation of the church. As early as 1532, influence was gained in Worcestershire with a grant of wardship and land in King's Norton during the minority of Anthony Norton. The coveted manor of Feckenham, cause of the extended correspondence with Thynne, was formerly part of the jointure of Queen Catherine Parr. The Duke of Norfolk sold Dudley a number of manors in Shropshire in 1541, and the manor of Birmingham was obtained through legal machinations.[43]

As the first Tudor Earl of Warwick, John Dudley acquired possessions in that country formerly belonging to the powerful fifteenth-century Beauchamp and Neville earls. Henry VII administered the so-called "Warwick's lands" and passed them on to his son and grandson. When Dudley received the famous Warwick Castle, many of its appurtenances had been disposed of; nevertheless, it had great symbolic importance, because he claimed descent from the Beauchamps through his mother. The castle was also the key to domination of the county, and by 1553 Dudley influence extended from Birmingham in the north to Stratford-on-Avon in the south. Lands from the college of St. Mary and the Friars Preachers, Warwick, Combe abbey, and Kenilworth monastery augmented the ancient earldom. In Coventry, the poor benefited from his gift of Cheylesmore. At the time of his marriage to Anne Seymour, Northumberland's eldest son was given the lordship of Balsall with rents worth £50 annually and was established in the county as heir apparent.[44] The total annual value of Northumberland's lands in Warwickshire at the death of Edward VI was approximately £1700.[45] Whether the Dudleys ever recognized it or not, their influence in the county paralleled the fifteenth-century earls in more ways than one. As kingmakers, they were consumed by the furies of political strife as completely as Richard Neville. Only the Dudleys had a second reign of power when Ambrose and Robert became the Elizabethan Earls of Warwick and Leicester.

Analyzed chronologically according to their acquisition or geographically, the estates of Northumberland add up to a princely sum; but they do not add up to a mathematical sum. For, alas, nowhere among the inventories is a complete valor of the estates. One of the inventories does contain the statement that Northumberland's lands were valued at £4300 annually. No explanation is given regarding the computation of the sum. Following this, are values of the estates of the others attainted: the Marquess of Northampton, £2800; Sir Andrew Dudley, £555; Sir John Gates, £796; and Sir Thomas Palmer, £309. If one is bold enough to assume these figures are accurate (and this is a reasonable conjecture, inasmuch as the inventory was prepared by commissioners of Queen Mary, who presumably had no motive for distortion), a number of comparisons are possible. To compare the income of Northumberland with the wealthier Elizabethan aristocracy studied by Professor Stone would be meaningless because of inflation. An apologist for Northumberland might draw comfort from contrasting his income of £4300 with the £7500, which Lord Hertford said in 1580 was the value of Somerset's estates; but Hertford's valuation could be challenged, even if the income of Northumberland were acceptable.[46]

Perhaps the least objectionable comparisons could be made with the early Tudor aristocracy. Professor Bean believed the clear income of Henry Percy, fifth Earl of Northumberland, was approximately £3900 in 1523. According to Dr. Charles Sturge, the income of Cuthbert Tunstall, Bishop of Durham, was in excess of £3000 in 1535, exclusive of an annual salary of £800 as president of the council of the North. In her study of the early Tudor peerage, Miss Miller placed the landed income of Edward Stafford, Duke of Buckingham, at £5000 and that of Henry Courtenay, Marquess of Exeter at £3000, and found the average income of the peerage from land about £1200.[47] Northumberland was obviously no average peer and, as the leading figure in the government of Edward VI after 1549, could reasonably expect a landed income equal to that of the wealthiest Henrician nobility. Unlike the Percys, the Staffords, and the

Courtenays, Northumberland had no vast inheritance of ancestral estates. After the death of Henry VIII, he acquired estates and offices at a rapid pace to support his increasing rank and responsibilities;[48] and for so doing, writers, who delighted in shocking their readers with accounts of extravagance and rapacity, branded him an upstart and a plunderer of the wealth of England.

Although by far the largest share of Northumberland's income came from land, he had commercial and industrial interests of several types. No personal accounts have survived to illuminate the importance of these activities, but isolated scraps of evidence afford brief glimpses into his business ventures. In December 1546, he purchased 3,000 fothers of lead from the King for £13,000 "to be paid at the six years and next after the delivery." The sale of lead was one of several financial expedients employed by Henry VIII to ease the economic distress of the government. It was believed that great profit could be made from sales on the Continent; however the negotiations of the King's financial agent, Stephen Vaughan, in Antwerp proved the contrary. Lisle's purchase of 3,000 fothers represented fully one-fourth of the total quantity at nine English ports awaiting shipment in 1544. The price of £4 6s. 8d. per fother paid by Lisle was well above the £4 11s. 0d. Flemish (£3 12s. 10d. English, if £ Flemish equals 16 English shillings), which Vaughan believed the entire lot would bring on the Continent in the event of a forced sale. Half of the purchase was not delivered to Lisle before the King's death and remained at Boston and Grimsby. What he did with the lead is not known, and there is no evidence that he ever paid the full £13,000. In May 1553, the Privy Council issued a warrant to Sir Richard Sackville signifying that the King had respited the payment of £1,333 until 1560, due from John Calthorpe, Anthony Merler, William Dale, and Walter Merler, for 400 fothers of lead from the 3000 sold to Lisle by Henry VIII. The inventories made after Northumberland's fall include small quantities of lead at Syon and Alnwick. If a portion sold by Queen Mary's commissioners at £5 6s. 8d. per fother represented market price, Northumberland may very well have enjoyed an excellent profit on his purchase.[49]

Besides his sizable investment in lead, Northumberland exported leather, owned fairs and markets, and operated a variety of mines and mills. In 1543, the King granted him a license to export 400 tons of tallow and 400 dikkers of calfskins (10 dozen equals one dikker). The value of two yearly fairs and a weekly market at Bishops Hatfield, Hertfordshire, and another fair at Aldington, Kent, is not known. Water, corn, and fulling mills in Nottinghamshire and Gloucestershire were retained only briefly. After receiving these in January 1550, they were regranted to John Beaumont in May 1551. A coal mine in Wrexham, Denbigh, had formerly belonged to Thomas Seymour. Northumberland was one of the pioneers in the iron industry. Contained among the inventories compiled in 1553 is a bill "received by me, William Uvedale, at my lord's grace's iron mills from the 20th day of November to the 1st day of May, 7 Edward VI [1553]." This fragment, referring to Northumberland's forge and furnace at Southfrith, Kent, lists wages and expenses amounting to more than £300.[50]

The profits of wardship contributed to the Dudley family wealth, as was the case in all families with political connections. Northumberland's eldest son received the wardship of Sir Edward Seymour, son of Somerset, with the keeping of all his manors, lands, and tenements in 1553. The keeping of one Thomas Philpot, alternatively described as "idiot" and "lunatic," was granted to Robert Dudley in 1552 and again the following year.[51]

Although the extent of Northumberland's activity as a promoter of the Willoughby and Chancellor expedition to discover the Northeast Passage has been a subject of dispute, there can be little doubt about the family's interest in geography and exploration. Northumberland utilized the services of leading French cosmographers and, with Sebastian Cabot, considered a possible raid on Peru in 1551. His son-in-law, Sir Henry Sidney, took personal charge of the maintenance of Chancellor, while the young Earl of Warwick was an intimate friend of John Dee, the mathematician and astronomer. In the preface to the *English Euclid*, Dee paid a touching tribute to Warwick and dedicated works on tides and astronomy to the Duchess of Northumberland. The economic purpose of these ventures was to find new markets for the declining cloth trade. Only after Northumberland's fall were the full benefits of his exertions realized by the Muscovy Company.[52]

The most important benefit a father could confer upon his children during his own lifetime was the arrangement of advantageous marriages. Two matches—Warwick and Anne Seymour, and Guildford and Jane Grey—were of the utmost political significance; in each case the desired objectives were not achieved. The love-match of Robert and Amy Robsart was ultimately a failure, but the financial arrangements surrounding it, if not spectacular, were at least typical for a younger son. The deed of settlement, drawn up May 24, 1550, settled Coxford priory and other land in Norfolk, formerly of the Duke of Norfolk, upon the couple and the heirs of Robert's body, if the "said Robert and Amy will thereunto condescend and agree." Northumberland also gave the pair and "the long-liver of them" an annuity of £50, with the curious stipulation that it would be void from the death of Princess Mary or the time that the princess married. A further payment of £200 was promised to Amy's father, Sir John Robsart, who, for his part, paid Robert £70 per year during the former's life. Furthermore, if Robert and Amy, "the heirs of their two bodies, or one of them" outlived Robsart and his wife, they would receive 3000 sheep. In 1553 Northumberland granted his manor of Hemsby, Norfolk, to the couple.[53]

More lucrative was the marriage between Henry Dudley and Margaret Audley, daughter and heir of Thomas, Lord Audley, who was lord chancellor from 1533 until his death in 1544. Margaret and her sister, Mary, remained co-heirs, until Mary herself died under age and unmarried leaving Margaret as sole heir to the Audley estates. When less than fourteen years of age, she was married to Dudley, who thereby acquired lands worth £1000 per year in London and Middlesex.

Attainted with the rest of his family, Henry was restored in 1556 and subsequently began proceedings with his wife in chancery to gain possession of land in Hertfordshire, claimed by Thomas Castell, Esq., of London. Shortly thereafter, Dudley was killed in military action, and his widow was remarried to Thomas Howard, fourth Duke of Norfolk. Ambrose Dudley was a widower in 1552 following the death of his wife, Anne, daughter of William Whorwood, attorney general between 1540 and 1545. From the moment of her death, Northumberland took steps to maintain control of the Whorwood inheritance. Possibly the most fruitful Dudley marriage was that between Mary and Sir Henry Sidney. The old Guildford estate of Halden, Kent, was given to the couple by the bride's father at the time of the wedding in 1551. This marriage helped atone for the sins of the Dudley family by giving to the world that most noble of Englishmen, Sir Philip Sidney.[54]

While the overthrow of the Dudleys in 1553 meant the utter ruination of the family fortune, with little more than an anguished hope of recovery in the future, the new regime of Queen Mary was faced with the immediate task of securing, inventorying, and disposing of their property. The inventories attest to the meticulous care taken by the Queen's commissioners and provide valuable insights into methods used and some of the difficulties encountered. No time was wasted in securing the family possessions. Before Mary herself entered London—indeed, only a few days after Northumberland's arrest at Cambridge on July 21—Sir William Petre and Sir John Baker began the preliminary surveys. Later, a commission composed of Lord Rich, Sir John Huddleston, Sir Robert Southwell, Sir Thomas Pope, and Sir Thomas Stradling was appointed to inventory goods of attainted persons or ones "who should be" attainted before the end of Mary's first parliament. Every effort was made to prevent any of the goods from being overlooked or from passing into private hands. Accordingly, Sir Edward North informed the commissioners in September that he heard Palmer had a house in Bedfordshire with "some stuff" in it and was concerned about its safety. In addition to the large inventories at Syon and Durham Place, surveys of family possessions in the houses of friends and associates in London were prepared. The commissioners were advised to examine a bill of goods Sir Andrew Dudley sent to Lady Margaret, daughter of the Earl of Cumberland, during his abortive courtship.[55]

Like vultures men of all ranks and degree swept in to claim various possessions of the Dudleys. Still vivid in the memory of John Coke was a "gown of taffeta furred with sable" worn by Dudley, when he was made a duke, which "appertained as fee unto me garter principal, king of arms." Coke said the men of the chamber and the barber could testify how the duke deferred "from time to time promising me to have either the same or else a gown as good" and hoped the commissioners would grant his request. Edward, Earl of Derby, one of the old nobility who had successfully weathered the Edwardian storms, received the council's permission to have part of Northumberland's goods at Durham Place. He told the commissioners that he was given "the choice of such as shall be for my purpose" and requested a reasonable price and time for payment.[56]

A woman who herself had known unhappiness and discomfiture, Queen Mary reserved some of the Dudley possessions for those who had suffered during her brother's reign. Imprisoned since 1538, Edward Courtenay was released by the Queen and created Earl of Devon. On September 4, the council ordered the commissioners to halt sales of Northumberland's goods "until such time as the Queen's highness having seen the inventories" decided what should be given to Courtenay and his mother, the Marchioness of Exeter. Courtenay also purchased considerable quantities of clothes and household goods. Whatever the personal failings of the Duchess of Somerset may have been, she was innocent of the charges made against her late husband; in recognition of this, Mary granted portions of Northumberland's household goods to the duchess and authorized the commissioners to make delivery.[57]

The Queen's generosity was even extended to the Duchess of Northumberland. Commendable as it was, favor toward the survivors of the fallen great was not unusual, for the Tudors ruled over an ordered society in which men's political power might be destroyed but not their social status. For her own part, the duchess undoubtedly adjusted to the loss of her husband more easily than she could have adjusted to economic privation, and Lord Ambrose Dudley was not surprised when his own mattress, bed, bolsters, and other goods were delivered to him "for his furniture at the Tower." The Queen's gifts to the duchess included 652 ounces of plate, carpets, tapestry, candlesticks, brass pots, a walnut table, and featherbeds from Syon and Durham Place—in all a list of goods filling more than two folio pages.[58] So that the duchess would suffer as little inconvenience as possible, the orders for delivery were among the first duties of Petre and Baker.

The task of inventorying the possessions of the Dudleys and other attainted persons was so large that the work of the commissioners continued into the spring of 1554. Besides the routine work, there were numerous delays and complications. Fees of 2s. 4d. were paid for opening stubborn locks at Durham Place; there were negotiations with people who owed money to Northumberland and purchased his goods, and wages for gardening at Syon. The Privy Council instructed the commissioners to pay the former servants of the family and "exhort them quietly to repair home to their friends or otherwise to provide for themselves, as they can by way of service." The wages of Northumberland's 246 servants totaled over £135. Other "necessary charges" of the commissioners, amounting to £195, included the hire of horses and barges, rewards given to laborers, smiths, carpenters, £13 for mowing hay at Syon, and costs "for making of a book concerning the affairs of the Commission." Thomas Turell, messenger of the Queen, presented a bill for 70s. "for riding and delivering of certain letters. . . ." His longest journey was from London to Cambridge, but there were frequent deliveries between London and Richmond over a period of thirty-five days in August and September. Special surveys of Northumberland's property in Warwickshire and Surrey were prepared in addition to the *inquisitions post mortem*, all adding to the crown's expense.[59] If Northumberland had no other consolation in his darkest hour of defeat and humiliation, he could draw some small comfort from the immense burden his family's wealth imposed upon the Queen's servants, who were required to survey and take possession of it.

Notes

CHAPTER I NOTES
(pp. 3–10)

1. J. J. Scarisbrick, *Henry VIII* (London, 1968), p. 20.

2. Chroniclers and historians have been almost unanimous in their condemnation of Dudley. For example, Antonio di Guaras, author of the contemporary account, *The Accession of Queen Mary*, trans. R. Garnett (London, 1892), pp. 80–109, held Northumberland responsible for the overthrow of the Howards under Henry VIII, the destruction of Protector Somerset and his brother Lord Seymour, and the death of Edward VI. John Hayward's *Life and Raigne of King Edward the Sixth* (London, 1636), p. 417, portrayed Northumberland as a man "sottishly mad with over-great fortune," who induced the dying Edward to will his throne to Lady Jane Grey. It was the modern scholar, A. F. Pollard, who called Northumberland "the subtlest intriguer in English history" in *England under Protector Somerset* (London, 1900), p. 244. W. K. Jordan's *Edward VI: The Young King* (London, 1968) is almost as unsympathetic to Northumberland as Pollard's study; cf. pp. 81, 304, 500, 501.

3. *Complete Peerage*. H. Sidney Grazebrook, "The Barons of Dudley," *Collections for a History of Staffordshire*, William Salt Archaeological Society, Birmingham, IX (1888), Part II, 71–77.

4. For further information see *Calendar of Inquisitions Post Mortem, Henry VII* (London, 1955), III, 489; M. A. Lower, *A Compendious History . . . with an Index to the First 20 Volumes of the Sussex Archaeological Society Collections* (Lewes, 1870), I, 117; *History of Parliament* (London, 1938), II, 443–696; D. M. Brodie, "Edmund Dudley, Minister of Henry VII," *Trans. R. Hist. Soc.* XV (1932), 157–58.

5. *Statutes of the Realm*, 3 Henry VIII, c. xix.

6. *Letters and Papers, Foreign and Domestic of the Reign of Henry VIII, 1509–1547*, ed. J. S. Brewer *et al.* (London, 1862–1910), 1 (1), 146 (425); Public Record Office: E.154/2/17, see also *L&P* 1 (2), g. 2055.

7. *L&P* 1 (1), g. 381; 1 (2), g. 3324; 3 (2), g. 3586.
8. For example see P.R.O.: C.1/498/19, 20 and S.C.12/23/45.
9. *L&P* 7, 788–89, 813, 823, 1026, 1251; P.R.O.: C.1/781, 42–43. There is a full account of these proceedings in my dissertation, "A Study of John Dudley, Duke of Northumberland and His Family," Northwestern University, 1965, pp. 89–94.
10. *L&P* 5, 1727; 6, 467; British Museum, Cotton MS, Vesp. F. XIII fo. 222/120; P.R.O.: St. Ch. 2, Vol. 13, fo. 120; *L&P* 12 (1), 1263.
11. For a detailed study of this problem see M. L. Bush, "The Lisle-Seymour Land Disputes: A Study of Power and Influence in the 1530's," *Historical Journal*, IX (1966), 255–274.
12. *L&P* 3 (2), 3288; Edward Hall, *The Union of the Two Noble and Illustre Famelies . . .* , ed. Henry Ellis, (London, 1809), pp. 670–71. Raphael Holinshed, *Chronicle* (London, 1807–1808), III, 688–90; *Calais Chronicle*, ed. J. G. Nichols (Camden Society, XXXV, 1846), 100.
13. Holinshed, III, 696.
14. *L&P* 4 (2), 3216.
15. *Calais Chronicle*, 41–42.
16. B. M. Add. MS, 6113, fos. 85v.–86v.
17. *L&P* 5, 909.
18. *L&P* 11, 580 (233), 632, 793.
19. James A. Froude, *History of England* (London, 1893), III, 69.
20. *Complete Peerage*; B. M. Eg. MS, 2642, fos. 8–9v; Holinshed, III, 686.
21. *Complete Peerage*; *L&P* 17, g. 2220; B. M. Add. MS, 6113, fos. 89f.; Eg. MS, 2642, fos. 9–10. Cf. John Stow, *The Annales of England* (London, 1615), p. 583, who states that Dudley was created in the right of his mother.

CHAPTER II NOTES
(pp. 11–42)

1. *Letters and Papers, Foreign and Domestic of the Reign of Henry VIII, 1509–47*, ed. J. S. Brewer, *et al.* (London, 1862–1910), 16, 169.
2. *L&P* 17, 318. For a detailed study of Henry VIII's Scottish policy see A. J. Slavin, *Politics and Profit* (Cambridge, 1966), pp. 68ff.; and R. B. Wernham, *Before the Armada* (London, 1966), pp. 149–163.
3. Edward Hall, *The Union of the Two Noble and Illustre Famelies . . .* , ed. Henry Ellis (London, 1809), p. 856; *Calendar of the Carew Manuscripts Preserved in the Archepiscopal Library at Lambeth, 1515–1574*, ed. J. S. Brewer and William Bullen (London, 1867), Nos. 173, 174; P. H. Brown, *History of Scotland* (Cambridge, 1908–1909), I, 392.
4. Historical Manuscripts Commission, *Marquess of Bath*, Vol. IV, *Seymour Papers*, 29.
5. Samuel Haynes and William Murdin, eds., *A Collection of State Papers . . . Left by William Cecil, Lord Burghley* (London, 1740–59), I, 1–3; H.M.C. *Marquess of Salisbury*, I, No. 79.
6. British Museum Microfilm M485/59, Vol. 231, fo. 48; H.M.C. *Salisbury*, I, No. 80.
7. *L&P* 17, 1048; cf. H.M.C. Salisbury, I, No. 83; *L&P* 17, 1080.
8. *The Hamilton Papers, Letters and Papers Illustrating the Political Rela-*

tions of England and Scotland in the 16th Century, ed. Joseph Bain (Edinburgh, 1890–92), I, No. 245.

9. *Seymour Papers,* 38–39, 40.

10. *Hamilton Papers,* I, Nos. 245, 261; *L&P* 17, 1180.

11. *L&P* 17, 1194; *Hamilton Papers,* I, No. 255.

12. *Hamilton Papers,* I, No. 299.

13. *L&P* 18, (1), 19.

14. *Hamilton Papers,* I, Nos. 315, 361.

15. *L&P* 18, (1), 36, Lisle to Hertford, January 11, 1543. The H.M.C. version (*Salisbury,* I, No. 99) is incorrectly dated 1543/44.

16. *Hamilton Papers,* I, Nos. 285–287.

17. *Ibid.,* Nos. 286–287.

18. *L&P* 18, (1), 450, 451. Cf. Bodleian MS, Ash. 1113, fo. 78.

19. *L&P* 18, (1), 468.

20. *Ibid.,* 867; (2), 348, 437.

21. The best studies of the last years of Henry VIII are L. B. Smith, "Henry VIII and the Protestant Triumph," *American Historical Review,* LXXI (July, 1966), 1237–1264; and *Henry VIII, The Mask of Royalty* (London, 1971).

22. *L&P* 21, (2), 139. Cf. J. J. Scarisbrick, *Henry VIII* (London, 1968), p. 486.

23. William Thomas, *The Pilgrim, A Dialogue of the Life and Actions of King Henry the Eighth,* ed. J. A. Froude (London, 1861), p. 19; *Calendar of State Papers, Spanish,* ed. M. A. S. Hume, *et al.* (London, 1862–1954), VIII, 208.

24. *L&P* 20, (2), 203.

25. *L&P* 21, (2), 554; Gilbert Burnet, *History of the Reformation* (Oxford, 1841), I, 252.

26. *L&P* 19, (1), 864.

27. Cf. Edward, Lord Herbert of Cherbury, *The Life and Raigne of King Henry the Eighth* (London, 1649), p. 511.

28. *L&P* 19, (1), 812, 87; (2), 606; 479, 507, 518.

29. *L&P* 20, (1), 513, 737, 834, 846, 857, 867, 883, 890; *C.S.P. Span.,* VIII, 91; (2), 683, 633, 533; (1), 846, 1031–32, 1121, 1222, 1284; 20, (2), 128, 225.

30. *L&P* 21, (1), 248, 488.

31. *L&P* 20, (2), 455, 738, App. 30.

32. M. Bryn Davies, "Surrey at Boulogne," *Huntington Library Quarterly,* XXIII (1960), 339–48. This article reprints extracts from the Gruffydd Chronicle at the National Library of Wales, Mostyn MS, 158 N.L.W.

33. *L&P* 21, (1), 248.

34. Herbert, 538.

35. S. R. Gammon III, "Master of Practices, A Life of William, Lord Paget of Beaudesert, 1506–63" (doctoral dissertation, Princeton University, 1953), pp. 11, 69; *L&P* 17, 1203; 18, (1), 183, 217.

36. Gammon, 31. A. L. Rowse, "Thomas Wriothesley, First Earl of Southampton," *Huntington Library Quarterly,* XXVIII (1965), 105–29.

37. Seymour was not appointed to the Privy Council until January 23, 1547; *L&P* 21, (2), 734. His amours are described in J. E. Neale, *Queen Elizabeth I* (New York, 1957), pp. 17ff.

38. C. Fenno Hoffman, Jr., "Catherine Parr as a Woman of Letters," *Huntington Library Quarterly,* XXIII (1960), 349–67. Cf. my rejoinder, "A Note on Queen Catherine Parr's Almoner," *op. cit.,* XXV (1962), 347–48. Catherine Parr

is also studied by J. K. McConica, *English Humanists and Reformation Politics* (Oxford, 1965), pp. 200–34.

39. *L&P* 21, (1), 969.

40. *Chronicle of King Henry VIII of England*, ed. M. A. S. Hume (London, 1889), p. 108.

41. Herbert, pp. 560–61; John Foxe, *Actes and Monuments*, 9th ed. (London, 1684), Bk. VIII, 491 ff. Cf. Scarisbrick, pp. 478–81.

42. W. G. Zeeveld, *Foundations of Tudor Policy* (Cambridge, Mass., 1948), pp. 119 ff.

43. John Strype, *The Life of the Learned Sir John Cheke* . . . (London, 1821), p. 20; Hester W. Chapman, *The Last Tudor King, A Study of Edward VI* (London, 1958), p. 63; W. K. Jordan, *Edward VI: The Young King* (London, 1968), pp. 40–45.

44. For a detailed history of the early Tudor navy see W. L. Clowes, *The Royal Navy, A History from the Earliest Times to the Present* (London, 1897–1903), I, 399–538.

45. *Hamilton Papers*, II, 159, 161, 7.

46. Hall, p. 860.

47. *Hamilton Papers*, II, Nos. 199, 200, 202.

48. *Ibid.*, No. 220.

49. Hall, p. 860. *Hamilton Papers*, II, Nos. 227, 228, 233. Cf. J. B. Paul, "Edinburgh in 1544 and Hertford's Invasion," *Scottish Historical Review*, VIII (1910), 113-31, who observed that no historian or chronicler made any mention of a general slaughter of the population; J. D. Mackie, *The Earlier Tudors* (Oxford, 1966), p. 407; Wernham, pp. 156–57.

50. *Hamilton Papers*, II, No. 237.

51. *Ibid.*, 241; cf. 247.

52. James A. Williamson, *The Tudor Age* (London, 1953), p. 179.

53. *L&P* 19, (2), 222; 799; 457, 473, 475, 491, 500, 536, 591–92, 629, 683.

54. *L&P* 20, (1), 121.

55. James A. Froude, *History of England* (London, 1893), IV, 130–31.

56. Hall, p. 863; *L&P* 20, (1), 987, 1023.

57. Froude, IV, 128; Clowes, I, 420, 463; *C.S.P. Span.*, VIII, Nos. 101, 187; Williamson, p. 183; Wernham, pp. 159–60; *L&P* 20, (2), 307.

58. *L&P* 21, (1), 693, 272; Froude, IV, 169.

59. *L&P* 21, (1), 507, 662, 682, 504.

60. *Ibid.*, 527, 553, 785.

61. *Calendar of State Papers, Venetian*, R. Brown, ed. (London, 1873), V, 320; *C.S.P. Span.*, VIII, 67.

62. *Ibid.*, 174.

63. *L&P* 21, (1), 235.

64. *C.S.P. Span.*, VIII, 224.

65. *L&P* 21, (1), 749, 761, 762, 682; *C.S.P. Span.*, VIII, 329, 254.

66. *L&P* 21, (1), 742, 763; 806; 816, 825, 830; 838; 850.

67. *Ibid.*, 904, 1007. Mackie, p. 410.

68. *Ibid.*, 1235, 1306, 1313, 1318–20, 1327, 1337–38; 1348, 1352.

69. *Ibid.*, 1405.

70. *Ibid.*, 1406.

71. *Original Letters Relative to the English Reformation*, ed. H. Robinson (Parker Society, Cambridge, 1846–47), I, 36.

72. *C.S.P. Span.*, VIII, 204, 238.

73. Foxe, VIII, 488; *L&P* 21, (1), 1181.
74. Cf. Philip Hughes, *The Reformation in England* (New York, 1954), II, 63; and Scarisbrick, pp. 478–82.
75. *L&P* 21, (1), 1452, 1463.
76. *C.S.P. Span.*, VIII, 308; *L&P* 21, (1), 1530; 21, (2), 15, 743; 63.
77. *C.S.P. Span.*, VIII, 316, 320. Cf. Hughes, II, 70.
78. *L&P* 21, (2), 1280; 122, 134, 149, 333; 346. Lisle was not present in the council during October. He and Gardiner were both present on November 1, 11, 12, 13, and 14. Lisle's illness has usually been ignored, and it has been assumed that he and Gardiner never met again in the council. The ambassadorial report is the only reference to the attack.
79. *Ibid.*, 381. Cf. J. A. Muller, *Stephen Gardiner and the Tudor Reaction* (New York, 1926), pp. 140–43; F. G. Emmison, *Tudor Secretary, Sir William Petre at Court and Home* (London, 1961), p. 64; Kenneth Pickthorn, *Early Tudor Government, Henry VIII* (Cambridge, 1951), pp. 539–40.
80. *C.S.P. Span.*, VIII, 370.
81. *L&P* 21, (2) , 1263, 555, 697; *Chronicle of King Henry VIII*, 147 ff. For a similar interpretation see Scarisbrick, pp. 482–83.
82. *C.S.P. Span.*, IX, 30–31. Van der Delft believed Paget to be "the person most in authority" as late as February 12, 1547. Hertford "produced certain letters patent sealed with the great seal of England under the late King, granting authority to him to assume the position [i.e., Protector], but these letters-patent were not examined by anyone."
83. *C.S.P. Span.*, VIII, 386.

CHAPTER III NOTES
(pp. 43–71)

1. A. F. Pollard, *England under Protector Somerset* (London, 1900), pp. 1–38; K. Pickthorn, *Early Tudor Government, Henry VIII* (Cambridge, 1934), pp. 518–43; L. B. Smith, "The Last Will and Testament of Henry VIII: A Question of Perspective," *Journal of British Studies*, II (November, 1962), 14–27.
2. Public Record Office: E.23/4.
3. *Letters and Papers, Foreign and Domestic of the Reign of Henry VIII, 1509–47*, ed. J. S. Brewer, *et al.* (London, 1862–1910), 20, (2), 427.
4. See Appendix.
5. The most recent study is W. K. Jordan, *Edward VI: The Young King* (London, 1968), pp. 78–124.
6. Quoted in Sir Lewis Namier, *The Structure of Politics at the Accession of George III* (2d ed., London, 1960), p. 1.
7. A. F. Pollard, *The Political History of England, 1547–1603* (London, 1919), p. 81. See also Jordan, pp. 17–50.
8. Term used by Pollard, *Somerset* and F. G. Emmison, *Tudor Secretary* (London, 1961).
9. *Calendar of State Papers, Spanish*, ed. M. A. S. Hume, *et al.* (London, 1862–1954), IX, 370, 386.
10. *Chronicle of King Henry VIII of England*, ed. M. A. S. Hume (London, 1889), pp. 152, 191; Charles Wriothesley, *A Chronicle of England*, ed. W. D. Hamilton (Camden Society, 1875–77), N.S. XI, I, 179; John Hayward, *The Life and Raigne of King Edward the Sixth* (London, 1636), p. 10.

11. John Strype, *Ecclesiastical Memorials* (Oxford, 1822), II, Pt. 1, 17; *L&P* 21, (2), 760; *C.S.P. Span.*, IX 6–7.

12. *Ibid.*, 370, 386.

13. *L&P* 21, (2), 760; *C.S.P. Span.*, IX, 6–8.

14. P. F. Tytler, *England under the Reigns of Edward VI and Mary* (London, 1839), I, 15–16. Cf. *Calendar of State Papers, Venetian*, ed. R. Brown *et al.* (London, 1864–1898), V, No. 703; Ambassador related that an altered version of the will was published.

15. British Museum, Harl. MS 353, fo. 3; Tytler, I, 15–16, 17–18. According to James A. Froude, *History of England* (London, 1893), IV, 247, Wriothesley spoke earnestly in opposition. Pollard, *Somerset*, p. 24, n. 2, said there was no authority for this assertion, but some support for Froude may be found in Van der Delft's letter of June 16, 1547, where he remarked that Hertford had not been given the title of protector in the will because of Wriothesley's opposition. *C.S.P. Span.*, IX, 100–101. Cf. Tytler, I, 168–73 and Jordan, p. 58.

16. *Acts of the Privy Council*, ed. J. R. Dasent (London, 1890), II, 7–8 ,63–64. J. G. Nichols, "The Second Patent Appointing Edward, Duke of Somerset, Protector . . . ," *Archaeologia*, XXX (1844), 463–89. Warwick's signature is also missing from this document of December, 1547.

17. For details of coronation arrangement see P.R.O.: L.C.2/3, Bk. 425; "Coronation Book of Edward VI."

18. B.M. Harl. MS 353, fos. lv, 2.

19. *A.P.C.*, II, *passim*; *C.S.P. Span.*, IX, 88, May 4; Antonio Di Guaras, *The Accession of Queen Mary*, trans. R. Garnett (London, 1892), p. 80.

20. *C.S.P. Span.*, IX, 340–41. Van der Delft to Emperor, February 8, 1549, "things heard from Paget."

21. *Ibid.*, 19–20, 122.

22. *Ibid.*, 19–20.

23. *Ibid.*, 30–31; cf. 48–51. P.R.O.: S.P.10/1, No. 28, fo. 100; No. 30, fo. 104 (Tytler, I, 28). Warwick to Paget, March 24, 1547. P.R.O.: E.315/475, fo. 52. Paget to Warwick, July 22, 1547.

24. Cf. Pollard, *Somerset*, pp. 30–33, esp. 33, n. 3, Jordan, pp. 69–72, and *C.S.P. Span.* IX, 48–51, 69, 197.

25. P.R.O.: S.P.68/13, Nos. 6, 41, 42, 59, 47 (*Calendar of State Papers, Foreign*, I, Calais Papers, ed. W. B. Turnbull [London, 1861]).

26. *A.P.C.*, II, 44. P.R.O.: S.P. 10/1, No. 29, fo. 102. Robert Fabyn, *Chronicle*, ed. Henry Ellis (London, 1811), p. 553. Pollard, *Somerset*, p. 153. *C.S.P. For.*, I, No. 128, cf. Nos. 129–31 p. 5. Cf. *Correspondence Politique de Odet de Selve, Ambassadeur de France en Angleterre* (Paris, 1888), p. 128.

27. For detailed studies of Anglo-Scottish relations during this period see Jordan, pp. 230–304; R. B. Wernham, *Before the Armada* (London, 1966), pp. 164–78; and Pollard, *Somerset*, pp. 144–76. Pollard's account is heavily colored by attitudes toward the Protector which verge on naivete. For example, the proposal of a united kingdom of Great Britain made to Huntley may have been enlightened, but coming *after* the holocaust of Pinkie, it can scarcely be used as an example of Somerset's liberality (pp. 148–49). Similarly, there is nothing notable or unique about "his dislike of coercion" (p. 149). Even Hitler and Stalin preferred negotiation to war if their objectives could be gained. In fact, twentieth-century diplomacy concerning Austria, Czechoslovakia, Poland, and the Baltic states resembles the sixteenth-century English attitudes toward Scotland, in at least one respect. That is to say, ideas of union or *anschluss* came as a *dictat*, not as the result of peaceful and friendly negotiations. Moreover, to cite

Somerset's pious prayer for "peace, unity, and quietness" as evidence of his humanitarianism and religious zeal rings rather hollow in the ears of those who live in the aftermath of two righteous world wars and in the midst of a cold ideological war. This is not to suggest that Somerset was an iniquitous monster or a hypocrite; quite the contrary. It would, however, be a mistake to assume that he fully divorced himself from long-established methods of dealing with the Scots. Somerset was, after all, nourished in the tradition of Flodden, and whether he liked it or not, was the disciple of Norfolk and Henry VIII in Border affairs.

28. Mary of Guise was not queen-regent until 1554; Pollard's error, p. 147. Cf. James Fergusson, "1547: The Rough Wooing," *Blackwood's Magazine*, CCLXII (1947), 183–94.

29. The French ambassador was not deceived by reports that Warwick was going to Warwick Castle rather than Scotland. Selve, p. 169, July 23, 1547.

30. *Calendar of State Papers, Scottish*, ed. J. Bain *et al.* (Edinburgh and Glasgow, 1898–), I, 64.

31. William Patten, "The Expedition into Scotland . . . ," in Edward Arber, *An English Garner* (London, 1877–1896), III, 80, 90, 91–92, 100–101.

32. *Ibid.*, 119, 123, 138.

33. E.g., *C.S.P. Span.*, IX, 150; Van der Delft, "The Earl of Warwick is greatly praised." Hayward, pp. 36 ff.

34. *Calendar of State Papers, Domestic*, ed. Robert Lemon and M. A. E. Green (London, 1856–1872), Addenda, Edward VI, I, 331. *C.S.P. Scot.*, I, 67.

35. William Patten, "The Expedition into Scotland," in Arber, III, 51–155. *C.S.P. Scot.*, I, 66. The castle fell September 21.

36. *C.S.P. Scot.*, I, 69, 67, 72.

37. *Ibid.*, 82. Edward's *Journal*.

38. On March 21, 1549, Sir Andrew Dudley was back at Broughty Craig; *C.S.P. Scot.*, I, 96. It was rumored that Warwick would go to Scotland to retake Hume Castle; Van der Delft to Emperor, February 20, 1549, *C.S.P. Span.*, IX, 345.

39. *Journal of the House of Lords* (London, 1846), I. A. F. Pollard, "The Authenticity of the Lords' Journals in the Sixteenth Century," *Trans. R. Hist. Soc.*, 3d ser., VIII (1914), 17–40.

40. Selve, pp. 307, 353; e.g., *C.S.P. Span.*, IX, 383.

51. P.R.O.: S.P.10/4, No. 17, June 14, 1548. Gosnold was solicitor of the augmentations and later solicitor general; W. C. Richardson, *History of the Court of Augmentations, 1536–1554* (Baton Rouge, 1961), pp. 155, 391, n. 41.

42. P.R.O.: S.P.10/4, No. 26, July 7. Cf. Warwick to Somerset, January 8, [1548], S.P.10/3, No. 1. Warwick to Somerset, September 17, 1548: British Museum Microfilm of Manuscripts of the Marquess of Salisbury at Hatfield, M485/59, Vol. 231, fo. 61. The editors of the Historical Manuscripts Commission, *Salisbury*, 50, give 1547 as the date for this letter. This is incorrect because Warwick was in Scotland on this date in 1547. The letter was written from Ely Place, Holborn, and I have assigned it to 1548.

43. Cf. Conyers Read, *Mr. Secretary Cecil and Queen Elizabeth* (London, 1962), p. 46.

44. P.R.O.: S.P.10/4, No. 11, No. 22, No. 26, No. 34.

45. B.M. M485/59, Vol. 231, fo. 54. Sir Henry Long to the Duke of Somerset, January 22, [1548]. H.M.C., Part I, 48, dates the letter 1546/7. Internal evidence suggests its date was 1548 or later.

46. Fabyn, p. 554. The plague is also mentioned by Wriothesley, II, 5.

B.M. M485/59, Vol. 231, fo. 61f; see note 45 above. B.M. Add. MS, 32, 657, fo. 49; Harl. MS 284, fo. 59.

47. *C.S.P. Span.*, IX, 221.

48. The debate is printed in Francis Gasquet and Edmund Bishop, *Edward VI and the Book of Common Prayer* (3rd ed. London, 1891), pp. 395–443; from B.M. Royal MS 17B XXXIX. This debate may not have taken place during a formal session of the House of Lords. It is nonetheless valuable for understanding Warwick's religious views.

49. Cf. Gasquet & Bishop, pp. 169–70.

50. Strype, *E.M.*, II, Pt. 1, 149–52; B.M. Lansd. MS 238, fos. 321v–25v; I.S. Leadam, *The Domesday of Inclosures 1517–18 . . . with Dugdale's MS Notes of Warwickshire Inquisitions* (Royal Historical Society, 1897), II, 656 f; S.P. 10/7, No. 35.

CHAPTER IV NOTES
(pp. 72–91)

1. E.g., John Maclean, *Life of Sir Thomas Seymour* (London, 1869), a very rare book, privately printed and not in British Museum Library; J. A. Froude, *History of England* (London, 1893), IV, 368 f.; A. F. Pollard, *England under Protector Somerset* (London, 1900), Chap. VII; W. K. Jordan, *Edward VI: The Young King* (London, 1968), Chap. XIII.

2. Samuel Haynes and William Murdin, eds., *A Collection of State Papers . . . left by William Cecil, Lord Burghley* (London, 1740–1759), I, 61.

3. P. F. Tytler, *England under the Reigns of Edward VI and Mary* (London, 1839), I, 102–04.

4. Anglesey MS, Box 2, Vol. II, fo. 1. Manuscripts from this collection were kindly loaned to me by the Marquess of Anglesey.

5. *Loc. Cit.*

6. *Calendar of State Papers, Spanish*, ed. M. A. S. Hume, *et al.* (London, 1862–1954), IX, 340–41; Public Record Office: S.P.10/6, No. 17; Haynes, 104–05, 77.

7. John Hayward, *The Life and Raigne of King Edward the Sixth* (London, 1636), p. 203. The most important collection of letters containing Paget's advice to Somerset is found in the Paget Letter Book at the Northamptonshire Record Office. John Foxe, *Actes and Monuments*, 9th ed. (London, 1684), Book 9, 93. See B. L. Beer, "The Paget Letter Book," *Manuscripta*, XIV (1970), 176–79, and "A Critique of the Protectorate," *Huntington Library Quarterly*, XXXIV (1971), 277–83.

8. Manuscripts of the Marquess of Bath, Longleat, Wiltshire; Thynne Papers, Vol. I, fos. 10–11. Cf. *C.S.P. Span.*, IX, 345. Thynne Papers, fos. 12, 15.

9. Thynne Papers, fo. 16

10. *Ibid.*, fos. 18, 19, 22. Manuscripts of the Inner Temple, Petyt MS 538, Vol. 46, fo. 438; (Nicholas Pocock, *Troubles Connected with the Prayer Book of 1549* [Camden Society, 1884], pp. 27–28). Cf. fo. 450v.; Sir Andrew Dudley appointed to Lord Russell's council by advice of Somerset and council, August 10, 1549. (*Prayer Book*, p. 52).

11. Thynne Papers, fo. 11. The reference is probably to Sir Edmund Peckham, a Privy Councillor.

12. P.R.O.: S.P.10/6, No. 23; Thynne Papers, fos. 20–21.

13. Historical Manuscripts Commission, *Marquess of Bath*, Vol. IV, *Seymour Papers*, 110; June 5.

14. Thynne Papers, fos. 24–25.

15. Petyt MS, Vol. 46, fos. 439–41, 438v., 442, 444–45, 446, 446v. Warwick attended Privy Council July 28.

16. Froude, IV, 433; Petyt MS, Vol. 46, fos. 449v., 450, 450v., 451v., 452, 456–57v.

17. *Ibid.*, fos. 451v., 452; Anglesey MS, fo. 5; Petyt MS, Vol. 46, fos. 452v., 455v.; (*Prayer Book*, pp. 56–60).

18. *Ibid.*, fos. 462–64v.

19. *Ibid.*, fos. 465 (September 12), 465v., 466, 466v. Cf. Anthony Fletcher, *Tudor Rebellions* (London, 1968), pp. 48–63. For a different interpretation see Jordan, pp. 453–77.

20. F. W. Russell, *Kett's Rebellion in Norfolk* (London, 1859), prints *inquisition post mortem* which refers to deed of 37 Henry VIII, pp. 230–31. Petyt MS, Vol. 46, fos. 452v.–55v. Warwick's movements: Signed Privy Council letter, July 28, Petyt MS, Vol. 46, fo. 439. Reported enroute to Wales, August 7, by Van der Delft, *C.S.P. Span.*, IX, 424. At Warwick, August 10, Tytler, I, 193. For Somerset's role, cf. Russell, pp. 114–19, Pollard, p. 241, Jordan, p. 488.

21. Tytler, I, 193.

22. Russell remains the best scholarly account of the Norfolk rebellion; the preceding paragraphs are based on this work. Cf. also S. T. Bindoff's pamphlet, *Ket's Rebellion, 1549*, Historical Association General Series, g. xii (London, 1949); Fletcher, pp. 64–77, Jordan, pp. 477–93.

23. British Museum, Harl. MS 523, fo. 53v. September 1. Cf. H.M.C. *Salisbury*, No. 322. Tytler, I, 195–96.

24. *C.S.P. Span.*, IX, 445; Gilbert Burnet, *History of the Reformation* (London, 1841), I, 378.

25. Paget Letter Book, Northamptonshire Record Office; Tytler, I, 185. See also Mary Dewar, *Sir Thomas Smith, A Tudor Intellectual in Office* (London, 1964).

26. Cf. Foxe, Book 9, 93.

27. A. J. A. Malkiewicz, "An Eye-Witness' Account of the Coup D'Etat of October, 1549," *E.H.R.*, LXX (1955), 600–609.

28. *C.S.P. Span.*, IX, 445–48, 454, 467–70; November 7.

29. P. L. Hughes and J. F. Larkin, *Tudor Royal Proclamations* (New Haven, 1964), I, 483. The proclamation was probably prepared several days earlier. Cf. Jordan, p. 508 and *C.S.P. Span.*, IX, 456–59.

30. Charles Wriothesley, *A Chronicle of England*, ed. W. D. Hamilton, (Camden Society, 1875–1877), N.S. XX, II, 24–26; *Prayer Book*, pp. 80–81; B. M. Cotton MS Titus B.II, fo. 55; Stowe MS 147, fo. 177–78, "copy"; also printed in Burnet; F. G. Emmison, *Tudor Secretary* (London, 1961), pp. 76–77; B. M. Cotton MS Titus B.II, fo. 55.

31. Records of the Corporation of London, Journal 16, fos. 36v., 37; Repertory 12 (1) fo. 151v. For further details see B. L. Beer, "London and the Rebellions of 1548–1549," *Journal of British Studies*, XII (1972), 15–38.

32. Petyt MS, Vol. 46, fos. 467, 467v., 469, 469v.

33. B. M. Harl. MS 353, fo. 77.

34. John Stow, *The Annales of England* (London, 1615), p. 598.

35. Tytler, I, 228–230; *Prayer Book*, pp. 106–07.

36. Tytler, I, 246.
37. Pollard, p. 244; B. M. Cotton MS Calig. B.VII, fo. 404; Tytler, I, 388–89.
38. B. M. M485/39, Vol. 150, fo. 137.

CHAPTER V NOTES
(pp. 92–123)

1. British Museum, Harl. MS 353, fo. 78f.; *Journals of the House of Lords* (London, 1846); *Edward's Journal*; J. G. Nichols, "The Second Patent Appointing Edward, Duke of Somerset, Protector," *Archaeologia*, XXX (1844), 463–89. Cf. A. F. Pollard, *England under Protector Somerset* (London, 1900), pp. 279–82, especially p. 282, n. 1.

2. The letter to Thynne was assigned to 1548 by the Historical Manuscripts Commission editors of the *Salisbury MSS* no. 246, p. 57. Internal evidence suggests November 1549 to be the more likely date: British Museum Microfilm M485/59, Vol. 231, fo. 76f. Thynne's answer to the council of November 28 is printed in H.M.C., *Marquess of Bath*, Vol. IV, *Seymour Papers*, 112. *Calendar of State Papers, Spanish*, ed. M. A. S. Hume *et al.* (London, 1862–1954), IX, 488–90, Van der Delft to the Emperor. The better side of the Duchess of Somerset appears in her letter of October 9, 1549, to Sir Thomas Smith in the Paget Letter Book.

3. *C.S.P. Span.*, X, 13; B.M. Lansd. MS 2, No. 34, fo. 85, Cheke to Duchess of Somerset.

4. Charles Wriothesley, *A Chronicle of England*, ed. W. D. Hamilton (Camden Society, 1875–1877), N.S. XX, II, 33. John Stow, *Annales of England* (London, 1615), p. 603. On February 22, 1549, Sir Thomas Smith, Sir John Thynne, Sir Michael Stanhope, Thomas Fisher, and William Gray were released on recognizances and "upon condition to be from day to day forthcoming and to abide all orders." *Acts of the Privy Council*, ed. J. R. Dasent (London, 1890), II, 398.

5. *C.S.P. Span.*, X, 60–64, April 12, 1550; 86–87, May 2, 1550.

6. E.g., dispatches of Van der Delft, October–January, 1549–1550, *C.S.P. Span.*, IX and X. According to a report from Paris even the King and Warwick were hearing mass: Simon Renard to Emperor, November 1, 1549, IX, 466. Cf. also Gilbert Burnet, *History of the Reformation* (London, 1841), *passim* and John Ponet, *A Short Treatise of Politike Power . . .* , in W. S. Hudson, *John Ponet, Advocate of Limited Monarchy* (Chicago, 1942).

7. *C.S.P. Span.*, X, 54–55, March 29, 1550.

8. Burnet, I, 390; Jasper Ridley, *Thomas Cranmer* (Oxford, 1962), pp. 302–303; *C.S.P. Span.*, IX, 476–78; B. M. Stowe MS 142, fo. 16.

9. Southampton was not listed as present in the Privy Council after October 21, 1549. Reports of his illness given by Van der Delft, *C.S.P. Span.*, X, 8, 44. Requests Privy Council to be in the country, *Acts of the Privy Council*, ed. J. R. Dasent (London, 1890), III, 59, 64–65. Wriothesley, II, 41. John Strype, *Ecclesiastical Memorials* (Oxford, 1822), II, Pt. I, 444.

10. *Lords' Journal*, 3rd session, 1st parliament, Edward VI, 1549–50. Act against Somerset: B.M. Harl. MS 353, fo. 78f. Cf. Burnet, I, 393f. and Ridley, *Crammer*, pp. 306f.

11. B.M. Cotton MS Calig. E. 1, printed by Burnet, II, ccxxxvii.

12. B.M. Lansd. MS 2, fo. 81f., February 22, 1550; B.M. Cotton MS Calig. E. I, printed in Burnet, II, ccxxxvii, February 27, 1550. Anglesey MS, Box 2, Vol. II, fo. 6. For further details on the negotiations see the damaged letter book, B.M. Cotton MS Calig. E. IV, fos. 201–19.

13. *C.S.P. Span.*, X, 47 (March 17, 1550), 54–55. Cf. R. B. Wernham, *Before the Armada* (London, 1966), pp. 177–78.

14. Edward's *Journal.*

15. *Loc. cit.*

16. *Original Letters Relative to the English Reformation*, ed. H. Robinson (Parker Society, Cambridge, 1846–47), I, 89. Hooper to Bullinger.

17. *C.S.P. Span.*, X, 94–96.

18. The marriage settlement is among the Dudley Papers at Longleat, Box II, No. 1.

19. *C.S.P. Span.*, X, 80–86.

20. *C.S.P. Span.*, X, 140f.

21. P. F. Tytler, *England under the Reigns of Edward VI and Mary* (London, 1839), II, 21–24. Misdated, should be 1550.

22. Inner Temple, Petyt MS 538, Vol. 47, fo. 418, July 8, 1550.

23. John Foxe, *Actes and Monuments* (London, 1684), III, 79ff. Edward's *Journal.*

24. The letters to Cranmer from Warwick and the council are printed by Foxe (1684 ed.), III, 120. Cf. Ridley, *Cranmer*, p. 309, who confuses the letter of Warwick with that of the council; and A. G. Dickens, *The English Reformation* (London, 1964), pp. 241–243.

25. B.M. Add. Charter 981. Cf. Pollard, *The Political History of England, 1547–1603* (London, 1919), p. 50; Edward's *Journal*, July 26, 1550; Wriothesley, II, 42.

26. *Grey Friars of London Chronicle*, ed. J. G. Nichols (Camden Society, 1852), p. 67.

27. Stow, p. 604; Wriothesley, II, 42.

28. *C.S.P. Span.*, X, 161–67, 167f.

29. *Ibid.*, 185–87; Tytler, I, 340.

30. Scheyfve claimed Edward was not only ill, but that the physicians had given him up, *C.S.P. Span.*, X, 185–87. The warrants are in the docquet book of the Privy Council, B.M. Royal MS 18C XXIV, fos. 4, 10v. Edward's *Journal* contains only three entries for November, 19, 20, 29. There are also gaps between October 24 and November 19, and between November 29 and December 15. In her labors to prove Edward a robust and healthy young man, Hester Chapman, *The Last Tudor King* (London, 1961), overlooked this important illness.

31. Conyers Read, *Mr. Secretary Cecil and Queen Elizabeth* (London, 1962), p. 63. Public Record Office: S.P. 10/10, No. 30, Warwick to Cecil. Cecil replaced Wotton as secretary on September 6; shortly afterwards the council granted an annuity of £100 "in consideration of his said office during the King's pleasure to be paid at the augmentations from Michaelmas last half yearly." Royal MS 18C XXIV, fo. 3v., October 29.

32. *C.S.P. Span.*, X, 213–19, 198; B. M. Add. MS 5756, fo. 261, Add. MS. 33,924, fo. 2; P.R.O.: S.P.68/9A, No. 286.

33. Ponet, *Treatise. . . .* For trial see J. A. Muller, *Stephen Gardiner and the Tudor Reaction* (New York, 1926), pp. 199, 357; Pollard's *England under Protector Somerset* omits reference to Somerset's role in the trial of Gardiner.

34. *C.S.P. Span.*, X, 225–30, March 1, 1551; Edward's *Journal.*

35. *C.S.P. Span.*, X, 251–61; Edward's *Journal.* Cf. Chapman, pp. 200–208.

36. *Grey Friars*, p. 69; Edward's *Journal.*

37. *Calendar of State Papers, Foreign*, ed. W. B. Turnbull (London, 1861), I, No. 461.

38. *Ibid.*, No. 375; P.R.O.: S.P.68/9A, p. 316; *C.S.P. For.*, I, No. 390 (P.R.O.: S.P. 68/7).

39. Edwards *Journal*; *C.S.P. Span.*, X, 371f.

40. *England under Protector Somerset*, pp. 279 f; Edward's *Journal*; B.M. Royal MS 18C XXIV, fo. 88v. Cf. G. Scott Thomson, *Lords Lieutenant in the Sixteenth Century* (London, 1923), pp. 24–35.

41. B.M. Cotton MS Titus B. II, fo. 57. Cf. Strype, *Ecclesiastical Memorials*, II, Pt. I, 436.

42. B.M. Cotton MS Titus B. II, fo. 48. Cf. *D.N.B.* "Whalley." W. K. Jordan, *Edward VI: The Threshold of Power* (London, 1970), p. 79, suggests that the letter was written by the Earl of Shrewsbury to the Earl of Huntingdon.

43. *A.P.C.*, III, 66, 244–46, 296, 391, 436, 478, 483–84, 486.

44. *C.S.P. Span.*, X, 261–66; *C.S.P. For.*, I, No 331; B.M. Royal MS 18C XXIV, fo. 80; *C.S.P. Span.*, X, 278f., 285f., Cf. also *C.S.P. For.*, I, No. 370.

45. *C.S.P. Span.*, X, 290f., 299–301, 318–22; Anglesey MS Nos. 9–11, fos. 12–14; *C.S.P. Span.*, X, 340.

46. B.M. Add. MS 6113, fos. 129–30 gives the ceremony. There is a discrepancy between the MS and Edward's *Journal* regarding the knights. Edward, who should have know whom he dubbed, listed Cheke, Neville, Sidney, and Cecil; the other version included Henry Dudley in place of Sidney. The council formally agreed to the promotions on October 4. Scheyfve speculated that Warwick would become Duke of Clarence, Lancaster, Buckingham, or Northumberland. Besides the modest annuity of 50 marks (Royal MS 18C XXIV, fo. 140) Northumberland received a huge endowment of land.

47. Especially the confession of Arundel, P.R.O.: S.P.10/13, No. 67 (Tytler II, 43–45).

48. See above. Pollard ignores this significant coincidence, pp. 288f.

49. *C.S.P. Span.*, X, 384–86.

50. *C.S.P. For.*, I, No. 481, November 13; P.R.O.: S.P.68/9 (*C.S.P. For.*, I, No., 488), November 18; No. 489, November 18; B.M. Cotton MS Galba B.XI, fo. 67. P.R.O.: S.P.68/9 (*C.S.P. For.*, I, No. 496), November 24.

51. B.M. Harl. MS 2194, fo. 20v.f. Pollard, p. 299. Jordan, p. 94, also rejects Pollard's view that the trial was packed.

52. Quoted in James A. Froude, *History of England* (London, 1893), V, 44. A slightly different translation in *Original Letters . . .*, II, 441.

53. *C.S.P. Span.*, X, 405f, 424, 452–54.

54. There is no evidence to prove that Northumberland was solely responsible for the alteration of a memorandum from the King to the Privy Council so that it became Somerset's death warrant. The alterations are in a hand resembling that of the King. One can only conjecture about Northumberland's involvement. B.M. Cotton MS Vesp. F. XIII, fo. 273.

55. Somerset's meditations are preserved in a "calendar": B.M. Stowe MS 1066.

CHAPTER VI NOTES
(pp. 124–146)

1. *Calendar of State Papers, Spanish,* ed. Royall Tyler (London, 1862-1954), X, 435–38, 492 ff.
2. Bodleian MS Smith 69, pp. 225–26, undated copy.
3. A. F. Pollard, *The Political History of England, 1547–1603* (London, 1919), p. 58; *England under Protector Somerset* (London, 1900), p. 275; W. K. Jordan, *Edward VI: The Threshold of Power* (London, 1970), p. 335.
4. Cf. J. E. Neale, *The Elizabethan House of Commons* (London, 1954), pp. 285–86. Pollard, *Somerset,* pp. 275–76.
5. *Journal of the House of Lords* (London, 1846); *Journal of the House of Commons* (London, 1852), p. 1552; *C.S.P. Span.,* X, 468. G. R. Elton, *The Tudor Constitution, Documents and Commentary* (Cambridge, 1960), pp. 59–60. T. F. T. Plucknett, *Taswell-Langmead's English Constitutional History* (11th ed., London, 1960), pp. 238–39.
6. British Museum, Harl. MS 284, fo. 123. Cf. W. C. Richardson, *History of the Court of Augmentations* (Baton Rouge, 1961), p. 163.
7. Public Record Office: S.P.10/14, No. 21. *Calendar of State Papers, Domestic,* ed. R. Lemon *et al.* (London, 1856–1872), I, 39, Nos. 29, 30. (S.P.10/14.) P.R.O.: S.P. 15/4, No. 5.
8. P.R.O.: S.P.10/14, Nos. 41, 45. E.g., S.P.10/14, No. 40; B.M. Lansd. MS 78, fos. 165–66.
9. B.M. Royal MS 18C. 24, fo. 191; P.R.O.: S.P.10/14, No. 32.
10. Edward's *Journal;* B.M. Royal MS 18C, 24, fo. 200v.
11. Arthur Collins, *Letters and Memorials of State . . .* (London, 1746), pp. 82 ff; B.M. Royal MS 18C, 24, fo. 218.
12. Richardson, pp. 355–56, November 4, 1549; B.M. Royal MS 18C, 24, fo. 27, January 2, 1551.
13. P. F. Tytler, *England under the Reigns of Edward VI and Mary* (London, 1839), II, 103–104. Cf. P.R.O.: S.P.10/15, No. 12.
14. Edward's *Journal,* October 6; B.M. Royal MS 18C, 24. fos. 265v, 261v. P.R.O.: S.P.68/15, No. 186.
15. Tytler, II, 111–16.
16. *Acts of the Privy Council of England,* ed. J. R. Dasent (London, 1891), III, 66. P.R.O.: S.P.10/14, No. 39.
17. Charles Wriothesley, *A Chronicle of England,* ed. W. D. Hamilton (Camden Society, 1875–1877), II, 67. Royal MS 18C, 24, fos. 183, 179.
18. Tytler, II, 108, 110–11; B.M. Lansd. 2, No. 78, fo. 165.
19. Edmund Lodge, ed., *Illustrations of British History . . .* (London, 1838), I, 170–75. The date, June 20, 1551, is incorrect. The manuscript, B.M. Microfilm M485/1, Vol. I, fos. 85–87, bears no date, but belongs to the summer of 1552.
20. Tytler, II, 108.
21. J. Hurstfield, *The Queen's Wards* (London, 1958), p. 203. Cf. also Hurstfield, "Corruption and Reform under Edward VI and Mary: The Example of Wardship," *E.H.R.,* LXVIII (1953), 22–36; Richardson, pp. 230–33; and Edward's *Journal.*
22. Conyers Read, *Mr. Secretary Cecil and Queen Elizabeth* (London, 1962), p. 77.

23. Tytler, II, 110–11; *The Diary of Henry Machyn*, ed. J. G. Nichols (Camden Society, 1848), p. 21.

24. B.M. Lansd. MS 2, No. 78, fo. 165; Historical Manuscripts Commission, *Manuscripts of the Marquess of Salisbury*, No. 386; Samuel Haynes and William Murdin, eds., *A Collection of State Papers . . . left by William Cecil, Lord Burghley* (London, 1740–1759), I, 120–21; June 21. John Strype, *Ecclesiastical Memorials* (Oxford, 1822), II, Pt. 1, 586.

25. P.R.O.: S.P.15/4, No. 4; May 30. Cf. S.P.10/14, No. 72, August 30, concerning difficulties with Lord Conyers. *C.S.P. Span*, X, 536–37

26. *C.S.P. Dom.*, I, 42. S.P.10/14, No. 50. B.M. M485/39, Vol. 151, fos. 39 ff. (Haynes, 122, H.M.C. *Salisbury*, No. 387).

27. P.R.O.: S.P.15/4, No. 8.

28. B.M. Royal MS 18C, 24, fo. 246; Edward's *Journal*; P.R.O.: S.P.15/4, No. 9, August 5.

29. P.R.O.: S.P.10/14, No. 72; 10/15, No. 1. Northumberland did not join the court at Shrewsbury as Scheyfve reported, *C.S.P. Span.*, X, 561–62, but he was very likely at Wilton on August 30, when Pembroke entertained the King with great pomp.

30. *C.S.P. Span.*, X, 546–48.

31. Tytler, II, 148–50, Northumberland to Cecil, December 7, 1552.

32. B.M. Harl. MS 353, fos. 121–23.

33. P.R.O.: S.P.10/14, No. 72, August 30. Cf. S.P.10/15, No. 7. S.P.10/15, No. 50, November 17

34. S.P.10/15, No. 39; S.P.10/15, No. 34.

35. Cf. S.P.10/15, No. 3.

36. S.P.10/15, No. 38.

37. *C.S.P. Span.*, X, 566–69.

38. S.P.10/15, No. 22. B.M. M485/39, Vol. 151, fo. 63; undated, ? November. (H.M.C. *Salisbury*, No. 407; Haynes, 132.) S.P.68/10, No. 584 (*Calendar of State Papers, Foreign,* Edward VI and Mary, ed. W. B. Turnbull [London, 1861], I). Another attempt of the French to deal directly with Northumberland: B.M. Cotton MS Cal. E.IV, fo. 315. B.M. M485/39, Vol. 151, fo. 40 (*Salisbury*, No. 388; 122).

39. S.P.10/15, No. 74; B.M. Royal MS 18C, 24, fo. 284v.; S.P. 68/10, No. 599; S.P.15/4, No. 24.

40. There were periodic rumors of discord in the council. E.g., *C.S.P. Span.*, X, 564–66; *Ambassades de Messieurs de Noailles en Angleterre*, Redigees par feu M. l'Abbe Rene Aubert der Vertot (Paris, 1763), II, 39–42.

41. Quoted in James A. Froude, *History of England* (London, 1893), V, 111.

42. Cf. statements of Northumberland to Gresham, June 16, 1551; B.M. M485/1, Vol. 1, fos. 83–84; *Salisbury*, No. 358.

43. S.P.10/10, No. 31. See Charles Sturge, *Cuthbert Tunstal* (London, 1938), pp. 288–92. Very little evidence about the proceedings has survived.

44. Tytler, II, 142–43. S.P.10/15, No. 57; B.M. M485/39, Vol. 151, fo. 58 (Haynes, 136–37); S.P.10/15, No. 62, December 3, 1552.

45. Tytler, II, 152–53, January 2, 1553; S.P.10/18, No. 3; January 6, 1553. Northumberland wrote again on January 19 showing concern for the appointment of a "learned man." S.P.10/18, No. 8. See Appendix.

46. Tytler, II, 142–43. For an account of Knox's activities in England, see Jasper Ridley, *John Knox* (New York, 1968), pp. 84–129. B.M. M485/39, Vol. 151, fo. 58. (*Salisbury*, No. 406; Haynes, 136–37.) Tytler, II, 148–50, 158–60.

John Knox, *Works*, ed. David Laing (Edinburgh, 1846–1864), III, 280–83. II Samuel 16:23.

47. R. B. Werhham, *Before the Armada* (London, 1966), pp. 179–192; J. D. Gould, *The Great Debasement* (Oxford, 1970), pp. 53–70, 197–98.

48. G. R. Elton, *The Tudor Revolution in Government* (Cambridge, 1959), p. 239.

49. Hurstfield, "Corruption and Reform"; F. G. Emmison, *Tudor Secretary* (London, 1961), pp. 100 ff.; F. C. Dietz, *Finances of Edward VI and Mary*, Smith College Studies in History, Vol. III, No. 2 (Northampton, Mass., 1918), 97. See also Richardson, *Court of Augmentations*, which takes an ambiguous position on the state of the administration under Edward VI.

50. P.R.O.: S.P.10/15, No. 73.

51. *Loc. cit.*

52. S.P.10/18, No. 6, footnote. B.M. M485/39, Vol. 151, fo. 30 (*Salisbury*, No. 424, pp. 108–109). Cf. B.M. Royal MS 18C, 24, fo. 292; Sir Andrew Dudley given warrant for cloth to make parliament gowns for the King, January 28.

53. Tytler, II, 160–63 (S.P.10/18, No. 6).

54. S.P.10/18, No. 8. Lord's *Journal*, 1553.

55. *Return of the Name of Every Member of . . . the Parliaments* (London, 1878). Parliamentary Papers LXII, Pt. I; B.M. Royal MS 18C, 24, fos. 289–90; Lansd. MS 3, fo. 36; Lansd. MS 94, fo. 19; Harl. MS 523, fos. 31, 31v.

56. H.M.C. *Salisbury*, No. 419 (Haynes, 201). B.M. Lansd. MS 3, fos. 75, 75v. Cf. Read, pp. 81–82.

57. Neale, p. 286. See also Vernon F. Snow, "Proctorial Representation in the House of Lords during the Reign of Edward VI," *Journal of British Studies*, VIII (1969), 1–27.

CHAPTER VII NOTES
(pp. 147–166)

1. *Calendar of State Papers, Spanish*, ed. Royall Tyler (London, 1862–1954), XI, 69–72.

2. Cf. speech attributed to Northumberland in Francis Godwin, *Annals of England* (London, 1630), p. 255.

3. *C.S.P. Span.*, XI, 10.

4. Public Record Office: S.P.68/12, No. 652; *C.S.P. Span.*, XI, 37–38; S.P.68/12, No. 684.

5. Original in Petyt MSS, Inner Temple.

6. S. T. Bindoff, "A Kingdom at Stake," *History Today*, III (1953), 642–48.

7. W. K. Jordan, *Edward VI: The Threshold of Power* (London, 1970), p 515.

8. Cf. Conyers Read, *Mr. Secretary Cecil and Queen Elizabeth* (London, 1962), pp. 91–93.

9. John Strype, *Ecclesiastical Memorials* (Oxford, 1822), II, Pt. 2, 505–506.

10. Inner Temple, Petyt MS No. 538, Vol. 47, fo. 534.

11. Bodleian MS, Ash. 1729, fo. 192.

12. Historical Manuscripts Commission, *Montagu of Beaulieu MSS*, 4–6. Montagu's petition was submitted after Mary ascended the throne. Cf. Jordan, pp. 516–17.

13. *Calendar of State Papers, Venetian*, ed. Rawdon Brown *et al.* (London, 1864–1898), V, 549. W. H. Dunham, Jr. gives the best explanation for the practice of granting licenses for retainers in *Lord Hastings' Indentured Retainers, 1461–1483: The Lawfulness of Livery and Retaining under the Yorkists and Tudors* (New Haven, 1955), pp. 110–11.

14. *The Chronicle of Queen Jane*, ed. J. G. Nichols (Camden Society, 1850), p. 8.

15. Bodleian MS, Tanner 90, fo. 187; R. Holinshed, *Chronicle* (London, 1586), II, 1088.

16. British Museum Microfilm M485/39, Vol. 151, fos. 124–25 (H.M.C. *Salisbury MSS*, No. 466). Cf. P.R.O.: E.101/631/44 1 bundle, further examination of Sir Andrew Dudley, September 9, 1553. Charles Wriothesley, *A Chronicle of England*, ed. W. D. Hamilton (Camden Society, 1875–1877), II, 96.

17. Antonio di Guaras, *The Accession of Queen Mary*, trans. R. Garnett (London, 1892), pp. 102–103; B.M. Harl. MS 2194, fos. 22, 22v.

18. Wriothesley, II, 100. *The Diary of Henry Machyn*, ed. J. G. Nichols (Camden Society, 1848), p. 42. *The Chronicle of Queen Jane*, p. 19. The inconclusive evidence concerning Northumberland's statements to the sons of the Duke of Somerset is reviewed by A. F. Pollard, *The Political History of England, 1547–1603* (London, 1919), p. 62, n. 4.

19. P.R.O.: L.R.2/118, fo. 115, Gage to Rich and Commissioners. J. A. Muller, *Stephen Gardiner and the Tudor Reaction* (New York, 1926), p. 222.

20. John Foxe, *Actes and Monuments* (London, 1684), Bk. 10, p. 13. *The Chronicle of Queen Jane*, p. 25.

21. B. M. Harl, MS 284, fo. 128v. *Grey Friars of London Chronicle*, ed. J. G. Nichols (Camden Society, 1852), p. 83.

22. B.M. Harl. MS 787, fo. 61v. Transcripts of letters said to have been found in the study of Mr. Dell, secretary to Archbishop Laud.

23. B.M. Harl. MS 2194, fo. 23.

24. Confession of Northumberland: (a) Notes of Mr. John Holmes, B.M. Add. MS 20,774, fos. 71–72. (b) Manuscript versions: B.M. Harl. MS 284, fos. 124 f.; Cotton MS Titus BII, fo. 162; Harl. MS 2194, fo. 23, third person; Royal MS 12A, 26, Latin; Add. MS 12,065, Latin and German. (c) Guaras' version is independent of the above manuscript versions. Cawood's version is reprinted in Guaras, pp. 145–48. (d) Other references: B.M. Harl. MS 353, fo. 142, Letter of John Rowe; *The Chronicle of Queen Jane*, p. 19, Letter of William Dalby. Other chroniclers followed the manuscript versions.

25. Harl. MS 284, fos. 127, 127v.

26. Guaras, p. 107.

27. Guaras, p. 109.

28. Cf. also *Ambassades de Messieurs de Noailles en Angleterre*, ed. Vertot (Paris, 1763), II, 117–119.

29. Foxe, Vol. 3, Bk. 10, p. 13.

30. For an example of a genuine "Roman" recantation see confession of Sir John Cheke, B.M. Harl. MS 353, fo. 182, October 4, 1556. Confession of Thomas Cromwell, Edward Hall, *The Union of the Two Noble and Illustre Famelies . . .* (London, 1809), p. 839.

31. P.R.O.: S.P.10/18, No. 4; S.P.68/10, No. 585.

32. Cf. Whitney R. D. Jones, *The Tudor Commonwealth, 1529–1559* (London, 1970), pp. 40–41, who believes that the contrast between the repression of the Northumberland regime and the liberalism of the Protectorate has been

overdrawn. He adds, "It was under Somerset that the most savage statute for repression of vagabondage had been passed, and under Northumberland that it was repealed. By 1552 a return to the traditional policy of preservation of tillage had taken place."

33. P.R.O.: S.P.46/124, No. 93, October 19, 1550.

34. Cf. P.R.O.: S.P.10/15, No. 24, October 15, 1552; *C.S.P. Span.*, X, 604–605, December 9, 1552; S.P.10/18, No. 11, ? January, 1553. Bodleian MS, Smith, 69 pp. 225–26, undated letter to Edward VI, copy.

35. P. F. Tytler, *England under the Reigns of Edward VI and Mary* (London, 1839), II, 154–56.

36. Arthur Collins, *Letters and Memorials of State* (London, 1746), *passim*; Collins, pp. 33 ff.; Longleat, Dudley Papers, Box 2, iii, Will of Sir Andrew Dudley, dated July 21, 1556; proved November 22, 1559.

37. Bodleian MS, Ash. 1133, fo. 2; cf. Ash. 1109, fo. 84; Ash. 1110, fo. 75. B.M. Add. MS 38,140, fo. 374/194.

APPENDIX NOTES
(pp. 167–198)

1. Public Record Office: L.R. 2/119, L.R. 2/118, E. 154/2/39.

2. Bodleian MS, Add. C94. There is no evidence to suggest that these books were confiscated by the crown.

3. P.R.O.: E. 154/6/42.

4. P.R.O.: L.R. 2/118.

5. *N.B.* small arithmetic error.

6. Cf. L.R. 2/119.

7. P.R.O.: E. 154/2/39; L.R. 2/119.

8. J. M. W. Bean, *The Estates of the Percy Family, 1416–1537* (Oxford, 1958); Alan Simpson, *The Wealth of the Gentry, 1540–1660, East Anglian Studies* (Chicago, 1961).

9. *Calendar of Patent Rolls, Philip and Mary* (London, 1936–1939), II, 116.

10. *Calendar of Patent Rolls, Edward VI*, ed. R. H. Brodie (London, 1924–1929), II. 87.

11. P.R.O.: S.P. 10/19.

12. See B. L. Beer, "The Rise of John Dudley, Duke of Northumberland," *History Today*, XV (1965), 269–77.

13. *Letters and Papers, Foreign and Domestic of the Reign of Henry VIII, 1509–47*, ed. J. S. Brewer, *et al.* (London, 1862–1910), 20 Pt. 2 No. 412.

14. *L&P* 20, (2), 427.

15. *L&P* 19, (1), 368, P.R.O.: E. 315/252, fo. 48. *L&P* 20, (1), 557, E. 315/252, fo. 43v. *L&P* 19, (2), 419, "The lord admiral's wages for one month £93 6s. 8d."

16. *L&P* 19, (1), g. 610 (8), May, 1544; *L&P* 21, (1), g. 970 (1), May 1546; P.R.O.: E. 318/715; *L&P* 18, (1), 436 (vii fo. 85); P.R.O.: E. 323/ 2B Pt. l. m. 73; *L&P* 21, (2), g. 476, p. 245.

17. *L&P* 16, g. 678 (47); P.R.O.: E. 318/392, E. 323/2B Pt. l. m. 27; *L&P* 20, (2), g. 1068 (41); P.R.O.: E. 318/393.

18. Helen Miller, "Subsidy Assessments of the Peerage in the Sixteenth Century," *B.I.H.R.* XXVIII (1955), 15–34. Historical Manuscripts Commission, *Marquess of Bath*, Vol. IV, *Seymour Papers*, 187.

19. *C.P.R.*, I, 174.

20. P. F. Tytler, *England under the Reigns of Edward VI and Mary* (London, 1839), I, 28; P.R.O.: S.P. 10/1, No. 30.

21. *C.P.R.* I, 252. Both Warwick's request for this grant (E. 318/2042) and the *Calendar of Patent Rolls* state the Henry VIII wished him to receive lands worth £300 annually. The particulars prepared by the Court of Augmentations (E. 318/2042) arrive at the same total value, but the register of gifts, exchanges, and purchases during the reign of Edward VI (S.P. 10/19) listed the grant at £498 18s. 8d., a sum which is closer to the values given in the *Calendar of Patent Rolls*.

22. P.R.O.: E. 315/475, fo. 52; *C.P.R.* I, 170 f.; P.R.O.: E. 318/2044 & 2052; *C.R.P.* II, 29ff, August 17, 1548; E. 318/2045 & 2051. Prices paid for individual parcels of land varied from 22 to 26 years' purchase.

23. P.R.O.: S.P. 10/3, No. 1, January 8, 1548. *C.P.R.* II, 254. Lisle was steward of Feckenham, August, 1543; *L&P* 19, (2), g. 107.

24. Longleat: Thynne Papers, Vol. I, fos. 10–23; *C.P.R.* III, 2 ff.; P.R.O.: E. 318/2048. The lands assigned to Warwick by the King exceeded the value of the lands assigned by Warwick by £15 6s. Warwick was to pay the difference to the court of augmentations. The particulars for the grant give a higher value for Feckenham than Warwick, £48 17s. 2d.

25. J. A. Youings, *Devon Monastic Lands: Calendar of Particulars for Grants, 1536–1558*, Devon and Cornwall Records Society, N.S. I (1955), xxiv, 102. *C.P.R.* III, 61. For career of Sackville, see W. C. Richardson, *History of the Court of Augmentations, 1536–1554* (Baton Rouge, 1931), 190ff.

26. Longleat: Dudley Papers, Misc. Nos. 4668, 4698, 4699. Other documents concerning Kenilworth, Nos. 4677, 4675. *C.P.R.* III, 58.

27. British Museum, Add. MS 34,893; B. Poole, *Coventry, Its History and Antiquities* (London, 1870), p. 124.

28. William Dugdale, *The Antiquities of Warwickshire* (London, 1730), 139–40.

29. *C.P.R.* III, 404; IV, 195 ff; 344. B.M. Royal MS 18C 24, fo. 196.

30. *C.P.R.* III, 71; P.R.O.: E. 318/2046. *Acts of the Privy Council of England*, ed. J. R. Dasent (London, 1891), III (1550–1552), 11. *C.P.R.* III, 370 ff., May 20, 1550; P.R.O.: E. 318/2049. *C.P.R.* III, 364 ff.

31. *C.P.R.* IV, 185. B.M. Royal MS 18C 24, fo. 157v, 170v. *C.P.R.* IV, 117 ff.; P.R.O.: E 318/1819.

32. B.M. Royal MS 18C 24, fo. 339v.; fees £50 13s. 4d. *C.P.R.* V, 175.

33 *Calendar of State Papers, Domestic*, ed. R. Lemon *et al.* (London, 1856–1872), I, 38, summarizes a letter from Northumberland to Cecil on April 7, 1552, in which the duke is said to have requested a grant of the palatine jurisdiction for himself. The original letter, S.P. 10/14, No. 18, is badly mutilated and in its present condition does not contain a clear, explicit request for such powers. Whether the letter formerly did permit the interpretation printed in the calendar is an unanswerable question. In fact, the powers granted Northumberland in May 1553, might be interpreted as *de facto* palatine jurisdiction.

34. Cf. Richardson, *passim.*

35. *C.S.P. Dom.*, I, 411; P.R.O.: S.P. 15/4, No. 6. *C.P.R.* IV, 347ff. B.M. Royal MS 18C 24, fo. 227.

36. See Chapter I.

37. P.R.O.: E. 318/1821; *C.P.R.* V, 171ff.

38. E. 318/2043. *C.P.R.* V, 173ff.

39. *C.P.R.* IV, 431; V, 179ff.
40. See Chapter I.
41. S. Shaw, *History and Antiquities of Staffordshire* (London, 1798–1801),
II, 140. Sampson Erdeswicke, *A Survey of Staffordshire*, ed. Thomas Harwood
(London, 1844), 337.
42. *L&P* 20, (2), 412. Cf. P.R.O.: C. 142/110, *inquisition post mortem* of
Duchess of Northumberland.
43. Dugdale, *Antiquities*, II, 902. Cf. P.R.O.: E. 36/167.
44. P.R.O.: E. 154/6/42, fo. 1. Cf. B.M. Royal MS 18C 24, fo. 372.
45. Computations are based on valuations given in *Calendar of Patent
Rolls; Abstract of the Bailiff's Accounts of Monastic and other Estates in the
County of Warwick, 1546–1547* . . . , ed. W. B. Buckley (Dugdale Society,
1923), II; the *Letters and Papers of Henry VIII*; and Dudley's correspondence.
46. P.R.O.: L.R. 2/118, fos. 12v., 13. *Seymour Papers*, 187.
47. Bean, 140. Charles Sturge, *Cuthbert Tunstal* (London, 1938), 388–90.
Helen Miller, "The Early Tudor Peerage, 1485–1547," *B.I.H.R.*, XXIV (1951),
88ff.
48. Calculation of Northumberland's total income, from landholding and office, would be rather like attempting to solve an algebraic equation with two
unknowns. At the time of his death, Northumberland held annuities and offices
worth at least £2,500 annually.
49. *L&P* 21, (2), 647. B.M. Harl. MS 284, fo. 105; Royal MS 18C 24, fo. 352.
P.R.O.: L.R. 2/118; L.R. 2/119; E. 154/2/39. 1 fother equals approximately
20 cwt. Cf. W. C. Richardson, "Some Financial Expedients of Henry VIII,"
Econ. Hist. Rev., N.S. VII (August, 1954), 33–48.
50. *L&P* 18, (1), g. 981; *C.P.R.*, I, 170ff.; III, 416, 71ff.; IV, 61; V, 174ff.;
III, 370 ff.; V, 174 ff. P.R.O.: E. 154/6/41, fo. 10. L. Stone, *The Crisis of the
Aristocracy* (Oxford, 1965), 344–51.
51. B.M. Royal MS 18C 24, fos. 224v., 225, 252v., 320, 330v. Cf. *L&P* 21,
(1), 963; *C.S.P. Dom.*, I, 41.
52. E.G.R. Taylor, *Tudor Geography, 1485–1583* (London, 1930), 89, 103.
T. S. Willan, *The Early History of the Russia Company* (Manchester, 1956), 2.
Cf. also Willan, *The Muscovy Merchants of 1555* (Manchester, 1953).
53. Longleat: Dudley Papers, Box II, No. 1. This copy of the marriage
settlement contains only the seal and signature of Warwick. No. 3192; grant of
Hemsby.
54. M. C. Rosenfield, "The Disposal of the Property of London Monastic
Houses with a Special Study of Holy Trinity, Aldgate," Ph.D. thesis, London,
1961, 104. Tytler, II, 112–14. *C.S.P. Dom.*, I, 41. B. M. Royal MS 18C 24, fos.
224v., 225. Collins, 82 ff.
55. P.R.O.: L.R. 2/120, fo. 83; E. 154/6/41; L.R. 2/118, fo. 131.
56. P.R.O: E. 101/631/44; L.R. 2/118, Derby to Commissioners, September 2, 1553.
57. P.R.O.: L.R. 2/118, fo. 129; fo. 146. Cf. E. 154/2/39.
58. P.R.O: E. 154/2/39; L.R. 2/118, fo. 93. Cf. Collins, 32.
59. P.R.O.: L.R. 2/118, fo. 100; E. 101/631/44; E. 36/167, 36/168; L.R.
2/118, fo. 152v.

Bibliography

I. MANUSCRIPT SOURCES
The following manuscript collections have been examined:

British Museum
    Additional MSS
    Cotton MSS
    Egerton MSS
    Harleian MSS
    Lansdowne MSS
    Royal MSS
    Salisbury MSS (Microfilm)
    Stowe MSS
    Wyatt Papers

Cambridge University Library
    Western MSS

Library of the Inner Temple, London
    Petyt MSS

London, Records of the Corporation
    Journals
    Repertories
    Letter Books

Longleat, Wiltshire. Manuscripts of the Marquess of Bath
  Dudley Papers
  Seymour Papers
  Thynne Papers

Middlesex County Record Office
  Paget Account Book

National Register of Archives
  Dudley Transcripts

Northamptonshire Record Office
  Paget Letter Book

Oxford, Bodleian Library
  Additional MSS
  Ashmolean MSS
  Locke MSS
  Smith MSS
  Tanner MSS

Plas Newydd, Llanfairpwll, Anglesey. Manuscripts of the Marquess of Anglesey.

Public Record Office
  Chancery (C.)
  Entries of Recognizances (IND. 8950)
  Exchequer (E.)
  Lord Chamberlain's Department (L.C.)
  Office of the Auditors of Land Revenue (L.R.)
  Privy Council (P.C.)
  Privy Seal Office (P.S.O.)
  Star Chamber (St. Ch.)
  State Papers (S.P.)
      Docquets
      Domestic
      Foreign
      Supplementary
      Various

Somerset House, Prerogative Court of Canterbury
  Wills

II. Printed Sources

Arber, Edward (ed.). *An English Garner.* 8 vols. London, 1877–96.

Bain, Joseph (ed.). *The Hamilton Papers, Letters and Papers Illustrating the Political Relations of England and Scotland in the Sixteenth Century.* 2 vols. Edinburgh, 1890–1892.

Beer, Barrett L. "A Critique of the Protectorate: An Unpublished Letter of Sir William Paget to the Duke of Somerset," *Huntington Library Quarterly*, XXXIV (1971), 277–283.

Buckley, W. B. (ed.). *Abstract of the Bailiffs' Accounts of Monastic and Other Estates in the County of Warwick, 1546–47.* Dugdale Society, 1923.

Burnet, Gilbert. *The History of the Reformation.* 2 vols. London, 1841. Includes *Journal* of King Edward VI and other documents.

Calendar of the Carew Manuscripts Preserved in the Archepiscopal Library at Lambeth, 1515–74. Eds. J. S. Brewer and William Bullen. London, 1867.

Calendar of the Inquisitions Post Mortem, Henry VII. 3 vols. London, 1898–1956.

Calendar of the Patent Rolls Preserved in the Public Record Office, Edward VI, 1547–53. 5 vols. and index. Ed. R. H. Brodie. London, 1924–1929.

Calendar of the Patent Rolls Preserved in the Public Record Office, Philip and Mary, 1553–58. 4 vols. Ed. M. S. Giuseppi. London, 1936–1939.

Calendar of State Papers, Domestic. Vol. 1. Ed. Robert Lemon *et al.* London, 1856–1872.

Calendar of State Papers, Foreign, Edward VI and Mary. 2 vols. Ed. W. B. Turnbull. London, 1861.

Calendar of State Papers Relating to Scotland and Mary, Queen of Scotts, 1547–1603. 12 vols. Ed. Joseph Bain *et al.* Edinburgh and Glasgow, 1898–1952.

Calendar of State Papers, Spanish. 13 vols. and 2 supplements. Eds. M. A. S. Hume, Royall Tyler *et al.* London, 1862–1954.

Calendar of State Papers, Venetian. 9 vols. Ed. Rawdon Brown *et al.* London, 1864–1898.

Collins, Arthur. *Letters and Memorials of State.* London, 1746.

Dasent, J. R. (ed.) *Acts of the Privy Council of England.* 32 vols. London, 1890–1907.

Deputy Keeper of the Public Records. *Reports*. London, 1840–.

Dudley, Edmund. *Tree of Commonwealth*. Ed. D. M. Brodie. Cambridge, 1948.

Elton, G. R. *The Tudor Constitution, Documents and Commentary*. Cambridge, 1960.

Fabyn, Robert. *Chronicle*. Ed. Henry Ellis. London, 1811.

Foxe, John. *Actes and Monuments*. London, 1684.

Guaras, Antonio di. *The Accession of Queen Mary*. Trans. R. Garnett. London, 1892.

Hall, Edward. *The Union of the Two Noble and Illustre Famelies, York and Lancaster*. London, 1550. Ed. Henry Ellis. London, 1809.

Haynes, Samuel and William Murdin (eds.). *A Collection of State Papers . . . Left by William Cecil, Lord Burghley*. 2 vols. London, 1740–1759.

Historical Manuscripts Commission. *Reports*. London, 1870–.

Holinshed, Raphael. *Chronicles*. 2 vols. London, 1586.

Hume, M. A. S. (ed.). *Chronicle of King Henry VIII of England*. London, 1889.

Inderwick, F. A. (ed.). *A Calendar of the Inner Temple Records*. 5 vols. London, 1896.

Jordan, W. K. (ed.). *The Chronicle and Political Papers of King Edward VI*. Cornell, 1966.

Journals of the House of Commons. Vol. 1. Eds. T. Vardon and T. E. May. London, 1852.

Journals of the House of Lords. 10 vols. London, 1846.

Knox, John. *Works*. 6 vols. Ed. David Laing. Edinburgh, 1846–1864.

Leadam, I. S. (ed.). *The Domesday of Inclosures, 1517–18 . . . with Dugdale's MS Notes of Warwickshire Inquisitions 1517, 1518, 1549*. 2 vols. Royal Historical Society, 1897.

Lefever-Pontalis, Germain (ed.). *Correspondence Politique de Odet de Selve, Ambassadeur de France en Angleterre*. Paris, 1888.

Letters and Papers, Foreign and Domestic of the Reign of Henry VIII, 1509–47, 21 vols. Ed. J. S. Brewer *et al*. London, 1862–1910.

Lodge, Edmund (ed.). *Illustrations of British History*. 3 vols. London, 1838.

Malkiewicz, A. J. A. "An Eye-Witness Account of the Coup D'Etat of

October, 1549," *English Historical Review*, LXX (1955), 600–609.

Nichols, J. G. (ed.). The *Chronicle of Calais in the Reigns of Henry VII and Henry VIII to the Year 1540*. Camden Society, XXXV. London, 1846.

———. *The Chronicle of Queen Jane and of Two Years of Queen Mary*. Camden Society, XLVIII. London, 1850.

———. *The Diary of Henry Machyn, Citizen and Merchant Taylor of London, 1550–63*. Camden Society, XLII. London, 1848.

———. *Grey Friars of London Chronicle*. Camden Society, LIII. London, 1852.

———. *Literary Remains of King Edward VI*. 2 vols. Roxburghe Club, 1857.

Nichols, J. G. "The Second Patent Appointing Edward, Duke of Somerset, Protector," *Archaeologia*, XXX (1844), 463–89.

Nott, G. F. (ed.) *The Works of Henry Howard, Earl of Surrey and Sir Thomas Wyatt, the Elder*. 2 vols. London, 1815–1816.

Pocock, Nicholas (ed.). *Troubles Connected with the Prayer Book of 1549*. Camden Society, XXXVII. London, 1884.

Return of the Name of Every Member of the Lower House of the Parliaments of England, Scotland and Ireland . . . 1213–1874. 3 vols. London, 1878.

Rice, R. G., and Godfrey, W. H. (eds.). *Transcripts of Sussex Wills as Far as They Relate to Ecclesiological and Parochial Subjects, up to the Year, 1560*. 4 vols. Sussex Record Society, 1935–1941.

Robinson, Hastings (ed.). *Original Letters Relative to the English Reformation, 1531–58, Chiefly from the Archives of Zurich*. 2 vols. Parker Society, Cambridge, 1846–1847.

Sidney, Sir Philip. *Works*. 4 vols. Ed. A. Feuillerat. Cambridge, 1922–1926.

Stow, John. *The Annales of England*. London, 1615.

Thomas, William. *The Pilgrim, A Dialogue of the Life and Actions of King Henry the Eighth*. Ed. James A. Froude. London, 1861.

Tytler, P. F. *England Under the Reigns of Edward VI and Mary*. 2 vols. London, 1839.

Vergil, Polydore. *Historiae Anglicae*. Ed. D. Hay. Camden Society, 3d Series LXXIV. London, 1950.

Vertot, Rene Aubert de. (ed.). *Ambassades de Messieurs de Noailles en Angleterre*. 5 vols. Paris, 1763.

Wriothesley, Charles. *A Chronicle of England*. 2 vols. Ed. W. D. Hamilton. Camden Society, N. S. XI., XX. London, 1875–1877.

Youings, J. A. (ed.). *Devon Monastic Lands: Calendar of Particulars for Grants, 1536–1558*. Devon and Cornwall Records Society, N. S. I, 1955.

III. SELECTED SECONDARY WORKS

Bean, J. M. W. *The Estates of the Percy Family, 1416–1537*. Oxford, 1958.

Beer, Barrett L. "London and the Rebellions of 1548–1549," *Journal of British Studies*, XII (1972), 15–38.

——. "A Note on Queen Catherine Parr's Almoner," *Huntington Library Quarterly*, XXV (1962), 347–48.

——. "The Paget Letter Book," *Manuscripta*, XIV (1970), 176–79.

——. "The Rise of John Dudley, Duke of Northumberland," *History Today*, XV (1965), 269–77.

——. "Sir William Paget and the Protectorate, 1547–1549," *Ohio Academy of History Newsletter*, II (1971), 2–9.

——. "A Study of John Dudley, Duke of Northumberland, and His Family," Ph.D. thesis, Northwestern, 1965.

Bindoff, S. T. *Ket's Rebellion, 1549*. Historical Association General Series. London, 1949.

——. "A Kingdom at Stake," *History Today*, III (1953), 642–48

Brodie, D.M. "Edmund Dudley, Minister of Henry VII," *Transactions of the Royal Historical Society*, 4th series, XV (1932), 133–61.

Brown, P. H. *History of Scotland*. 3 vols. Cambridge, 1908–1909.

Bush, M. L. "The Lisle-Seymour Land Disputes: A Study of Power and Influence in the 1530's," *Historical Journal*, IX (1966), 255–74.

Chapman, Hester. *The Last Tudor King, A Study of Edward VI*. London, 1961.

Clowes, W. L. *et al*. *The Royal Navy, A History from the Earliest Times to the Present*. 5 vols. London, 1897–1903.

Cokayne, G. E. *Complete Peerage of England, Scotland, Ireland*. 13 vols. London, 1910–1949.

Cooper, J. P. "Henry VII's Last Year's Reconsidered," *Historical Journal*, II (1959), 103–29.

Davies, M. Bryn. "Surrey at Boulogne," *Huntington Library Quarterly*, XXIII (August, 1960), 339–48.

Dickens, A. G. *The English Reformation*. London, 1964.

Dewar, Mary. *Sir Thomas Smith*. London, 1964.

Dictionary of National Biography. Eds. Sir Leslie Stephen and Sir Sidney Lee. 63 vols. London, 1885–1900.

Dietz, F. C. *Finances of Edward VI and Mary*. Smith College Studies in History, III, No. 2. Northampton, Massachusetts, 1918.

Dugdale, William. *The Antiquities of Warwickshire*. 2 vols. Ed. William Thomas. London, 1730.

———. *Baronage of England*. 2 vols. London, 1675–1676.

Elton, G. R. *England under the Tudors*. London, 1955.

———. "Henry VII: Rapacity and Remorse," *Historical Journal*, I (1958), 21–39.

———. "The Political Creed of Thomas Cromwell," *Transactions of the Royal Historical Society*, 5th series, VI (1956), 69–92.

———. *The Tudor Revolution in Government*. Cambridge, 1959.

Emmison, F. G. *Tudor Secretary, Sir William Petre at Court and Home*. London, 1961.

Erdeswicke, Sampson. *A Survey of Staffordshire*. Ed. Thomas Harwood. London, 1844.

Ferguson, James. "1547: The Rough Wooing," *Blackwood's Magazine*, CCLXII (1947), 183–94.

Froude, James A. *History of England*. 12 vols. London, 1893.

Fussner, F. Smith. *The Historical Revolution: English Historical Writing and Thought, 1580–1640*. New York, 1962.

Gammon, S. R., III. "Master of Practices: A Life of William, Lord Paget of Beaudesert, 1506–63," Ph. D. thesis, Princeton, 1953.

Gasquet, Francis A., and Bishop, Edmund. *Edward VI and the Book of Common Prayer*. 3rd ed. London, 1891.

Godwin, Francis. *Annals of England*. London, 1630.

Gould, J. D. *The Great Debasement*. Oxford, 1970.

Grazebrook, H. Sidney. "The Barons of Dudley," *Collections for a History of Staffordshire*. William Salt Archaelogical Society, (1888), IX, Part II.

Hasted, Edward. *A History and Topographical Survey of the County of Kent*. 12 vols. Canterbury, 1797–1801.

Hayward, John. *The Life and Raigne of King Edward the Sixth.* London, 1636.

Herbert of Cherbury, Edward, Lord. *The Life and Raigne of King Henry the Eighth.* London, 1649.

Hoffman, C. Fenno., Jr. "Catherine Parr as a Woman of Letters," *Huntington Library Quarterly,* XXIII (1960), 349–67.

Hudson, W. S. *John Ponet, Advocate of Limited Monarchy.* Chicago, 1942. Prints *A Short Treatise of Politike Power.*

Hughes, Philip. *The Reformation in England.* 3 vols. London, 1950–1954.

Hume, David. *History of England.* 8 vols. London, 1811.

Hurstfield, Joel. "Corruption and Reform under Edward VI and Mary: The Example of Wardship," *English Historical Review,* LXVIII (1953), 22–36.

———. *The Queen's Wards.* London, 1958.

Hutchinson, William. *The History and Antiquities of the County Palatine of Durham.* 3 vols. Newcastle and Carlisle, 1785–1794.

Jones, Whitney R. D. *The Tudor Commonwealth, 1529–1559.* London, 1970.

Jordan, W. K. *Edward VI: The Young King.* London, 1968.

———. *Edward VI: The Threshold of Power.* London, 1970.

Lehmberg, Stanford E. *The Reformation Parliament, 1529–1536.* Cambridge, 1970.

Lindsay, Philip. *The Queenmaker: A Portrait of John Dudley, Viscount Lisle, Earl of Warwick, and Duke of Northumberland, 1502–1553.* London, 1951.

Lingard, John. *History of England.* 10 vols. London, 1849.

Lower, M. A. *A Compendious History of Sussex.* 2 vols. Lewes, 1870.

MacCaffrey, Wallace T. "Elizabethan Politics: The First Decade, 1558–1568," *Past and Present,* No. 24, (1963), 25–41.

Mackie, J. D. *The Earlier Tudors, 1485–1558.* Oxford, 1952.

Mattingly, Garrett. *Catherine of Aragon.* New York, 1960.

Miller, Amos C. *Sir Henry Killigrew, Elizabethan Soldier and Diplomat.* Leicester, 1963.

Miller, Helen. "The Early Tudor Peerage, 1485–1547," *Bulletin of the Institute of Historical Research,* XXIV (1951), 88–91.

———. "Subsidy Assessments of the Peerage in the Sixteenth Century," *Bulletin of the Institute of Historical Research,* XXVIII (1955), 15–34.

Muller, J. A. *Stephen Gardiner and the Tudor Reaction.* New York, 1926.

Namier, Lewis B. *The Structure of Politics at the Accession of George III.* 2nd ed. London, 1960.

Neale, J. E. *The Elizabethan House of Commons.* London, 1954.

Paul, J. B. "Edinburgh in 1544 and Hertford's Invasion," *Scottish Historical Review*, VIII (1910), 113–31.

Plucknett, T. F. T. *Taswell-Langmead's English Constitutional History.* 11th ed. London, 1960.

Pickthorn, Kenneth. *Early Tudor Government, Henry VIII.* Cambridge, 1934.

Pollard, A. F. "The Authenticity of the Lord's Journals in the Sixteenth Century," *Transactions of the Royal Historical Society*, 3rd series VIII (1914), 17–40.

———. *England under Protector Somerset.* London, 1900.

———. *Henry VIII.* London, 1925.

———. *The Political History of England, 1547–1603.* London, 1919.

Poole, Benjamin. *Coventry, Its History and Antiquities.* London, 1870.

Read, Conyers. *Mr. Secretary Cecil and Queen Elizabeth.* London, 1962.

Richardson, W. C. *History of the Court of Augmentations, 1536–1554.* Baton Rouge, 1961.

———. *Tudor Chamber Administration, 1485–1547.* Baton Rouge, 1952.

———. "Some Financial Expedients of Henry VIII," *Economic History Review*, N. S. VII (1954), 33–48.

Ridley, Jasper. *John Knox.* New York, 1968.

———. *Thomas Cranmer.* Oxford, 1962.

Rosenfield, M. C. "The Disposal of the Property of London Monastic Houses, with a Special Study of Holy Trinity, Aldgate," Ph.D. thesis, London, 1961.

Roskell, J. S. *The Commons and Their Speakers in English Parliaments, 1376–1523.* Manchester, 1965.

Rowse, A. L. "Thomas Wriothesley, First Earl of Southampton," *Huntington Library Quarterly*, XXVIII (1965), 105–29.

Russell, F. W. *Kett's Rebellion in Norfolk.* London, 1859.

Scarisbrick, J.J. *Henry VIII.* London, 1968.

Shaw, Stebbing. *History and Antiquities of Staffordshire.* 2 vols. London, 1798–1801.

Simpson, Alan. *The Wealth of the Gentry, 1540–1660.* Chicago, 1961.

Simpson, A. W. B. *An Introduction to the History of Land Law.* London, 1961.

Slavin, A. J. "The Fugitive Folio and Other Problems: A New Edition of Edward VI's Writings," *Manuscripta,* XI (1967), 94–101.

————. *Politics and Profit, A Study of Sir Ralph Sadler, 1507–1547.* Cambridge, 1966.

Smith, Lacey Baldwin. "Henry VIII and the Protestant Triumph," *American Historical Review,* LXXI (1966), 1237–64.

————. *Henry VIII, The Mask of Royalty.* London, 1971.

————. "The Last Will and Testament of Henry VIII: A Question of Perspective," *Journal of British Studies.* II (1962), 14–27.

————. *Tudor Prelates and Politics.* Princeton, 1953.

————. *A Tudor Tragedy, The Life and Times of Catherine Howard.* London, 1961.

Somerville, R. "Henry VII's 'Council Learned in the Law,'" *English Historical Review,* LIV (1939), 427–42.

Stone, Lawrence. *The Crisis of the Aristocracy, 1558–1641.* Oxford, 1965.

Strype, John. *Ecclesiastical Memorials.* 3 vols. Oxford, 1822.

————. *The Life of the Learned Sir John Cheke.* Oxford, 1821.

————.*The Life of the Learned Sir Thomas Smith.* Oxford, 1820.

Sturge, Charles. *Cuthbert Tunstal.* London, 1938.

————. "The Life and Times of John Dudley, Viscount Lisle, Earl of Warwick, and Duke of Northumberland." Ph.D. thesis, London, 1927.

Taylor, E. G. R. *Tudor Geography,* 1485–1583. London, 1930.

Wernham, R. B. *Before the Armada.* London, 1966.

Willan, T. S. *The Early History of the Russia Company, 1553–1603.* Manchester, 1956.

————. *The Muscovy Merchants of 1555.* Manchester, 1953.

Williamson, J. A. *The Tudor Age.* London, 1953.

Zeeveld, W. G. *Foundations of Tudor Policy.* Cambridge, Massachusetts, 1948.

Index